BE A BETTER READER

READER

EIGHTH EDITION

NILA BANTON SMITH

PEARSON

Pronunciation Key

Symbol	Key Word	Respelling
a	act	(akt)
ah	star	(stahr)
ai	dare	(dair)
aw	also	(AWL soh)
ay	flavor	(FLAY vər)
e	end	(end)
ee	eat	(eet)
er	learn	(lern)
	sir	(ser)
	fur	(fer)
i	hit	(hit)
eye	idea	(eye DEE ə)
y	like	(lyk)
ir	deer	(dir)
	fear	(fir)
oh	open	(OH pen)
oi	foil	(foil)
	boy	(boi)
or	horn	(horn)
ou	out	(out)
	flower	(FLOU ər)
oo	hoot	(hoot)
	rule	(rool)
yoo	few	(fyoo)
	use	(yooz)

Symbol	Key Word	Respelling
u	book	(buk)
	put	(put)
uh	cup	(kuhp)
ə	a *as in*	
	along	(ə LAWNG)
	e *as in*	
	moment	(MOH mənt)
	i *as in*	
	modify	(MAHD ə fy)
	o *as in*	
	protect	(prə TEKT)
	u *as in*	
	circus	(SER kəs)
ch	chill	(chil)
g	go	(goh)
j	joke	(johk)
	bridge	(brij)
k	kite	(kyt)
	cart	(kahrt)
ng	bring	(bring)
s	sum	(suhm)
	cent	(sent)
sh	sharp	(shahrp)
th	thin	(thin)
th	then	(*then*)
z	zebra	(ZEE brə)
	pose	(pohz)
zh	treasure	(TREZH ər)

Acknowledgments: Grateful acknowledgment is made to the following for copyrighted material: **Gyldendal Norsk Forlag:** "Kon Tiki" by Thor Heyerdahl from *Kon-Tiki*. Reprinted by permission of Gyldendal Norsk Forlag. **National Wildlife Magazine:** "The Ingredients of Expedience" by Henry Gibson from *National Wildlife December–January 1971*. **United Media:** "This is News…" from *Another View*. Copyright © United Feature Syndicate, Inc. Reprinted by permission of United Media. **John Wiley & Sons, Inc.:** "Eel, Eelgrass, Eelpout, Eelworm, E'en, E'er, -Eer, Eerie, Efface, Effective, Effectual, Effectuate, Effeminate, Effendi, Efferent, Effervesce, Effete, Efficacious, Efficacy, Efficiency, Efficiency Apartment, Efficient, Effort, Effortless, Effrontery, Effulgence" from *Webster's New World Dictionary, Basic School Edition*. Copyright © 1989 by John Wiley & Sons, Inc. Reprinted by permission of John Wiley & Sons, Inc. Note: Every effort had been made to locate the copyright owner of material reproduced in this component. Omissions brought to our attention will be corrected in subsequent editions.

Photo Credits: Cover images, clockwise from top left: © Anatoliy Meshkov/Shutterstock, © Getty Images, © Getty Images, © Getty Images, © Tootles/Shutterstock, © Lexy Sinnott/Shutterstock, Charmaine Whitman/Pearson, © Getty Images, © Getty Images, © Getty Images; Cover background: © JuiceDrops; Lesson and unit opener: © Stockbyte; p. 13: © Kon-Tiki Museum; p. 42: © Duncan Gilbert/Shutterstock; p. 43: © David Muench/CORBIS; p. 101 (left): © Gary Braasch/CORBIS; p. 101 (right): © Indranil Mukherjee/AFP/Getty Images; p. 102 (left): © Alvis Upitis/Brand X Pictures/Jupiter Images; p. 102 (right): © Phil Degginger/Carnegie Museum/Alamy; p. 103 (left): © Sean Locke/iStockphoto; p. 103 (right): © Michael Fuller/iStockphoto; p. 117: © Mike Flippo/Shutterstock; p. 118: © Comstock Select/Corbis; p. 146: Clay Bennett/© 2001 The Christian Science Monitor—All rights reserved; p. 150 (main): © Lü Zhi/National Geographic Image Collection; p. 150 (inset): © Mike Flippo/Shutterstock; p. 151: © Merlin D. Tuttle, Bat Conservation International; p. 152: © AP Images; p. 157: © Julio Etchart/Alamy; p. 164: © NASA Johnson Space Center (NASA-JSC); p. 165: © AP Images.

Staff Credits: Joshua Adams, Melania Benzinger, Karen Blonigen, Laura Chadwick, Andreea Cimoca, Katie Colón, Nancy Condon, Barbara Drewlo, Kerry Dunn, Marti Erding, Sara Freund, Daren Hastings, Ruby Hogen-Chin, Mariann Johanneck, Julie Johnston, Mary Kaye Kuzma, Mary Lukkonen, Carol Nelson, Carrie O'Connor, Marie Schaefle, Julie Theisen, Chris Tures, Mike Vineski, Charmaine Whitman, Sue Will

ISBN-13: 978-0-7854-6661-1

ISBN-10: 0-7854-6661-4

3 4 5 6 7 8 9 10 V0UD 20 19 18 17 16

1-800-992-0244
www.pearsonschool.com

Contents

Contents
continued

How to Use *Be A Better Reader*

For more than thirty years, **Be A Better Reader** has helped students improve their reading skills. **Be A Better Reader** teaches the comprehension and study skills that you need to read and enjoy all types of materials—from library books to the different textbooks that you will encounter in school.

To get the most from **Be A Better Reader**, you should know how the lessons are organized. As you read the following explanations, it will be helpful to look at some of the lessons.

In each of the first four lessons of a unit, you will apply an important skill to a reading selection in literature, social studies, science, or mathematics. Each of these lessons includes the following nine sections.

▶ BACKGROUND INFORMATION

This section gives you interesting information about the selection you are about to read. It will help you understand the ideas that you need in order to learn new skills.

▶ SKILL FOCUS

This section teaches you a specific skill. You should read the Skill Focus carefully, paying special attention to words that are printed in boldface type. The Skill Focus tells you about a skill that you will use when you read the selection.

▶ CONTEXT CLUES OR WORD CLUES

This section teaches you how to recognize and use different types of context and word clues. These clues will help you with the meanings of the underlined words in the selection.

▶ STRATEGY TIP

This section gives you suggestions about what to look for as you read. The suggestions will help you understand the selection.

▶ SELECTIONS

There are four kinds of selections in **Be A Better Reader**. A selection in a literature lesson is similar to a selection in a literature anthology, library book, newspaper, or magazine. A social studies selection is like a chapter in a social studies

textbook or an encyclopedia. It often includes maps or tables. A science selection, like a science textbook, includes special words and sometimes diagrams. A mathematics selection will help you acquire skill in reading mathematics textbooks.

▶ COMPREHENSION QUESTIONS

Answers to the questions in this section can be found in the selection itself. You will sometimes have to reread parts of the selection to complete this activity.

▶ CRITICAL THINKING ACTIVITY

The critical thinking activity includes questions whose answers are not directly stated in the selection. For these questions, you must combine the information in the selection with what you already know in order to infer the answers.

▶ SKILL FOCUS ACTIVITY

In this activity, you will use the skill that you learned in the Skill Focus section at the beginning of the lesson to answer questions about the selection. If you have difficulty completing this activity, reread the Skill Focus section.

▶ READING-WRITING CONNECTION

In this writing activity, you will have a chance to use the information in the selection you read about, by writing about it. Here is your chance to share your ideas about the selection.

Additional Lessons

The remaining lessons in each unit give you practice with such skills as using a dictionary, an encyclopedia, and other reference materials; using phonics and syllabication in recognizing new words; locating and organizing information; and adjusting your reading rate. Other reading skills that are necessary in everyday life, such as reading a bus schedule, are also covered.

Each time you learn a new skill in **Be A Better Reader**, look for opportunities to use the skill in your other reading at school and at home. Your reading ability will improve the more you practice reading!

LESSON 1

Skill: Character

BACKGROUND INFORMATION

In "Silent World," two students cooperating on a project—one deaf and one hearing—must learn how to communicate in ways they both can understand. Today more than 28 million Americans have irreversible and permanent hearing damage, and about 2 million are profoundly deaf. Technology, such as closed captioning for television and TTYs (Text Telephone Yokes), makes communication easier.

SKILL FOCUS: Character

Every fictional character can be classified as static or dynamic. A **static character** is the same at the end of a story as he or she was at the beginning. A **dynamic character** undergoes a permanent change in some aspect of his or her personality or outlook.

An author can reveal how the character changes in a combination of ways.

1. the character's actions and speech
2. the character's thoughts and feelings
3. the opinions and comments of other characters

▌ Read the paragraphs below. Then fill in the chart in the next column to show how the author reveals the emperor's personality and how he changes.

The emperor paraded proudly through the streets, believing he was superior to all in his invisible clothes when, in fact, he wore nothing. The crowd thought he was a fool, but only when a young lad pointed out his lack of clothing did the emperor's pride take a tumble.

"I am a conceited fool!" he thought to himself, seizing a blanket from a nearby stand. To the relief of the crowd, he wrapped the blanket around himself and humbly lowered his head, considering the child's wisdom compared to his own.

	Character's Actions and Speech	Character's Thoughts and Feelings	Opinions and Comments of Others
At first			
At the end			

CONTEXT CLUES: Dictionary

When you read a word that you don't know, and there are no context clues to help you, use a **dictionary** to look up the word. Read the following sentences.

*Elliot evaded his partner's glances. He was disgusted. What a terrific weekend this was going to be, he thought, with more than a trace of **sarcasm**.*

If you don't know the meaning of the word *sarcasm*, look it up in a dictionary. It means "a taunting or ironic remark."

▌ Use a dictionary to find the meaning of the underlined word below. Write the meaning on the line.

*"He didn't understand your words because you haven't learned to **enunciate** clearly yet."*

_____

In "Silent World," look up the underlined words *mattock, knoll,* and *pantomimed* in a dictionary.

> ### Strategy Tip
>
> As you read "Silent World," try to determine if the characters are static or dynamic.

Silent World

Elliot evaded his partner's glances. He was disgusted. *What a terrific weekend this was going to be,* he thought, with more than a trace of sarcasm. He'd thought that it would be exhilarating to clear last winter's debris from the hiking trails with all the local high school conservation clubs. How was he to know that he would be working with a student from the Madison School for the Deaf?

✔ Elliot made numerous attempts to talk to Caroline, but the situation was hopeless. He couldn't understand a word she said, although he pretended that he did. He smiled and nodded, but he no longer cared what she was saying.

✗ As Elliot swung his <u>mattock</u> angrily, Caroline observed him out of the corner of her eye. *Just because they can hear*, she thought, *they think they know everything.* She knew that she could show Elliot how to use that mattock properly, but why bother? He'd just smile, nod ignorantly, and continue using it incorrectly. *They think that we don't know anything because we're deaf.*

Caroline swung her mattock easily. As the hard sod crumbled beneath her blows, Caroline relished thinking about how Elliot's arms would ache by the end of the day.

At lunch, Caroline and her friends sat on a grassy <u>knoll</u>. They "talked" animatedly, lip reading and using finger spelling and sign language. Her hands flew as she discussed the events of the morning. Caroline <u>pantomimed</u> Elliot's clumsy efforts for the benefit of her friends, and everybody laughed. The hearing students sitting nearby glanced up, startled, and pretended not to notice. Yet the deaf teenagers noticed.

"Who wants to talk to them anyway?" Caroline's friends signed to Mr. Soong, their counselor. Mr. Soong wasn't deaf, but he used manual communication as fluently as they did. "It's easier not talking to them, isn't it?" he said.

"I talked," Caroline scowled. "He didn't understand me."

"He didn't understand your words because you haven't learned to enunciate clearly yet. It takes time and some people won't ever understand you—but there are other ways to communicate."

"How? He doesn't understand signs or finger spelling."

"It's a problem, I know," signed Mr. Soong, "but I'm sure you can think of something."

After lunch, Elliot collected trash in the brush off the trail. He looked up, saw Caroline walking toward him, and looked away again. Caroline tramped through the brush to where Elliot was working. When she finally got there, she couldn't believe her eyes—Elliot was standing knee-deep in poison oak.

Caroline burst out laughing—she couldn't help it . . . until she remembered the time that she had had an extremely bad reaction to poison oak. It was a horrible and painful ordeal.

As Elliot bent down to extract a stubborn bit of trash from the brush, Caroline, exasperated, yelled, "That's poison oak!"

However, Elliot couldn't understand her. "Yeah, sure," he said, shrugging. Caroline glared at him. Then she gestured at the brush and yelled. Elliot ignored her.

Suddenly Caroline began to pantomime. She pantomimed somebody whose body is itching all over. As Elliot stared at her, fascinated with her performance, Caroline pointed at the brush again. This time Elliot turned and looked where she was pointing.

✔ "Hey!" he said. "That's poison oak!" He leaped away. "I didn't even see it—is that what you were attempting to tell me? I'm so allergic to that stuff, you wouldn't believe it. Listen, thanks, Caroline." He turned and stopped, realizing that Caroline was staring blankly at him, uncomprehending.

Later Elliot approached Mr. Soong and told him what had happened. As Elliot turned to leave, he said, "So would you tell her thanks for me?"

Mr. Soong just looked at him. "Why don't you tell her yourself? Caroline doesn't hear," said Mr. Soong. "That doesn't mean you can't communicate. She can definitely read lips. If you enunciate clearly, speak slowly, and look at her when you talk, she can understand you."

Elliot hesitated for a moment, and then he said, "Would you show me something?"

Later Elliot went back to where Caroline was working. He felt extremely foolish, but he realized that undoubtedly Caroline occasionally felt foolish, too. Caroline looked up, and Elliot smiled at her. Then putting his fingertips to his lips, palms flat, he attempted the gesture that Mr. Soong had said meant "thank you."

For an instant, Caroline looked quite astonished. She peered suspiciously at Elliot, looking in his face for a sign of a joke or betrayal. Uncomfortable but determined, Elliot continued beaming at her. Slowly Caroline's face relaxed. She broke into a smile.

✖ When Elliot picked up the mattock again, Caroline took it from his hands. Wordlessly, she demonstrated the correct way to hold it.

COMPREHENSION

1. Where do the events in this story take place?

   _____

   _____

   _____

2. Explain why Elliot is angry at the beginning of the story.

   _____

   _____

   _____

   _____

3. Describe what Caroline and Elliot have in common.

   _____

   _____

   _____

   _____

4. List two ways in which deaf people can communicate.

   _____

   _____

   _____

   _____

5. Why does Caroline tell Elliot about the poison oak?

   _____

   _____

   _____

   _____

6. Draw a line to match each word with its meaning.

   mattock   **a.** expressed by actions or gestures instead of words

   pantomimed   **b.** a mound or small hill

   knoll   **c.** a cutting and digging tool similar to an axe

1. Identify the following statements as fact or opinion by writing *F* or *O* on the line.

   _____ Trying to communicate with people who cannot hear is a hopeless effort.

   _____ People who cannot hear have many ways of communicating with others.

   _____ Sign language can be learned quickly.

2. The people in this story communicate in many ways.

   a. Which ways are deliberate? _____

   _____

   b. Which ways are unconscious? _____

   _____

3. Explain why Elliot and Caroline distrust each other at first.

   _____

   _____

4. Assess why Elliot's embarrassment makes Caroline so angry.

   _____

   _____

5. Explain why Caroline looks suspicious when Elliot uses sign language.

   _____

   _____

6. Describe how you think deafness has influenced Caroline's personality.

   _____

   _____

7. Some people become deaf after they have learned a language. Others are born deaf. Explain how life would be different for you if you were born deaf and didn't know what spoken language was.

   _____

   _____

   _____

1. An author can reveal the personality of a character in a combination of ways:

   a. the character's actions and words;

   b. the character's thoughts and feelings;

   c. the opinions and comments of other characters.

   Read the following passages about the main characters in the story. On the line in front of each passage, write the letter of the technique that the author uses. On the line provided after each passage, tell what the passage reveals about the character.

   _____ After lunch, Elliot collected trash in the brush off the trail. He looked up, saw Caroline walking toward him, and looked away again.

   _____

   _____ She … could show Elliot how to use that mattock … but … he'd just smile, nod ignorantly, and continue using it incorrectly.

   _____

2. Reread the two paragraphs with ✔ next to them. Together, what do these paragraphs reveal about the kind of person Elliot is?

   _____

3. Read the two paragraphs with ✘ next to them. What do these paragraphs reveal about the kind of person Caroline is?

   _____

4. Are Elliot and Caroline static or dynamic characters? Write a paragraph of four or five sentences for each character. Explain how each character does or doesn't change during the story.

   Elliot _____

   _____

   _____

   Caroline _____

   _____

   _____

Reading-Writing Connection

On a separate sheet of paper, write a short message that you would like to pass along to someone who cannot hear. Then pair off with another student and try to pass along that message without speaking or letting the other person see the written words.

Skill: Using Primary and Secondary Sources

BACKGROUND INFORMATION

The next selection is about a unique voyage across the Pacific Ocean on a log raft. It was led by Norwegian anthropologist Thor Heyerdahl. The first part of the selection is called "A Voyage on a Raft." It was written by someone who did not participate in the voyage. The second part of the selection, "From *Kon-Tiki*," is Heyerdahl's own account of the voyage, taken from his book, *Kon-Tiki*, published in 1950. Both parts of the selection describe Heyerdahl's voyage.

SKILL FOCUS: Using Primary and Secondary Sources

Information about an event can be found in both primary and secondary sources. **Primary sources**, meaning first or original sources, are accounts that give firsthand information. They are written by eyewitnesses to history, usually at the time an event occurs. **Secondary sources** are descriptions or interpretations of an event by someone who does not witness the event. Often these are written long after the event occurs. When comparing information from two different sources, follow these guidelines.

1. **Identify the source.** Who wrote the information? When was it written? How was the author involved in the event? Is it a primary or a secondary source?

2. **Analyze the information.** What event is described? Which time period? How reliable is the information?

3. **Evaluate the information.** Why might one source be more accurate or more biased than the other? What conclusions can you draw based on both sources?

▶ Decide whether each source below would more likely be a primary source or a secondary source. Then fill in the chart at the top of the next column with a source from the list below. encyclopedia, diary, newspaper, biography, autobiography, history book

Primary Source	Secondary Source

CONTEXT CLUES: Details

Often the meaning of a word is made clear by **details** provided in the surrounding text. As you read the sentence below, look for detail context clues that explain the meaning of the underlined word.

Finally, in one __surge__, the sea rose and lifted them inside the reef.

The word *surge* is explained by the words that follow it, *the sea rose* and *lifted them*. These words give details that help you understand that *surge* means "a swelling or sweeping forward like that of a wave or series of waves."

▶ Read the sentence below. Then circle the details that help you understand the underlined word.

As the __troughs__ of the sea gradually grew deeper, it became clear that we had moved into the swiftest part of the Humboldt Current.

In "A Voyage on a Raft" and "From *Kon-Tiki*," the words *valid*, *chaos*, and *cessation* are underlined. As you read these accounts, look for details that help you figure out the meanings of the words.

Strategy Tip

As you read these primary and secondary sources, compare the information in them. Which selection is the primary source? Which is the secondary source? Use the guidelines for comparing sources in the Skill Focus to help you compare them.

A Voyage on a Raft

While visiting Fatu Hiva, a Polynesian island in the Pacific Ocean, Thor Heyerdahl heard a fascinating legend—a tale about an ancient god and chief named Tiki, who had brought people to the islands many centuries ago. Before that time, they had inhabited "a big country beyond the sea."

The old legend seized Heyerdahl's scientific curiosity. He wondered where these people might have come from and how they had crossed the ocean. Heyerdahl went to Peru, where he heard a legend about Kon-Tiki, the sun king, who once led a group of people across the Pacific Ocean. This legend was similar to the Polynesian story about the god Tiki. Could the two legends be descriptions of the same event?

After years of research and speculation regarding these questions, Heyerdahl formulated a startling theory. He proposed that the first settlers on the Polynesian Islands had traveled over 4,000 miles (6,400 kilometers) from Peru.
✗ The facts supported Heyerdahl's theory. First, the wind blows constantly toward the west from South America. Second, the Polynesian settlers had once carved huge stone statues similar to statues found in South America. Third, the ancient Incas of Peru had gone to sea in rafts, sailing over 50 miles (80 kilometers) from the coast to catch fish. At that distance, they were in the Humboldt Current, which runs north along the coast of Peru and then swings west just below the equator to join the South Equatorial Current, which goes straight to the Polynesian Islands. Tiki could have reached those islands on a raft.

Heyerdahl was determined to test his theory, even if he had to cross the Pacific on a raft himself. ✗ With five other men, he built a raft exactly like those described in ancient records. They chose nine of the thickest balsa logs that they could find. They cut deep grooves into the wood to prevent the ropes holding the whole raft together from slipping; not a single spike was used. In the middle of the raft, they erected a small, open bamboo cabin. The men then set up a sail and a steering oar. When the raft was completed, they stocked it with a four-month supply of food.

On April 28, 1947, the six men and their parrot began their voyage from Callao, Peru. A tug towed them about 50 miles (80 kilometers) from shore into

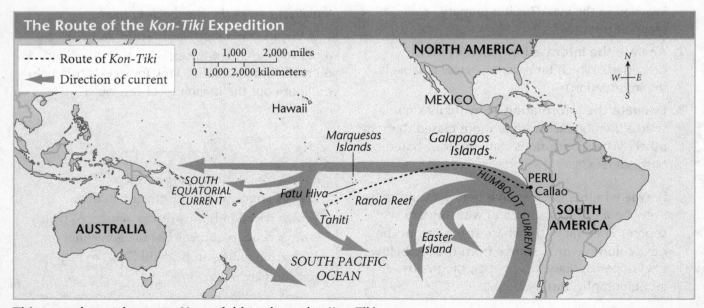

The Route of the *Kon-Tiki* Expedition

- - - - Route of *Kon-Tiki*
◄——— Direction of current

0   1,000   2,000 miles
0 1,000 2,000 kilometers

NORTH AMERICA

MEXICO

Hawaii

Marquesas Islands

Galapagos Islands

PERU
Callao

HUMBOLDT CURRENT

SOUTH
EQUATORIAL
CURRENT

Fatu Hiva

Raroia Reef

Tahiti

Easter Island

SOUTH
AMERICA

AUSTRALIA

SOUTH PACIFIC
OCEAN

This map shows the route Heyerdahl took on the *Kon-Tiki*.

the Humboldt Current. For almost four months, they would not encounter another human being.

At first, the raft tossed about in the treacherous sea. When the water became calm, the men caught fish for food. At night, they charted their progress by the stars and found that the current was carrying them—just as Heyerdahl had predicted—westward toward the Polynesian Islands.

On July 3, 1947, the crew saw land birds for the first time. Several weeks later, they saw a small cloud on the horizon. It did not move with the wind but rose steadily like a column of smoke. It was caused by the warm air rising from an island.

On July 30, the crew saw land, but they couldn't reach it because the wind and currents carried them away from it. They soon passed another remote island and headed toward it. The raft hit the coral wall of the reef innumerable times. Finally in one surge, the sea rose and lifted them inside the reef. Although the raft was severely damaged, the men were not injured.

Maps showed that they had landed on Raroia Reef in the Polynesian Islands. Their voyage did not prove that such a voyage had been made centuries ago. It did prove, though, that it could have been made. Thor Heyerdahl, however, was satisfied that his theory was <u>valid</u>.

FROM *KON-TIKI*

As the troughs of the sea gradually grew deeper, it became clear that we had moved into the swiftest part of the Humboldt Current. This sea was obviously caused by a current and not simply raised by the wind. The water was green and cold and everywhere about us; the jagged mountains of Peru had vanished into the dense cloud banks astern. When darkness crept over the waters, our first duel with the elements began. We were still not sure of the sea; we were still uncertain whether it would show itself a friend or an enemy....

About midnight, a ship's light passed in a northerly direction. At three, another passed on the same course. We waved our little paraffin lamp and hailed them with flashes from an electric torch. But they did not see us, and the lights passed slowly northward into the darkness and disappeared. Little did we on board the raft realize that this was our last ship and the last trace of men we should see till we had reached the other side of the ocean.

We clung like flies, two and two, to the steering oar in the darkness and felt the fresh seawater pouring off our hair while the oar hit us, and our hands grew stiff with the exertion of hanging on. We had a good schooling those first days and nights; it turned landlubbers into seamen. For the first 24 hours, every man, in unbroken succession, had two hours at the helm and three hours' rest. We

arranged that every hour a fresh man should relieve one of the two steersmen who had been at the helm for two hours.

✔ The next night was still worse; the seas grew higher instead of going down. Two hours of struggling with the steering oar was too long. A man was not much use in the second half of his watch, and the seas got the better of us and hurled us around and sideways, while the water poured on board. Then we changed over to one hour at the

***Kon-Tiki*, shown leaving Callao Harbor, Peru, was named after the Peruvian sun god, Kon-Tiki.**

helm and an hour and a half's rest. So the first sixty hours passed, in one continuous struggle against a <u>chaos</u> of waves that rushed upon us, one after another, without <u>cessation</u>....

After a week or so, the sea grew calmer, and we noticed that it became blue instead of green. We began to go west-northwest instead of due northwest and took this as the first faint sign that we were out of the coastal current and had some hope of being carried out to sea.

The very first day we were left alone on the sea, we had noticed fish around the raft, but we were too much occupied with steering to think of fishing. The second day, we went right into a thick shoal of sardines, and soon afterward an eight-foot blue shark came along and rolled over with its white belly uppermost as it rubbed against the raft's stern.... It played around us for a while, but disappeared when we got the hand harpoon ready for action.

The next day, we were visited by tunnies, bonitos, and dolphins. When a big flying fish thudded on board, we used it as bait and at once pulled in enough food for several days. On steering watch, we could see many fish we did not even know. One day, we came into a school of porpoises which seemed quite endless. The black backs tumbled about, packed close together, right in to the side of the raft, and sprang up here and there all over the sea as far as we could see from the masthead.

COMPREHENSION

1. According to Peruvian legend, who was Kon-Tiki and what did he do?

   _____

   _____

   _____

2. Heyerdahl and his men kept the raft going in the right direction by which of the following methods? Check two items.

   _____ **a.** charting their movement according to the stars

   _____ **b.** always looking for the equator

   _____ **c.** sailing with the Humboldt Current

3. Sequence the events below in the order in which they happened.

   _____ *Kon-Tiki* travels on the Humboldt Current.

   _____ After research in Peru, Heyerdahl formulates his theory.

   _____ *Kon-Tiki* leaves Peru.

   _____ Heyerdahl first visits Polynesia.

   _____ *Kon-Tiki* arrives at a Polynesian island.

4. What ocean current moves in a northwest direction along the coast of South America?

   _____

   _____

   _____

5. What was the name of the place that the *Kon-Tiki* landed on?

   _____

   _____

   _____

   _____

6. Reread the two paragraphs that have ✘ next to them. Then in each paragraph, underline the sentence that states the main idea of the paragraph.

7. Draw a line to match each word with its meaning.

   cessation   **a.** based on evidence

   chaos   **b.** stopping

   valid   **c.** confusion

1. Identify each of the following statements as fact or opinion. Write *F* or *O* on the line.

   _____ The crew of the *Kon-Tiki* risked their lives to make the voyage.

   _____ Heyerdahl was wrong to risk the lives of his crew members.

2. The crew sighted land birds and a small cloud that did not move with the wind but rose steadily like a column of smoke. What did the crew conclude?

   _____

3. Reread the paragraph with a ✔ next to it. Write a sentence describing its main idea.

   _____

4. Describe Thor Heyerdahl from what you have read about his character.

   _____

5. Write a generalization based on the three facts below.

   Facts: a. The crew of the *Kon-Tiki* was alone on the vast Pacific Ocean.

   b. The ocean waves crashed across the small raft with great force.

   c. Sharks swam up close to the raft.

   Generalization: _____

6. Look at the photograph of the *Kon-Tiki* and its caption on page 13.

   a. What country was the *Kon-Tiki* leaving from?

   _____

   b. Why do you think Heyerdahl named the raft *Kon-Tiki*?

   _____

SKILL FOCUS: USING PRIMARY AND SECONDARY SOURCES

Compare the information presented in "A Voyage on a Raft" and "From *Kon-Tiki*."

1. Identify the source.

   a. Who wrote the information?

   "A Voyage on a Raft" _____

   "From *Kon-Tiki*" _____

   b. When was the information written?

   "A Voyage on a Raft" _____

   "From *Kon-Tiki*" _____

c. How was the author involved in the event?

"A Voyage on a Raft" _____

"From *Kon-Tiki*" _____

d. Is it a primary or a secondary source?

"A Voyage on a Raft" _____

"From *Kon-Tiki*" _____

2. Analyze the information given.

    a. What event is described?

"A Voyage on a Raft" _____

"From *Kon-Tiki*" _____

    b. What time period does the source cover?

"A Voyage on a Raft" _____

"From *Kon-Tiki*" _____

    c. How reliable is the source's information?

"A Voyage on a Raft" _____

"From *Kon-Tiki*" _____

3. Evaluate the information given.

    a. Why is one source apt to be more accurate than the other?

_____

_____

    b. Why is one source apt to be more biased than the other?

_____

_____

    c. What conclusions can you draw about Heyerdahl's theory based on both sources of information?

_____

_____

Reading-Writing Connection

Find a firsthand and a secondhand account of an event reported in your local newspaper. On a separate sheet of paper, write a paragraph in which you compare the two accounts. Describe how they are similar and how they are different.

Skill: Cause and Effect

BACKGROUND INFORMATION

"Earthquakes and Tsunamis" examines two explosive and destructive natural forces—earthquakes and tsunamis. The surface of the Earth consists of giant chunks, or plates. When these plates move, earthquakes and tsunamis can occur, causing a ripple effect so strong that they can topple buildings and crack streets.

SKILL FOCUS: Cause and Effect

A **cause** is a reason, condition, or situation that makes an event happen. An **effect** is the result of a cause. For example, earthquakes may uproot trees. Earthquakes are the cause, and uprooted trees are the effect. When an effect becomes the cause of another effect, a chain of causes and effects is formed.

Read the following sentences.

An earthquake caused gas lines in the ground to break. The gas that was released caused a fire.

The earthquake is the cause, and the uprooted gas lines are the effect. Then the uprooted gas lines become the cause, and the fire is the effect.

▶ Read the sentences below. Record the chain of causes and effects in the chart that follows.

As 30-foot (9-meter) waves crashed into the coast, houses were washed into the sea. As a result, 13,000 people were left homeless.

CONTEXT CLUES: Appositive Phrases

Sometimes the meaning of a new word is made clear by a phrase that follows it. This is called an **appositive phrase**. An appositive phrase is usually set apart by commas and starts with the word *or*.

Read the sentences below. Look for an appositive phrase that helps explain the underlined word.

When an earthquake occurs on the ocean floor, vibrations cause waves to form. These waves have a long __wavelength__, or distance from the crest of one wave to the crest of another.

The appositive phrase *or distance from the crest of one wave to the crest of another* explains what *wavelength* means.

▶ Read the sentence below. Circle the appositive phrase that explains the meaning of *tsunamis*.

In September 1992, a mild undersea earthquake in the eastern Pacific Ocean triggered __tsunamis__, or seismic sea waves, that rushed with jet-plane speed toward Nicaragua.

In "Earthquakes and Tsunamis," the words *preceding, susceptible,* and *calculates* are underlined. Look for appositive phrases as you read to figure out the meanings of these words.

Strategy Tip

As you read "Earthquakes and Tsunamis," look for causes and effects of earthquakes and tsunamis. Think about how a chain of causes and effects relate to these natural phenomena.

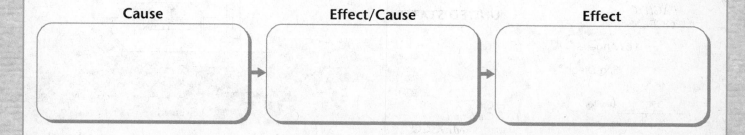

Cause	Effect/Cause	Effect

EARTHQUAKES AND TSUNAMIS

On January 17, 1995, a powerful earthquake hit the city of Kobe, Japan. Although the quake lasted only 20 seconds, it killed more than 5,000 people and injured 26,000 more. Over 50,000 buildings were destroyed or severely damaged, leaving 310,000 people—one-fifth of the city's population—without homes. In January 1994, an earthquake struck Northridge, California, a suburb of Los Angeles. This quake killed more than 50 people, injured 7,000, and left 20,000 homeless.

In December 2004, a huge undersea earthquake in the Indian Ocean triggered seismic sea waves, or **tsunamis** (tsoo NAH meez), that rushed with jet-plane speed toward South Asia and East Africa. As 30-meter (100-foot) waves crashed into the coasts, 157,577 people drowned; 26,763 people were missing; and more than 1 million people throughout the affected areas were left homeless.

What Are Earthquakes?

If you throw a pebble into a pond, you see waves moving outward in all directions. When rocks in the Earth break, something similar happens; waves travel through the Earth in all directions, causing the ground to shake. During a severe earthquake, the ground may rise and fall in a way that is similar to the movement of waves in the ocean. The motion of the ground causes trees and buildings to sway and fall.

Most earthquakes are caused by **faulting**, which occurs when sections of the Earth's crust are pushed or pulled in different directions. During faulting, rocks break and slide past one another, releasing energy. The movement in an earthquake is caused both by the movement and the vibration of rocks. As the rocks move or vibrate, they cause nearby rocks to move or vibrate. This chain reaction continues until all the energy is expended, or used up.

A break in the Earth's surface where faulting occurs is called a **fault**. The San Andreas Fault runs north and south from the Gulf of California to San Francisco. As the map named San Andreas Fault shows, the land west of this fault is slowly moving north, and the land east of it is slowly moving south. However, the rocks along the fault do not all move simultaneously, or at the same time, nor do they all necessarily move at the same pace. During a severe earthquake in San Francisco in 1906, rocks on both sides of the San Andreas Fault moved.

Faults can be close to the Earth's surface or up to 74 kilometers (243 feet) deep. The point beneath the surface where rocks break and move is called the

San Andreas Fault

CALIFORNIA
Sacramento
San Francisco · San José
PACIFIC OCEAN
San Andreas Fault
UNITED STATES
Los Angeles
San Diego
N W E S

0   150   300 miles
0   150   300 kilometers

Gulf of California
MEXICO

The San Andreas Fault runs through California.

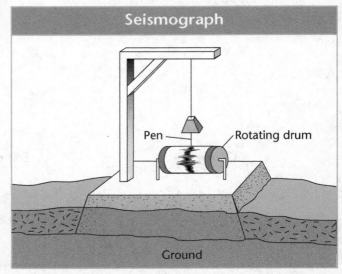

Seismograph

Pen — Rotating drum

Ground

FIGURE 1. A seismograph measures an earthquake's strength.

focus of an earthquake. The point on the Earth's surface directly above the focus is called the **epicenter** (EP ə sen tər). The most violent movement during an earthquake is at its epicenter.

Detecting and Measuring Earthquakes

Rock movement and vibration can be measured by an instrument called a **seismograph** (SYZ mə graf), shown in Figure 1 on page 18. This instrument has a recording sheet on a rotating drum. Above the drum, a pen is attached to a heavy object. When all is quiet, the pen draws a straight line on the recording sheet. When the Earth moves, the base vibrates, but the weighted pen does not. As a result, the pen leaves a wavy line on the drum. The degree of side-to-side movement of the wavy line depends on the strength of the earthquake. Figure 2 shows recordings under both normal and earthquake conditions.

The Richter scale, which was designed in 1935 by Charles F. Richter, an American scientist, is used to measure how much energy an earthquake releases.

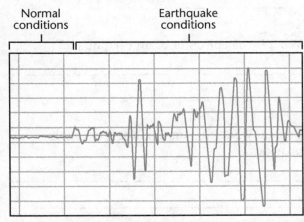

FIGURE 2. This recording sheet from a seismograph shows a straight line when the Earth is not moving and a wavy line during an earthquake.

This scale numbers earthquakes from 1 to 10, based on how violent they are. Each number indicates an earthquake that is ten times stronger than the <u>preceding</u> number, or the number that comes before. For example, an earthquake that registers 2 on the scale is ten times stronger than an earthquake that registers 1. Any quake registering more than 6.0 on the Richter scale is termed destructive. The Kobe, Japan, earthquake registered 7.2. The Northridge, California, quake registered 6.7.

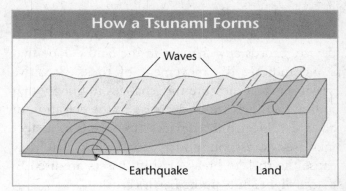

How a Tsunami Forms

FIGURE 3. This diagram shows that an earthquake on the ocean floor causes waves that can cause a tsunami.

What Is a Tsunami?

When an earthquake occurs on the ocean floor, an area of the ocean floor may rise. If, for example, an area the size of Indiana or Ohio rises about 2 meters (7 feet), it sends vibrations through the water, and the waves caused by the vibrations form a tsunami. Tsunamis move very fast—1,000 to 1,300 kilometers (620 to 800 miles) per hour! Their waves have a long wavelength, or distance from the crest of one wave to the crest of another. As long as the waves are over the deep ocean, however, they are not very high. Figure 3 shows a tsunami forming.

As tsunamis rush toward land, the shallow water slows them down. This slowdown, in turn, causes the water to pile up, forming a towering wave that may be over 30 meters (98 feet) high. The power behind the wave sends it crashing against the shore and makes the water flood the land.

Predicting Earthquakes and Tsunamis

Scientists can quickly determine the epicenter of a quake that has occurred, but they still don't understand earthquakes well enough to predict them. However, every earthquake that occurs provides scientists with data that brings them closer to understanding these natural disasters. From such data, scientists hope to find a pattern of natural events that are related to earthqukes and that take place before the actual quake. If scientists can identify such a pattern, perhaps they can predict earthquakes. Certain areas are more <u>susceptible</u> to, or easily affected by, earthquake activity, and scientists are studying these areas carefully.

In their studies, scientists use various instruments, one of which is called a **tiltmeter**. This device records any changes in the land's slope that could indicate the movement of rocks. Sensitive gravity meters measure tiny changes in gravity that indicate an increase or decrease in the elevation of an area. Electronic devices are used to detect increased stress on underground rock that may cause the rock to break or shift. Lasers are used to detect slight shifts in the Earth's crust.

In addition to these scientific methods, scientists are also examining folklore about earthquakes. Animals have been reported as behaving strangely hours before a quake, and strange lights and loud sounds have supposedly occurred before an earthquake. Scientists are trying to find out how reliable these signs are.

Because tsunamis occur after earthquakes, they are less difficult to predict. Earthquakes occurring on the ocean floor usually produce tsunamis, but strong quakes on land can also produce tsunamis if they disturb the ocean floor.

The most important aim in the study of tsunamis is a warning system to let people in coastal areas know when these waves are coming. Such a warning system operates in Hawaii. It sends information to the entire Pacific area. This station receives seismograph readings from many other stations. Equipped with a computer, the station determines the position of the earthquake's epicenter and <u>calculates</u>, or figures out, the time that the tsunami is expected to arrive at land bordering the Pacific Ocean.

The study of earthquakes is a relatively young area of science. Yet scientists around the world are working hard to learn how to predict these disasters and reduce the loss of lives.

COMPREHENSION

1. What causes the Earth's movements in an earthquake?

   _____

   _____

2. What is a fault?

   _____

   _____

3. What causes most earthquakes?

   _____

   _____

   _____

4. What is the focus of an earthquake?

   _____

   _____

5. What is the epicenter of an earthquake?

   _____

   _____

6. Explain what information a seismograph provides.

   _____

   _____

7. What does the Richter scale measure?

   _____

   _____

8. Explain what causes a tsunami.

   _____

   _____

9. Explain what makes the low ocean waves of tsunamis become towering waves near a coast.

_____

_____

10. What two means are scientists using to study earthquakes? Give an example of each.

_____

_____

_____

11. Complete each sentence with the correct word below.

preceding   susceptible   calculates

a. A computer _____ faster than a person.

b. He slept late because he had worked hard the _____ day.

c. If you don't eat properly, you are more _____ to colds.

CRITICAL THINKING

Circle the letter next to the correct answer.

1. An earthquake that registers 5.5 on the Richter scale is ten times weaker than a quake that registers _____.
   a. 4.5   b. 6.5   c. 55   d. 6.0

2. An earthquake registering 8.0 would _____.
   a. do little damage
   b. cause extensive damage
   c. be the strongest earthquake known
   d. cause leaves to flutter

3. Aftershocks are felt in an area for weeks, months, and sometimes even years after an earthquake occurs. Although they can cause damage, they usually register lower on the Richter scale than the earthquake itself. Aftershocks are an indication that
   a. the rocks around the earthquake's focus are still using up released energy.
   b. the rocks around the epicenter of the earthquake are stable again.
   c. the rocks in areas where earthquakes occur are always stable.
   d. another earthquake will not occur.

4. In which of the following areas is an earthquake most likely to result in a tsunami?
   a. Colorado   b. central Canada   c. the Pacific Ocean   d. Arizona

5. Why can't scientists predict earthquakes?
   a. Since earthquakes have not occurred for very long, scientists have not had much time to study them.
   b. Earthquakes occur in more than just one part of the world, so scientists don't know where a quake will hit.
   c. Scientists have not been able to find a pattern that is common to all earthquakes that would help them make predictions.
   d. Scientists do not have the instruments necessary to measure the vibrations of the Earth's crust.

Create the correct chain of causes and effects by underlining one of the two causes and one of the two effects shown. The sentence in the middle column should be an effect of the cause you have chosen, as well as a cause of the effect you have chosen.

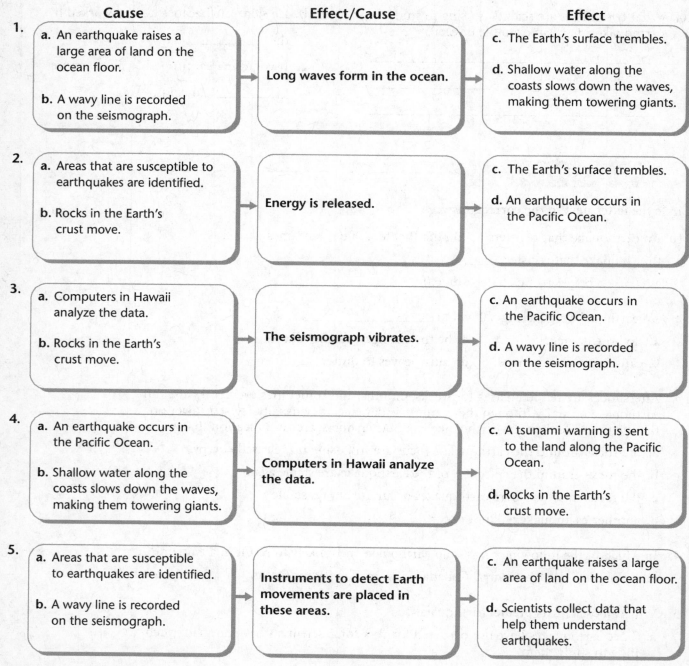

Cause	Effect/Cause	Effect
1. **a.** An earthquake raises a large area of land on the ocean floor. **b.** A wavy line is recorded on the seismograph.	Long waves form in the ocean.	**c.** The Earth's surface trembles. **d.** Shallow water along the coasts slows down the waves, making them towering giants.
2. **a.** Areas that are susceptible to earthquakes are identified. **b.** Rocks in the Earth's crust move.	Energy is released.	**c.** The Earth's surface trembles. **d.** An earthquake occurs in the Pacific Ocean.
3. **a.** Computers in Hawaii analyze the data. **b.** Rocks in the Earth's crust move.	The seismograph vibrates.	**c.** An earthquake occurs in the Pacific Ocean. **d.** A wavy line is recorded on the seismograph.
4. **a.** An earthquake occurs in the Pacific Ocean. **b.** Shallow water along the coasts slows down the waves, making them towering giants.	Computers in Hawaii analyze the data.	**c.** A tsunami warning is sent to the land along the Pacific Ocean. **d.** Rocks in the Earth's crust move.
5. **a.** Areas that are susceptible to earthquakes are identified. **b.** A wavy line is recorded on the seismograph.	Instruments to detect Earth movements are placed in these areas.	**c.** An earthquake raises a large area of land on the ocean floor. **d.** Scientists collect data that help them understand earthquakes.

Reading-Writing Connection

On a separate sheet of paper, write a short essay about what you would do if an earthquake struck nearby. Be sure to include tips on safety, things to do, and things to avoid.

Skill: Word Problems

BACKGROUND INFORMATION

"Solving Word Problems" provides a five-step process that you can follow to successfully solve word problems that involve numbers. Word problems have existed for as long as people have used numbers. A word problem is really a mathematical situation that has been put into words and about which a question is asked.

SKILL FOCUS: Word Problems

It helps to solve **word problems** in a systematic way. Use the following five steps to guide you.

1. **Read the problem.** Think about the question. Try to picture the information in your mind. Read the problem again. It may help to draw a diagram.

2. **Decide how to find the answer.** It may help to write a sentence that describes the problem. Often there are two or more steps to a problem. When a problem involves three steps, you will need to write three equations. Key words, such as *in all*, *were left*, and *for each*, help you decide which operations to use.

3. **Estimate the answer.** Use rounded numbers to make an estimate for each equation.

4. **Carry out the plan.** Solve each equation.

5. **Reread the problem.** Write the complete solution. Be careful to label the numbers with the correct units. Check your solution. Is it logical? How close is it to your estimate?

▶ Read this word problem below and answer the questions that follow to figure out how to solve it.

The ancient temple mound at Cuicuilco in Central America is a stepped pyramid. From top to bottom, the steps are 14 meters, 7.3 meters, 1.2 meters, and 1.5 meters. How tall is the pyramid?

1. Which math operation should you use?

_____

_____

2. What do you estimate the answer to be?

_____

_____

3. Solve the equation.

_____

_____

4. Does your answer make sense? Why?

_____

_____

WORD CLUES

Be alert for key words as you read mathematical problems. The word *per,* for example, is often used to signal division in mathematics problems. To find kilometers per hour, you divide the total number of kilometers by the total number of hours. Similarly, to find one amount per another amount, you divide the first amount by the second. The word *difference* often signals that subtraction is the operation needed to find the answer. The words *entire*, *total*, or *sum* often signal addition.

> ### Strategy Tip
>
> As you read "Solving Word Problems," use the five steps to help you solve the problems. When you write the solution to each problem, be sure to include the correct unit in the statement of the answer.

Solving Word Problems

The Europeans who explored the New World found sophisticated Native American civilizations and the remains of earlier cultures. These explorers wrote accounts of their discoveries. The accounts include mathematical descriptions. Word problems about these discoveries are often based on these accounts.

Use the following five steps in solving word problems.

1. Read the problem.
2. Decide how to find the answer.
3. Estimate the answer.
4. Carry out the plan.
5. Reread the problem, and write the complete solution.

Read the Problem

When Alexander von Humboldt, a German naturalist, visited South America in the early nineteenth century, he was amazed by the roads built by the Incas. One stretch of the main road crossed a pass that was 4,041 meters above sea level. The road rose over a course of 295 kilometers from an elevation of only 1,084 meters. How many meters did the road rise per kilometer traveled?

Reread the problem. Be sure that you know the unit label that is used for each number in the problem. Are there any words that you do not know? If so, look those words up in a dictionary to find their meanings. Does the problem ask a question, or does it call for you to supply some information? What question does the problem ask? Often the last sentence of a problem asks the question. *How many meters did the road rise per kilometer traveled?*

Decide How to Find the Answer

In this problem, you need to use more than one operation to obtain the solution. First list the facts

that you know as separate sentences. Then decide on the operations to use.

1. The high pass crossed by the road was 4,041 meters above sea level.
2. The point where the road started to rise was 295 kilometers from the pass.
3. The point where the road started to rise was 1,084 meters above sea level.

Be sure that you know how the rise of a road per kilometer is calculated. The amount of the rise is divided by the number of kilometers over which it rises. You need to do two mathematical operations to find the answer. First you must find the difference between the elevations of the high pass and the place where the road started to rise. Then you must divide this difference by the total distance between the two places.

Each operation can be shown as an equation. Let d be the difference between the two elevations and m be the rise per kilometer.

$$4,041 - 1,084 = d$$
$$d \div 295 = m$$

Estimate the Answer

You can estimate this answer easily with rounded numbers.

$$4,000 - 1,000 = 3,000$$
$$3,000 \div 300 = 10$$

Your estimate, 10, is the estimated number of meters per kilometer. Do you think that a rise of 10 meters per kilometer is reasonable? Another way to state this estimate is 10 meters per 1,000 meters, which is equivalent to a rise of 1 meter for every 100 meters. This rise is not unreasonably steep.

Carry Out the Plan

First operation: $4,041 - 1,084 = 2,957$
Second operation: $2,957 \div 295 = 10.02$

The answer of 10.02 is given to the nearest hundredth.

Reread the Problem

After rereading the problem, write the complete solution. *The road rises at a rate of 10.02 meters per kilometer.*

Notice that the solution is very close to the estimate. You should expect it to be close, since 4,041 is close to 4,000, 1,084 is close to 1,000, and 295 is close to 300.

Now use the five steps to solve the following problem. With problems of this type, it may be helpful to draw a diagram like the one shown below.

Read: *The temple mound at Cuicuilco, in the Valley of Mexico, may be the oldest large building still standing in the Americas. It was covered by a hill of ash from a volcano thousands of years ago. Like many ancient temples in Central America, it is a stepped pyramid. From top to bottom, the steps are the following heights: 14 meters, 7.3 meters, 1.2 meters, and 1.5 meters. The hill that was excavated to find the temple was only 18.5 meters higher than the surrounding area. The top of the temple was found 2.1 meters beneath the top of the hill. A more recent lava flow had raised the area surrounding the base of the hill. Find out the thickness of the later lava flow.*

Make sure that you know what all the words in the problem mean. If you do not know the meanings of the words *lava* or *stepped pyramid*, look them up in a dictionary.

Decide: You are asked to supply the depth of a lava flow using the dimensions of the stepped pyramid as a guide. First list the facts. Then decide what you will do to reach the answer. From the information about the pyramid, you can calculate how tall the pyramid is. From the information about the hill, you can find out how far the pyramid extends beneath the lava flow that surrounds the hill. This depth is the same as the depth of the lava flow around the hill.

The problem can be solved with equations. You could find the height of the pyramid h, the distance from the lava layer to the top of the pyramid e, and the thickness t of the lava layer, which is the difference between h and e. Those equations are as follows:

$$14 + 7.3 + 1.2 + 1.5 = h$$
$$18.5 - 2.1 = e$$
$$h - e = t$$

Estimate: You can make a good estimate by rounding all the decimals to whole numbers.

$$14 + 7 + 1 + 2 = 24$$
$$18 - 2 = 16$$
$$24 - 16 = 8$$

Carry Out: $14 + 7.3 + 1.2 + 1.5 = 24$
$$18.5 - 2.1 = 16.4$$
$$24 - 16.4 = 7.6$$

Reread: *The later lava flow is 7.6 meters thick.*

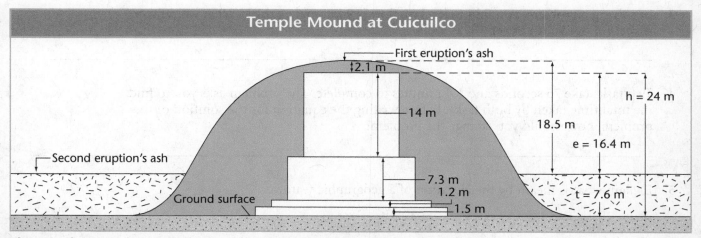

Temple Mound at Cuicuilco

First eruption's ash
2.1 m
14 m
h = 24 m
18.5 m
e = 16.4 m
Second eruption's ash
7.3 m
1.2 m
Ground surface
1.5 m
t = 7.6 m

The temple mound at Cuicuilco was covered by ash thousands of years ago.

1. Identify the mathematical operation that is indicated by the word *per*.

   _____

2. Name the last step you should perform in solving a word problem.

   _____

3. If you do not understand some words in a word problem, what should you do?

   _____

4. What is a good way to estimate the solution to a word problem?

   _____

5. When you arrive at an estimate, what should you ask yourself?

   _____

6. In the "decide," step, how do you express your plan of action?

   _____

   _____

7. What do you call the step in which you solve the equations that describe a problem?

   _____

CRITICAL THINKING

1. If you estimate the answer to the sum of 5,430 and 9,397 and 3,486 by rounding to the nearest thousand, would you expect your estimate to be close to the actual sum or fairly far from it? Explain.

   _____

2. If a problem calls for you to find the number of temple ruins per hundred square kilometers in Yucatan, what mathematical operation is required?

   _____

3. In solving a problem, you find that a lava flow is 9 kilometers thick. What would you suspect about your answer?

   _____

4. Two tasks take 75 seconds and 1.4 minutes to complete. The problem asks you to find the total time taken by both tasks. Before writing the equation for the solution of the problem, how should you change the problem?

   _____

5. Explain what is meant by the elevation of a geographic feature.

   _____

1. **Read:** In the mid-1920s, the explorer Thomas W. F. Gann discovered that the Mayas, like the Incas, built extensive roads. The road from Cobá to a point near Chichen Itzá stretches for 97 kilometers. It is 9.75 meters wide and built with stone and rubble to an average height of 1.5 meters above the ground. In cubic meters, what is the volume of stone used in making such a road? (There are 1,000 meters in a kilometer. The formula for volume is length × width × height.)

Decide: _____

Estimate: _____

Carry Out: _____

Reread: _____

_____

2. **Read:** Every 3 kilometers along the Incan roads was a *chasqui,* a small hut where messengers could rest or sleep. It is estimated that the Incan road system included 16,000 kilometers of roads. About how many *chasquis* were there?

Decide: _____

Estimate: _____

Carry Out: _____

Reread: _____

_____

3. **Read:** The archaeologist Sylvanus G. Morley discovered an ancient Mayan inscription whose date in the Mayan system is equivalent to April 9, A.D. 328. On that date, 266 days remained in the year. He discovered the inscription on May 10, 1916, which was the 131st day of the year 1916. How many days had passed since the inscription had been made until it was discovered? (Ignore leap years, and simply count every year as 365 days. Include the days in the year that came before the discovery and the days remaining in the year 328.)

Decide: _____

Estimate: _____

Carry Out: _____

Reread: _____

_____

Reading-Writing Connection

If you want to find the number of cars per square kilometer in your school parking lot, what mathematical operations would you use? On a separate sheet of paper, draw a diagram of your school parking lot. Then measure it and label the dimensions on your diagram.

Skill: Syllables

To help you pronounce long words, divide the words into **syllables**. There are several different ways of deciding how a word should be divided.

RULE 1: Compound Words

Always divide a compound word into syllables by separating it between the two smaller words first. If one or even both of the smaller words in a compound word have more than one syllable, it may also be necessary to use another rule. However, you can easily pronounce most compound words if you divide them into two words.

snowstorm   snow storm

A. Divide the following compound words into two syllables. Write the two smaller words separately on the line next to the word.

1. doghouse _____
2. highway _____
3. downtown _____
4. bedspread _____
5. sidewalk _____
6. toothpaste _____

RULE 2: Words With Double Consonants

Another rule to use is for words with double consonants. Divide the word into two syllables between the two consonants and read each syllable.

lettuce   let tuce

B. Use this rule to divide the following two-syllable words into syllables. Write each syllable separately on the line next to each word.

1. common _____
2. muffin _____
3. kitten _____
4. tunnel _____
5. splatter _____
6. pillow _____

RULE 3: Words With a Prefix or Suffix

A prefix or suffix always has at least one sounded vowel. Therefore, a prefix or suffix always contains at least one syllable. You can divide a word that has a prefix or suffix between the prefix or suffix and the base word.

preheat   pre heat
cloudy   cloud y

C. Divide the following words into two syllables between the prefix or suffix and the base word. Write the syllables separately on the line next to the word.

1. rethink _____
2. pitcher _____
3. monthly _____
4. unfair _____
5. misplace _____
6. worthless _____

RULE 4: Words With Two Consonants Between Two Sounded Vowels

A word that has two consonants between two sounded vowels is usually divided into syllables between the two consonants.

helmet   hel met

D. Divide the following words into two syllables. Write the syllables separately on the line next to the word.

1. cactus _____
2. picture _____
3. chapter _____
4. pencil _____
5. magnet _____
6. plaster _____

RULE 5: Words With One Consonant Between Two Sounded Vowels

Rule 5a: A word that has one consonant between two sounded vowels, with the first vowel long, is usually divided into syllables before the consonant.

robot   ro bot

Rule 5b: A word that has one consonant between two sounded vowels, with the first vowel short, is usually divided into syllables after the consonant.

venom   ven om

E. Say the following words to yourself. If the first vowel is long, use Rule 5a to divide it into two syllables. If the first vowel is short, use Rule 5b. Write the syllables separately on the line next to the word.

1. canine _____
2. seven _____
3. flavor _____
4. critic _____
5. closet _____
6. climate _____

RULE 6: Words With Blends

The word *trophy* has two consonants between two sounded vowels. Because *ph* is a consonant digraph, you do not divide the word between the two consonants. The letters *ph* are treated as one consonant. When dividing the word *trophy* into syllables, use Rule 5a.

trophy   tro phy

If three consonants are in the middle of a word, two of the consonants may be a blend, or digraph. You treat the blend, or digraph, as one consonant. For example, *complex* has a *pl* blend. You divide the word between the consonant and the blend.

complex   com plex

F. Circle the blend, or digraph, in each of the following words. Then divide the word into two syllables. Write the syllables separately on the line next to the word.

1. panther _____
2. complaint _____
3. lichens _____
4. farther _____
5. menthol _____
6. degree _____

When a word ends in -*le*, the -*le* and the consonant before it make up a syllable, as in *han dle*.

G. Divide the following words into two syllables. Write the syllables separately on the line next to the word.

1. trample _____
2. noble _____
3. marble _____
4. stable _____
5. trouble _____
6. uncle _____

Skill: Prefixes

A **prefix** is a word part that is added to the beginning of a word to change its meaning. Ten prefixes and their meanings are given below.

Prefix	Meaning	Prefix	Meaning
bi-	having two, or happening every two times	non-	not
de-	undo	pre-	before
dis-	away or opposite of	re-	again or do over
mid-	middle	tri-	having three
mis-	wrong or badly	uni-	having one

A. Read each word below and the meaning that follows it. Then write the correct prefix on the line before each word.

1. _____ monthly — happening once every two months

2. _____ trust — to trust wrongly

3. _____ angles — shapes that have three angles

4. _____ cautions — cautions taken beforehand

5. _____ code — undo a code

6. _____ possess — to possess again

7. _____ cycle — one-wheeler that is used for riding

8. _____ connect — the opposite of connect

9. _____ fiction — not fiction

10. _____ day — the middle of the day

B. Use the correct word above to complete each sentence below.

1. The spy was able to _____ the secret message from the head of state.

2. On weekdays, we eat our _____ meal in the school cafeteria.

3. Maria Alonzo publishes a(n) _____ magazine that comes out six times a year.

4. The automobile company will _____ your car if you do not make payments on time.

5. Sarah had to _____ the CD player because the wire looked worn.

6. Geometry includes measurement of squares, _____, and circles.

7. Carla took _____ against burglary by installing an alarm in her house.

8. The acrobat in the circus rode a red _____.

9. _____ is a form of writing that deals with real people and events.

10. _____ is a natural attitude to have toward someone who lies.

Skill: Main Idea

The **main idea** often appears in the first or last sentence of a paragraph. However, the main idea can be found in any sentence in a paragraph.

To find the sentence with the main idea, you first need to read the paragraph carefully. Try to figure out what most of the sentences are about. Then look for the sentence that tells the main idea.

Each of the following paragraphs is about a different subject. Read each paragraph. Then underline the sentence that tells its main idea.

Paragraph 1

In February 1987, grave robbers dug a pit into a mud-brick platform near the village of Sipán in Peru. They found an ancient tomb and looted it of gold and silver ornaments. Scientists learned of the tomb when the robbers sold their loot. Peruvian archaeologist Walter Alva began excavating the looted tomb and others he found later. The tombs of Sipán proved to be one of the richest archaeological finds in the New World.

Paragraph 2

Africa's population includes many distinct peoples and cultures. The northern part of the continent is primarily Arabic. South of the Sahara desert, the population is predominantly black African. Not counting European languages introduced by colonists, about 1,000 different languages and distinct dialects are spoken. Most people in North Africa speak Arabic. Major languages south of the Sahara include Swahili, Amharic, Yoruba, Hausa, and Xhosa.

Paragraph 3

Edwin L. Drake drilled an oil well near Titusville, Pennsylvania, in 1859. This oil well was the first successful oil well to be drilled in our country. Using a steam-operated drill and a wooden rig, Drake struck oil at a depth of 69.5 feet (20.9 meters). His well produced approximately 10 to 35 barrels of oil a day. Soon wells were drilled in other parts of the country. The sticky black petroleum was taken to refineries, where kerosene oil was extracted from it. When the automobile came into use, the refineries began making gasoline.

Paragraph 4

Do you know the origin of the word *cereal*? The ancient Romans prayed to Ceres, the goddess of agriculture. They believed that Ceres guarded their food plants and was responsible for the growing season. Once a year, they held a festival in her honor, called the *Cerealia*. From the names of the goddess and of her festival came the word *cereal*. The word is now used to describe various kinds of grain from plants such as oats, corn, wheat, and rice.

Paragraph 5

A firefly blinks its light in the summer night. A bird migrates thousands of miles to its winter home in the South. A dolphin swims fast enough to outrace some boats. An ape uses a stick to draw out ants from an anthill that cannot be captured otherwise. Each of these animals can do something that people can do. A firefly creates light; people do the same thing with fire or with electric light bulbs. A bird can travel great distances—so can people with their airplanes or ships. A dolphin speeds through water, just as people speed through water in a motorboat. An ape makes a tool for food gathering, just as humans make tools to perform functions that they cannot do otherwise.

Skill: Main Idea—Stated or Unstated

When you read a chapter in a textbook, the **main idea** of each paragraph is often stated in a sentence. However, sometimes the main idea of a paragraph is not stated in one of the sentences. You need to use the information in the paragraph to **infer,** or figure out, the main idea. To do so, you need to ask yourself what the paragraph is about.

Read the following paragraph about deaf people interacting in a hearing world. Because the main idea is not stated, you will need to infer it.

> Deaf people do not wear signs that identify them as people who cannot hear. They function in a sound-oriented world. Sometimes, though, when others learn that someone is deaf or hearing-impaired, they scream at the deaf person. They seem to think that shouting will solve the communication problem. Others ignore deaf people's attempts to be included in conversation. They turn away lips that might be read.

Underline the phrase below that tells what this paragraph is about.

    a. methods of coping for deaf people

    b. a basic problem that deaf people encounter

    c. lessons that people need to teach each other

If you chose *b*, you are correct. The paragraph tells about a basic problem that deaf people have. The following sentence is a main idea sentence for this paragraph.

A main problem that deaf people have is the insensitivity of the hearing community.

Read the following selection about deaf individuals.

Help for Those Who Cannot Hear

1. People who are deaf have unique challenges. Unlike blind people with seeing-eye dogs or white walking sticks, deaf people do not show any outward signs that they cannot hear. Drivers may use their horns without any effect. Trains may be announced over public address systems, but people without hearing never hear the announcements. Sirens go unnoticed. Hearing people who try to communicate with those who do not hear may be cruel without meaning to be because they think that these people are not paying attention. A ringing phone, a blaring alarm clock, an oven timer going off—all these things may be meaningless to those who do not hear.

2. Many deaf individuals use lip reading as an aid in receiving information from others. Deaf people learn to watch a person talking and understand what that person is saying from mouth movements. Deaf people actively and carefully watch others' lips to "get the message." Sometimes, however, other people talk in such a way that reading their lips may be very difficult. Following a conversation between two or more other people is also difficult for a deaf person if the conversation bounces back and forth very quickly. Part of what is said gets lost because it is never seen. A person whose lips are being read may carelessly turn his or her head away. The entire process is then suddenly halted for the deaf person.

3. Signing is a two-way conversation and communication process that deaf people use. It is a language that is expressed by use of the hands. The positioning of the fingers and the movement of the hands give the meaning. Fingers and hands can spell out entire words and phrases. A single sign can also give a complete word or phrase. Signing is a good method, but it has its limitations. Signers can communicate only with other people who know how to sign. Unlike lip reading, signing does not help deaf people understand individuals who cannot sign. On the other hand, signers can often communicate where hearing people cannot—such as on a noisy bus.

4. Two important electronic devices—TTY and TDD—are available to enable deaf people to communicate over long distances. TTY stands for *Text Telephone Yoke*. TDD stands for *telephone device for the deaf*. Both devices are basically variations of the same machine. A TTY is a device that has a keyboard and a readable display. Just as a telephone links up with other telephones, a TTY links up with other TTYs. Deaf people type what they want to say, and the message comes up on someone else's readable display. The other person types a response and sends it back to the first person.

5. Deaf people used to sit in front of a television and try to figure out what was going on by watching the movements of the people and by trying to read their lips. This method was haphazard at best. Most of what happens on television is conveyed by the dialogue. Lip reading television conversations is very difficult, because the speakers often turn their backs or talk off-camera. Then closed-caption television was developed. Through the use of a decoding device, deaf people can display the dialogue in printed subtitles on their television screens so they can read what is being said. In 1992, Congress passed a law that all television sets with screens 13 inches or larger sold after July 1, 1993, must include a built-in decoding device.

6. Seeing-eye dogs are no longer the only canine aids for people with disabilities. Trained hearing-ear dogs are also now in use. These dogs are trained to respond obediently to silent hand signals. They alert their deaf owners to such sounds as doorbells, smoke alarms, crying babies, whistling teakettles, oven timers, alarm clocks, auto horns, and any unusual sounds at night. Hearing-ear dogs give their deaf owners freedom to live independently. The dogs are good companions, too.

In paragraphs, 1, 3, and 4, the main idea is stated. Underline the main idea sentence in each of these paragraphs. In paragraphs 2, 5, and 6, the main idea is unstated. For each of these paragraphs, underline one of the phrases in the list below that tells what the paragraph is about. Then write a main idea sentence on the lines provided.

Paragraph 2

  a. numbers of people who use lip reading

  b. advantages and disadvantages of lip reading

  c. how to lip read

  _____

Paragraph 5

  a. how deaf people can enjoy television

  b. getting more deaf people on TV

  c. producing television shows about deaf people

  _____

Paragraph 6

  a. the companionship provided by hearing-ear dogs

  b. the training of hearing-ear dogs

  c. how hearing-ear dogs help their owners

  _____

Skill: Reading a Health Insurance Application

Most people buy **health insurance** to help pay some of the costs for doctors, hospitals, and medicine. When choosing a health insurance policy, be sure that you understand how much coverage, or protection, it provides and how much it costs. Most importantly, be sure you answer all the questions correctly before you sign the application.

Study the part of a completed health insurance application on page 35.

A. Determine if the health insurance application asks for each of the following items of information. Write *yes* or *no* on the line next to the number of each item. For each *yes* response, find the section on the form that contains the required information. Then write the section number on the line following the item.

_____   1. the applicant's employer's address _____

_____   2. what the applicant does at his job _____

_____   3. the eye color of the applicant's child _____

_____   4. if any insurance policy has been denied to the applicant or to any of his dependents

_____

_____   5. if the applicant or any of his dependents ever made a claim for an illness _____

_____   6. whether the applicant or any of his dependents has ever been treated for a broken arm

or leg _____

_____   7. the amount of money that must accompany the application _____

_____   8. the name of the doctor who treated the applicant or any of his dependents for a

disease during the past five years _____

B. Complete each sentence using the information from the health insurance application.

1. The person applying for health insurance is _____.

2. The applicant works at the _____.

3. The applicant has _____ dependents.

4. You can tell that the applicant wishes his dependents to be covered by the health insurance policy

because _____.

5. The oldest person on the applicant's policy is _____.

APPLICATION TO: ☐ **UNITED CASUALTY COMPANY**   ☑ **VALLEY HEALTH INSURANCE COMPANY**

1. APPLICANT

(PRINT) Arthur E. Lewis	HEIGHT 5'-10"	WEIGHT 155	SEX M AGE 41

ADDRESS 120 Waverly Drive   CITY Linwood   STATE & ZIP CODE NJ 08221   BIRTH DATE 6/11/66

EMPLOYER Holiday Hotel   OCCUPATION tennis coach   DUTIES give tennis lessons

SEND PREMIUM NOTICE TO: Arthur E. Lewis   ADDRESS: 120 Waverly Drive, Linwood, NJ 08221

2. IF YOU ARE APPLYING FOR FAMILY DEPENDENTS TO BE COVERED, COMPLETE THIS SECTION.

FIRST NAME	RELATIONSHIP	BIRTH DATE	AGE	HEIGHT	WEIGHT	FIRST NAME	RELATIONSHIP	BIRTH DATE	AGE	HEIGHT	WEIGHT
Jennifer	wife	12/26/69	38	5'5"	119						
Martin	son	11/14/94	13	5'11"	138						

3. To the best of your knowledge and belief, have you or any dependent named ever made application for, or had issued, any type of insurance which has been declined, postponed, withdrawn, modified or rated up?   ☐ Yes ☑ No

4. To the best of your knowledge and belief, do you or any dependent named now carry any disability income, hospital, surgical insurance or service plan or have an application pending for such insurance or plan?   ☐ Yes ☑ No

5. To the best of your knowledge and belief, have you or any dependent named ever made a claim for, or received indemnity on account of an injury or illness? (If Yes to Questions 3, 4, or 5 complete the following.)   ☐ Yes ☑ No

Question No.	Name of Company	TYPE (Income, Hosp., etc.)	Date	Reason & Amount Paid	Person Pertaining to

6. To the best of your knowledge and belief, have you or any dependents named ever been medically treated for or medically advised for any of the following:

a) Alcoholism, epilepsy, or any nervous, mental, or emotional disorder.   ☐ Yes ☑ No

b) Abnormal blood pressure, heart attack, stroke or any other blood or circulatory disorder.   ☐ Yes ☑ No

c) Asthma, emphysema, or any other lung or respiratory disorder.   ☑ Yes ☐ No

d) Ulcer of the stomach or duodenum, rectal disorder, liver disorder, gallbladder disorder, or any other digestive disorder.   ☐ Yes ☑ No

e) Kidney disorder or any other urinary disorder, prostate disorder, or female disorder.   ☐ Yes ☑ No

f) Thyroid disorder, diabetes, gout, or any eye or ear disorder.   ☐ Yes ☑ No

g) Arthritis, rheumatism, any disorder of the back, spine, bones, muscles, or joints.   ☐ Yes ☑ No

h) Cancer, tumor, growth, or any skin disorder   ☐ Yes ☑ No

7. To the best of your knowledge and belief, have you or any dependents named, been a user of marijuana, amphetamines, barbiturates, hallucinogens, or narcotics, except upon a physician's prescription?   ☐ Yes ☑ No

8. To the best of your knowledge and belief, have you or any dependent named had medical or surgical advice or treatment, or been hospital confined during the past 5 years, other than admitted in answer to question 6?   ☐ Yes ☑ No

9. To the best of your knowledge and belief, have you or any dependent named ever had any physical impairment, deformity or disease during the past 5 years other than admitted in question 6? (If Yes to question 6 a-h, 7, 8, or 9 complete the following.)   ☐ Yes ☑ No

Question No.	First Name	Med. Condition	Dates	Results	Doctors or Hospitals
6C	Martin	asthma	since 2004	on medication	Dr. Sherman

10. If you are applying for disability income protection complete the following.

What portion of your average monthly earnings does the disability indemnity under all policies you have or are applying for represent?   ☐ Less than 50%   ☐ 50% to 66 $^2/3$%   ☐ More than 66 $^2/3$%

I understand and agree that no coverage shall be in force unless the policy is issued, and if issued, that coverage will be in force as of the effective date shown on the issued policy. Dated 1/6/08 At Valley Health-Linwood office

Signature of applicant X   *Arthur E. Lewis*

I hereby certify that information supplied me by the applicant has been truly and accurately recorded hereon.

Agent or Broker *Maria Soto*   code 6247009

CHECK OR CURRENCY MUST ACCOMPANY APPLICATIONS

Time Future, Time Past

LESSON 10

Skill: Plot

BACKGROUND INFORMATION

"Ask MIKE" is about a high school senior who wishes that someone else would make his decisions for him. The last year of high school has always been potentially stressful for students. Many important decisions must be made, including whether to get a full-time job, work part-time and continue school, or apply to a four-year college.

SKILL FOCUS: Plot

Plot is the plan of action or the series of events that an author uses in a story. The plot in most stories follows a basic pattern consisting of five parts. These are the **beginning**, the **rising action**, the **climax**, the **falling action**, and the **conclusion**. They are shown in the diagram below.

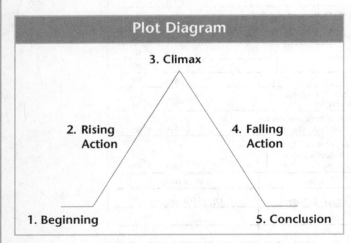

Plot Diagram

3. Climax
2. Rising Action
4. Falling Action
1. Beginning
5. Conclusion

Sometimes an author gives clues about events that will happen in the plot. This technique is called **foreshadowing**.

The questions below will help you understand plot.

- What are the main events in the story's plot?
- Does the author hint at an event before it occurs in the story? If so, which event?
- Is the story's conclusion expected or unexpected?

▶ Read the following passage. The dialogue foreshadows an event that is likely to happen later. On the lines, write what you think might happen.

"I've always been afraid of spiders," laughed Carl, "but I don't imagine we'll find any around here." "Probably not!" answered Peter.

_____

_____

CONTEXT CLUES: Definitions

Sometimes the meaning of a new word is made clear by a **definition** that is found in the same or next sentence. Read the sentences below. Look for the definition that explains the underlined word.

Nothing about my life these days seemed to be __synchronized__ with anything else. Nothing runs at the same time.

If you don't know the meaning of the word *synchronized*, read on. The next sentence explains that *synchronized* means "running at the same time."

▶ Read the sentences below. Circle the words that provide a definition for the underlined word.

The voice startled me. It was calm and reassuring, and it __emanated__ from the computer. The voice came out of the computer!

In "Ask MIKE," look for the underlined words *procrastinating*, *anteroom*, and *genial*. Find words or phrases that provide definitions to figure out the words' meanings.

> **Strategy Tip**
>
> As you read, "Ask MIKE," look for the five parts of a plot pattern. Pay special attention to the twist in the story's ending.

Ask MIKE

I was ready to give up. I'd been curled up on the canvas sling chair in my room for so long that my knees felt permanently locked into position. I was becoming increasingly aware that, for the past half hour, I'd been staring at a nearly microscopic speck on the ceiling. Nothing about my life these days seemed to be synchronized. Nothing was running at the same time with anything else. I was in my last year in high school, the deadline for college applications was approaching, and I still hadn't decided about going on to college.

"Frank! Still <u>procrastinating</u>, putting off finishing your applications? You can't do that forever!" My mother had caught me wasting time again.

"I just wish I had a computer that was programmed to make all the important decisions for me!"

Mom wasn't impressed—I could tell. "Would you be satisfied with a decision that was made for you? I wouldn't want a machine to control everything in my life. Looks like you need more time to contemplate your future—by yourself." With that, she left me alone.

I surveyed the piles of college brochures around my room. Halfheartedly, I sat down with an application and stared at the first question: Why do you wish to attend Appleton University?

Before long, I was staring at that speck on the ceiling again. Suddenly, the speck grew larger and began to change color. Soon it turned into a pinwheel of spiraling colors, pulling me into its center with the force of a whirlpool. The next thing I knew, I was in a brightly lit and immaculate <u>anteroom</u>, a reception area, filled with waiting teenagers.

By the door, a man was stationed at a touch-screen display terminal. I cautiously approached him.

"Name?" he inquired pleasantly when he saw me.

"Frank Olsen," I responded.

He attempted to scroll it up on the computer display, as if my name should be in the records.

"Don't see it here. Are you sure you have the date right—November 12, 2108?"

I gasped—"2108? I've just lost an entire century! Where am I?"

"Well, young man," he said snappishly, "right now you're in the Life Determination Resources Center." He continued. Now let me see. Olsen . . . Olsen . . . I don't have you here, but I think MIKE—the Micro Interviewer for Career Evaluation—could see you in a few moments. Have a seat."

I sat down and watched as one student after another entered a room and came out a few minutes later, smiling contentedly.

The next instant, my name was called. I found myself entering the room. I was alone in the hushed atmosphere, except for a computer terminal that faced me.

"Mr. Olsen, sit down please."

The voice completely startled me. It was calm and reassuring, and emanated from the computer.

"It will take just a few nanoseconds—ah, yes—here we are. Sorry for the delay, but a hundred years is a bit out of the ordinary."

I nodded dumbly.

"My clients call me MIKE," the computer continued in its genial, friendly tone. "We're here to determine your future. Let's see . . . math four years . . . science-fair winner . . . mmm . . . very admirable, if a bit dated. You tinker with motorcycles and once fixed your parents' dishwasher. All right. Now let's see what's available for you. Yes. You'll study microelectronics at Future Tech for two years, then take a position as a robotic repair technician. In seven years, you'll be earning enough to support a family, and you'll be allowed to take out a marriage license. At that time, SAM—that's an acronym for Standardized Acquisition of Mate—will find you a suitable mate."

I began to stammer. "I don't . . . ."

The computer interrupted. "Is there a problem? Perhaps your file is incorrect—a human error during input, of course."

I interrupted. "I don't want to be a technician, and I'm not interested in robotics—at least, not now. I might want to be something else—maybe a construction engineer! I had been thinking of graduating from a four-year college. . . ."

"That's impossible," MIKE interrupted. "Technicians do not require four years of school. As for engineering, we cannot have an excess of workers in any field. We don't need any more engineers. You must understand that, in your day, people made all their own life decisions and all their own mistakes. Some people were unemployed because they were trained in fields with no future. In other areas, jobs went begging for workers. People married for all the wrong reasons, and the divorce rate skyrocketed. We have figured out these problems by removing human error from the decision-making process."

"But I don't know if I even want to be a technician," I repeated, "and I certainly don't want a computer choosing a wife for me!"

"Oh, we do very well in that regard. It takes all the tension and stress out of dating."

I was getting increasingly more upset.

"There is no further recourse," MIKE said. The light blinked, and the room grew dimmer. "Your appointment time is up. Your life decisions have been made in their entirety."

"Wait!" I screeched. "I don't want a computer to control my life!"

Suddenly, I found myself back in my room. I realized that I had just experienced a bad dream. In my panic, I had knocked over a pile of college brochures. On top of the pile was a catalog for Future Tech. Perhaps I'd take a two-year course; perhaps not. It was a possibility to think about. As I started to contemplate the decisions that I had to make, the phone rang.

"Hello," I said.

"Is this Frank Olsen?" the caller inquired.

"Yes, it is."

"Well, congratulations, Frank. You're the lucky winner of our new personal decision-making microcomputer. It will be delivered tomorrow. We know you will enjoy letting the computer make your decisions for you. Congratulations, Frank!"

"No, no, I don't want it," I responded, but before I finished, the caller hung up. When the microcomputer was delivered the next day, no one could understand why I would not accept it.

1. a. Where does the story begin?

_____

b. Where does the action move to?

_____

2. a. Who is the narrator of the story?

_____

b. Is the narrator a participant in the events or an outside observer?

_____

c. From which point of view is the story told— first person or third person?

_____

3. Explain why Frank wishes he had a computer to make important decisions for him.

_____

4. Complete each sentence with the correct word.

genial   anteroom   procrastinating

a. It's time to stop _____ and finish your assignment.

b. Visitors are met in the _____ and then escorted into the office.

c. Jessica is a warmhearted and _____ friend.

CRITICAL THINKING

1. a. Circle two words below that best describe Frank's character in the beginning of the story.
undecided   procrastinating   forceful

b. Circle two words below that best describe Frank's character after his dream.
decisive   carefree   determined

c. Is Frank a static or a dynamic character? Explain.

_____

_____

2. Explain why Frank decides he'd rather not have MIKE make his career decisions.

_____

_____

3. Contrast the way Frank and the others respond to MIKE.

_____

_____

4. Infer why some people might like having MIKE make their decisions.

_____

_____

5. Does Frank understand why he must make his own decisions about college? Explain.

_____

1. On the diagram below, identify the five parts of the plot structure. Then fill in the letter of the appropriate event from the list below.

3. _____ _____

2. _____ _____   4. _____ _____

1. _____ _____   5. _____ _____

   a. Frank wishes that a programmed computer would make all his important decisions.

   b. Upset when the computer makes decisions that affect his future, Frank decides he doesn't want a computer to control his life.

   c. Frank doesn't accept the microcomputer when it's delivered.

   d. Frank wakes up from his dream, only to learn that he has won his own personal decision-making computer.

   e. In the Life Determination Resources Center, MIKE makes decisions for Frank: Frank will go to the Future Tech for two years, and a suitable mate will be selected for him seven years later.

2. **a.** Which event does the author hint at before it occurs in the story?

   _____

   b. Go back to the story and circle the statement that foreshadows this event.

3. Is the story's conclusion expected or unexpected? Explain.

   _____

   _____

4. Here are some sentences from a very short story. In this story, one event foreshadows another that occurs later in the story. Circle the letter of the foreshadowing event. Then, on the lines below, rewrite the story so that the ending is unexpected.

   a. Junior forgot to feed the dog and to put it outside.

   b. "Dinner time!" sang Mrs. Carson.

   c. While the Carsons ate their dinner, the dog enjoyed their dessert—the ice cream cake.

   d. Junior is grounded and will have no desserts for a week.

   _____

   _____

Reading-Writing Connection

On a separate sheet of paper, write a persuasive paragraph for or against using a computerized program to help you make decisions.

Skill: Cause and Effect

BACKGROUND INFORMATION

"The Ancient Ones" tells about the Anasazi, ancestors of the modern Pueblo Native Americans, who once inhabited parts of the American Southwest. The archeological sites in Mesa Verde National Park preserve the culture of these people, who built cliff dwellings and villages in the canyon walls, where they lived for centuries before vanishing mysteriously.

SKILL FOCUS: Cause and Effect

A **cause** is an underlying reason, condition, or situation that makes an event happen. An **effect** is the result, or outcome, of a cause. Sometimes a cause brings about an effect that, in turn, becomes the cause of another effect. This results in a chain of causes and effects.

For example, rain might be the cause that creates a flood. The flood is the effect. In turn, the flood may cause people to lose their homes. The flood has become the cause, with the effect now being the homeless victims. As you read, look for cause-and-effect relationships to help you understand not only what happens but also why it happens.

▌ Read the paragraph below. Then determine the cause-and-effect relationships. Write the chain of events in the boxes.

Stones heated in a fire were dropped into a basket containing water and food. The hot stones made the water boil, which then cooked the food. However, this method was slow and often cooked the food unevenly.

CONTEXT CLUES: Appositive Phrases

Sometimes the meaning of a new word is made clear by a phrase that follows it. This is called an **appositive phrase**. It is usually set apart by commas and may start with the word *or*.

Read the sentence below. Look for an appositive phrase that helps explain the underlined word.

Wetherill had discovered cliff __dwellings__, or homes, built by people who had vanished from the area more than 500 years earlier.

The appositive phrase *or homes* explains what *dwellings* are.

▌ Read the sentence below. Circle the appositive phrase that defines the underlined word.

As more land was cleared for fields, hunters had to search farther for __game__, or animals to hunt.

In "The Ancient Ones," the words *nomads*, *foraged*, and *alcoves* are underlined. As you read, look for appositive phrases that can help you figure out the meanings of these words.

Strategy Tip

As you read "The Ancient Ones," try to understand how ideas are connected. When you think about causes of particular actions, think about their effects. Also think about how some of these effects become causes that result in other effects.

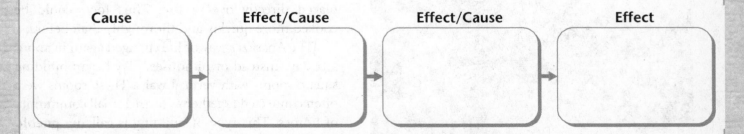

Cause	Effect/Cause	Effect/Cause	Effect

THE ANCIENT ONES

One cold winter day in 1888, Colorado rancher Richard Wetherill was trying to find some cattle that had strayed. As he stood on the rim of Mesa Verde and looked at the canyon wall on the opposite side, he spotted what seemed to be the ruins of an ancient town. Wetherill had discovered cliff dwellings, or homes, built by people who had vanished from the area more than 500 years earlier.

Who were these ancient people? What were their lives like? Why did they build their towns high on cliff walls? Why did they abandon their homes?

The First Settlers

The earliest Americans living in the Southwest were <u>nomads</u>, people who had no permanent homes. They moved from place to place as they hunted animals and <u>foraged</u>, or searched, for food. Then almost 2,000 years ago, these nomadic people learned how to grow corn and squash, and their way of life changed. Although they still hunted, they could now settle in one place with a reliable supply of food.

The Cliff Palace at Mesa Verde National Park in Colorado is the largest Anasazi pueblo ruin in North America. It has 217 rooms and 23 kivas.

One group of people settled in what is today the Four Corners region of southern Colorado. The region is named Four Corners because Colorado, Arizona, New Mexico, and Utah meet there. No one knows what these early people called themselves. Today we call them the **Anasazi** (a nə SAH zee), from a Navajo word meaning "the ancient ones."

Changing Ways of Life

When the Anasazi first settled in the Four Corners region, small family groups lived in rock <u>alcoves</u>, or shallow recesses. Because these early settlers made finely crafted baskets, archaeologists named them the Basket Makers. The tightly woven baskets were used for carrying and storing food and water and even for cooking. Stones heated in a fire were dropped into a basket containing water and food. The hot stones made the water boil, which then cooked the food. However, this method was slow and often cooked the food unevenly.

About A.D. 550, some Anasazi moved to Mesa Verde. There they began to build permanent houses. Archaeologists call these structures **pithouses** because the floors were formed by digging shallow pits in the ground. The sloping walls and the roof were made of wooden poles covered with mud. Archaeologists have found the remains of several pithouses close together.

Another important change during this time was that the people learned to make pottery. Clay pots and bowls improved the way food was cooked. Unlike baskets, which burn, clay containers could be placed directly over a fire. Thus food could be cooked more quickly and thoroughly than before.

The Anasazi's way of life changed again in about A.D. 750. Instead of pithouses, they began building square rooms with vertical walls. These rooms were often connected together to form a small community of homes. This type of building is called a **pueblo** (PWEB loh), from the Spanish word for "village."

Pueblos at Mesa Verde were constructed on top of the mesa. A mesa is a raised, flat land form often found in the Southwest. The walls and roofs were built from wooden posts covered with **adobe** (ə DOH bee), which is sun-dried mud. Some buildings had a row of stones around the base. Later the Anasazi built the entire walls of stone, which made the buildings sturdier and more permanent.

In about 1100, small villages began to join together to form large towns. Pueblos were built with many connected rooms used for sleeping, storage, and social gatherings. The people stored water in ditches and reservoirs for drier times.

In front of each pueblo was a single room dug into the ground, much like the earlier pithouses. This room, called a **kiva** (KEE və), was used for community meetings and religious ceremonies. People would gather in the kiva to conduct healing ceremonies and to pray for rain, a good harvest, and success in hunting.

Between 1150 and 1200, the Anasazi began building their pueblos in large alcoves in the canyon walls. Many pueblos consisted of hundreds of rooms built in rows on top of one another. The roof of one room formed a porch for the room above it. The families who lived in the upper rooms had to climb ladders to reach them.

This keyhole kiva, found near the Balcony House at Mesa Verde, is typical of the kivas that the Anasazi built for meetings and ceremonies.

In the canyon alcoves, the cliff ledges offered protection against the weather. Pueblos were often built on south-facing cliff walls. During the summer, when the sun is higher in the sky, the cliff's shadow helped keep the buildings cool. In the winter, when the sun is lower in the sky, its light would strike the buildings directly and keep them warmer.

A major disadvantage of the cliff pueblos was that the people had to climb up and down the steep cliff walls to tend their fields on the mesa top and in the canyon below. Perhaps, some archaeologists suggest, the Anasazi moved to the cliffs because pueblos there would be easier to defend in case of an enemy attack. During their final years at Mesa Verde, the Anasazi began to build towers, which may have been used for sending signals or watching for approaching enemies.

Daily Life

The Anasazi planted and tended fields of corn, squash, and beans. They gathered wild plants—roots, berries, nuts, seeds, and fruits—and hunted deer, rabbits, and other animals. They also raised turkeys, but not for food. Instead, the feathers were wrapped around fibers used to weave warm robes and blankets for the chilly nights and cold winters.

Animal skins also provided coverings. Fibers from the yucca plant were twisted into cords to make baskets, sandals, ropes, and snares for catching small animals.

Although some tasks, such as harvesting crops, were shared by all the people, men and women generally had different roles in Anasazi society. Women were responsible for preparing and cooking food. They made cornmeal by grinding dried corn with a hand-held stone called a **mano** (MAH noh) against a flat stone slab called a **metate** (mə TAHT ee). Some Pueblo Indians of today still grind corn in this way. The coarse cornmeal was mixed with water and baked in flat cakes on a stone griddle or formed into small balls and boiled in soups or stews. Beans and squash were cooked alone or with meat. Foods were flavored with salt and wild plants.

Women also cared for the young children. Babies were tucked snugly into cradleboards that their mothers wore on their backs or propped up nearby as they worked. Girls learned how to prepare food, weave baskets, and make clothing, while boys practiced hunting with smaller versions of the men's bows and arrows.

Men were responsible for clearing land and building houses and other structures. They cut logs with stone axes to make wooden supports for floors and roofs. The axes were also used to chip large sandstone chunks into rectangular blocks for building.

Desperate Times

By the 1200s, several thousand Anasazi were living in the cliff pueblos of Mesa Verde. All the available land was being used to grow crops, and nutrients in the soil were becoming depleted, or used up. As more land was cleared for fields, hunters had to search farther for game, or animals to hunt. It was also more difficult to find wood to use for building and fuel.

In 1276, a disastrous 23-year period of drought began. Year after year, crops failed because there was not enough rain. The climate also became cooler, which made the growing season shorter. Skeletons unearthed at Mesa Verde show evidence of malnutrition among the Anasazi people. Conflicts also arose as people competed for scarce food. As conditions worsened, groups of people began to move away. Some pueblos seemed to have been abandoned suddenly, with pots, baskets, and tools simply left behind. By the time the drought finally ended, no Anasazi remained at Mesa Verde.

What Happened to the Anasazi?

When they abandoned their pueblos at Mesa Verde and other locations in the Four Corners region, the Anasazi moved south and east. Some groups settled along the Rio Grande in what is today northern New Mexico. Other groups joined the Hopi, Zuni, and Tewa peoples of Arizona and western New Mexico.

As the Anasazi merged with other peoples, they lost many of their old customs and adopted new ones. The present-day Pueblo Indians of the American Southwest are descendants of the Anasazi. However, it is difficult to tell which of their traditions are derived from the Anasazi and which are derived from other cultures.

Mesa Verde Today

After Wetherill discovered the Mesa Verde cliff pueblos, many people worked to convince the U.S. government to protect the ruins. Finally in June 1906, President Theodore Roosevelt signed a bill establishing Mesa Verde as a national park. Today more than 600,000 visitors tour the ruins every year. Mesa Verde is one of the only national parks in the United States created specifically to preserve the works of an ancient people. This park is a monument to the skill of the Anasazi who built this early, authentically American architecture.

COMPREHENSION

1. Match each word in the left column with a description in the right column.

___ adobe

___ pueblo

___ mano

___ kiva

a. handheld stone used to grind corn

b. community of connected homes

c. underground room used for meetings and ceremonies

d. sun-dried mud

2. Number the following events in the order in which they occurred.

_____ **a.** Small villages on top of the mesa joined to form large towns.

_____ **b.** Small family groups lived in rock alcoves.

_____ **c.** The Anasazi built their pueblos in large alcoves in the canyon walls.

_____ **d.** The Anasazi built connected houses with square rooms and vertical walls.

_____ **e.** The Anasazi built permanent pithouses on top of the mesa.

3. Reread the paragraph with an ✗ next to it. Underline the sentence that states the main idea.

4. For each sentence that follows, fill in the circle with the correct meaning of the underlined word.

   a. Desert <u>nomads</u> herd their sheep and goats to find grass and water.

      ○ people who raise crops

      ○ people who move from place to place

      ○ people who eat meat

      ○ people who stay in one place

   b. The bear <u>foraged</u> for berries as it roamed the forest.

      ○ searched   ○ competed

      ○ dug down   ○ found

   c. <u>Alcoves</u> near the main entrance held statues of the library's founders.

      ○ shallow recesses   ○ hallways

      ○ platforms   ○ deep caves

CRITICAL THINKING

1. Identify each of the following statements as fact or opinion. Write *F* or *O* on the line.

   _____ a. The Anasazi built cliff pueblos to escape enemy attacks.

   _____ b. Pueblos in south-facing cliff walls were cooler in the summer and warmer in the winter.

   _____ c. More than 600,000 people visit Mesa Verde National Park every year.

   _____ d. Too many people visit Mesa Verde National Park every year.

2. Explain why there were different activities for Anasazi girls and Anasazi boys.

   _____

   _____

3. Reread the paragraph with a ✔ next to it. Write a sentence describing its main idea.

   _____

   _____

SKILL FOCUS: CAUSE AND EFFECT

A. Use the items listed below to complete the cause-and-effect chains on the next page.

   • Food became scarce.

   • All the available land was being used to grow crops.

   • The Anasazi abandoned Mesa Verde.

   • The growing season became shorter.

   • A 23-year drought began.

   • People suffered from malnutrition.

   • Nutrients in the soil were being depleted.

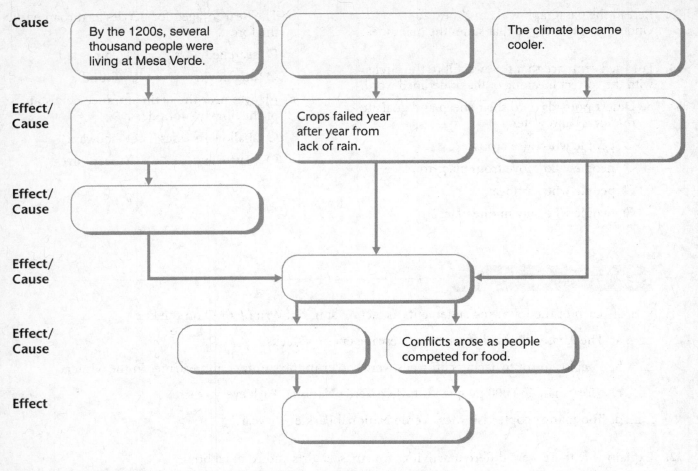

Cause

By the 1200s, several thousand people were living at Mesa Verde.

The climate became cooler.

Effect/ Cause

Crops failed year after year from lack of rain.

Effect/ Cause

Effect/ Cause

Effect/ Cause

Conflicts arose as people competed for food.

Effect

B. Answer the following questions by inferring a cause or an effect.

1. Why did the Anasazi leave belongings behind when they abandoned their pueblos?

_____

_____

_____

2. How did making Mesa Verde a national park help protect the ruins?

_____

_____

_____

Reading-Writing Connection

Which parts of the Anasazi culture would you like to learn more about? On a separate sheet of paper, make a list. Tell why you are interested in each part of the culture.

Skill: Reading a Diagram

BACKGROUND INFORMATION

"The Electromagnetic Spectrum" is about electromagnetic radiation that surrounds us. Except for visible light, humans cannot see this radiation. There are different kinds of radiation, including microwaves, radar, infrared, visible radiation, ultraviolet, X-rays, and gamma rays. The theory of electromagnetic radiation originated in the 1860s with the Scottish physicist James Clerk Maxwell. His theory united the phenomena of electricity, magnetism, and light.

SKILL FOCUS: Reading a Diagram

Textbooks often contain **diagrams** to show what is being explained. A diagram can help you visualize this scientific material. Read a diagram's **captions** and then its **labels** for important information.

Follow these steps for reading text with diagrams.

1. Read the paragraph before each diagram. Then study the diagram. Be sure to read the labels and caption. Then read the paragraph after the diagram, which may also explain what is pictured.

2. Read the rest of the selection. Look back at the diagrams whenever you think they will help you.

3. After reading, look away from the text. Try to picture what you have read and the details in the diagrams. Read the material again, if necessary.

4. Follow this method until you understand all the ideas in the selection.

▶ Read the paragraph below and study the diagram in the next column. Then use both to answer the question below the paragraph.

Electromagnetic radiation from space reaches Earth's surface at only a few wavelengths, such as radio frequencies and the visible spectrum. At higher altitudes, more kinds of electromagnetic radiation can be observed. Some microwave radiation can be observed from mountaintops.

Which three kinds of radiation from space are visible at altitudes above 20 kilometers?

_____

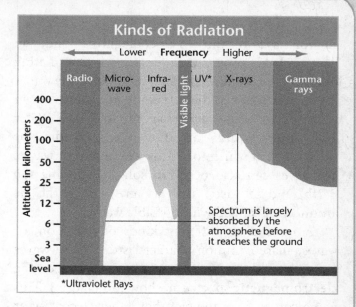

Kinds of Radiation

←— Lower **Frequency** Higher —→

Radio | Micro-wave | Infra-red | Visible light | UV* | X-rays | Gamma rays

Altitude in kilometers
400
200
100
50
25
12
6
3
Sea level

Spectrum is largely absorbed by the atmosphere before it reaches the ground

*Ultraviolet Rays

CONTEXT CLUES: Definitions

Sometimes the meaning of a word is made clear by a **definition** that is found in the next sentence. Read the sentences below. Look for the definition that explains the underlined word.

*This movement forms **alternating** crests and troughs. Alternating means "one coming after the other."*

Based on the definition in the second sentence, you know that the movement forms crests and troughs that come one after the other.

▶ Read the sentences below. Circle the definition that explains the underlined word.

*If you have ever thrown a pebble into a pond, you have probably observed **ripples** radiating out from the point where the rock entered the water. Ripples are waves.*

In "The Electromagnetic Spectrum," use definition context clues for the underlined words *emitted, potentially,* and *modulated.*

Strategy Tip

While reading "The Electromagnetic Spectrum," study the diagrams, including the captions and labels.

The Electromagnetic Spectrum

If you have ever thrown a pebble into a pond, you have probably observed ripples, or waves, radiating out from the point where the rock entered the water. If you ever watched the tide come in, you have seen wave after wave of water crash onto the beach. Water and other liquids are the easiest media, or substances, in which to see the movement of waves. Yet waves can also occur in solids, including the Earth, and in gases, such as air. In fact, the air around you is filled with invisible waves.

A number of different kinds of radiation, or waves, share common characteristics. These waves are grouped together in what is called the **electromagnetic spectrum**, shown in Figure 1. This name comes from the fact that either electricity or magnetism can produce these waves. The waves of the electromagnetic spectrum include radio waves, television waves, light, and X-rays.

Characteristics of Waves

One characteristic of electromagnetic radiation is that all these waves travel at the same speed—about 300,000 kilometers (186,420 miles) per second, which is the speed of light.

All waves in the electromagnetic spectrum share another characteristic: They are **transverse** waves. If you have ever watched a bottle bob up and down in

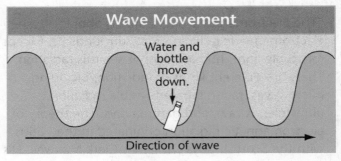

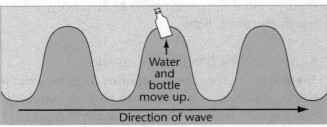

FIGURE 2. The water and the bottle move up and down as the wave moves from left to right.

water, you have watched transverse waves in action. The bottle goes up and down at right angles to the movement of the wave over the surface of the water. See Figure 2. As the energy of the wave passes through a medium, or substance, the medium moves up and down perpendicular to the wave movement. This movement forms alternating crests and troughs. *Alternating* means "one coming after the other." The crests are formed by the upward movement of the water, and the troughs are formed by the downward movement of the water. The distance from the crest of one wave to that of the next wave is called the **wavelength**. See Figure 3 on the next page.

The radiations, or waves, in the electromagnetic spectrum share some characteristics with all other waves. For example, different types of waves have different wavelengths. **Frequency** is the number of complete wavelengths that pass a given point in a specific amount of time. Frequency is measured in **hertz**, abbreviated Hz. One hertz is the passage of one complete wavelength per second. If a wave has a frequency of 1,000 Hz, then 1,000

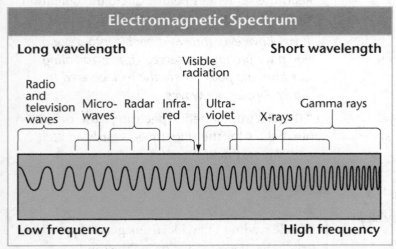

FIGURE 1. The electromagnetic spectrum includes many forms of radiation, or waves.

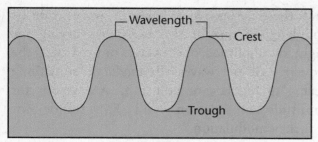

FIGURE 3. **A wavelength is measured from crest to crest.**

wavelengths pass a given point every second. The frequency of sound waves is also measured in hertz.

The frequency and the wavelength of a wave have an **inverse** relationship. The higher the frequency of a wave, the shorter its wavelength is, and vice versa. If, for example, the frequency is doubled, the wavelength is cut in half. The reverse is also true: The lower the frequency of a wave, the longer its wavelength is.

Types of Radiation

The shortest waves in the electromagnetic spectrum are **gamma rays**, which are <u>emitted</u> by the nuclei of certain atoms. *Emitted* means "given out." Because their wavelengths are so short, gamma rays have a very high frequency. They are so powerful that they can travel through 60 centimeters of concrete or 30 centimeters of steel. They can also pass through the bones and tissues of living organisms, which makes gamma rays <u>potentially</u> dangerous. *Potentially* means "having the possibility of doing or being something." Under controlled conditions, however, gamma rays can be used for the medical purpose of killing cancer tissue because this tissue is destroyed more easily than healthy tissues.

The next most powerful type of electromagnetic radiation are **X-rays**. These waves are produced when high-speed electrons strike a heavy metal, such as tungsten. X-rays can penetrate soft body tissues, but they do not pass through bones and teeth. As a result, when an X-ray picture is taken of the human body, the bones and teeth form a shadow on the film. Although X-rays can be very useful, they can, like gamma rays, be dangerous. People who work around X-rays often wear protective clothing, including lead aprons, to protect their bodies from this radiation.

Ultraviolet waves can cause sunburn. They can also be used to sterilize materials and to preserve food. Scientists can figure out the composition of certain rocks and minerals that glow when placed under ultraviolet light. There is evidence that certain insects have sense receptors for detecting ultraviolet light.

Visible light is the portion of the electromagnetic spectrum whose waves produce the colors that humans can detect. Visible light forms a spectrum of color from red to violet. See Figure 4. Humans see these colors because their eyes have special receptors that are sensitive to this part of the electromagnetic spectrum. Because visible light waves have less energy than other waves in the spectrum, they are not dangerous.

Infrared radiation is made up of waves that carry heat. Most substances produce infrared waves, but hot objects produce more of these waves than do cold objects. One useful application of infrared radiation is heat-efficiency studies of houses. A picture can be taken of a house on film that is sensitive to infrared rays. The result is a picture showing the various temperatures of the structure, thereby identifying areas of heat loss.

Microwaves are used in radar to determine the speed and location of a distant object. They are also produced by microwave ovens to cook food and by transmitters that send messages between the Earth and space. Satellite broadcasts of television programs are, in part, made possible by microwaves.

Television and radio transmissions also depend on radiation in the electromagnetic spectrum. Radio and television waves are among the longest waves in the spectrum. When you set a television or radio to a channel or station, you set that device's

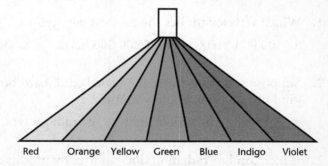

Red Orange Yellow Green Blue Indigo Violet

FIGURE 4. **Visible light forms a spectrum of color from red to violet.**

tuner to pick up only certain wave frequencies. These waves carry the sound and picture signals from the selected station.

The waves used in communication, such as radio and television broadcasts, are coded before they are transmitted. You may know that radio stations are either AM or FM, but do you know what these letters mean? Radio waves can be modulated in one of two ways: by varying the height, or amplitude, of the waves or by varying the frequency of the waves. To *modulate* something means "to regulate or adjust it." AM stands for amplitude modulation, and FM stands for frequency modulation.

COMPREHENSION

1. Identify four types of radiation in the electromagnetic spectrum.

   _____

   _____

   _____

2. Describe two characteristics that all forms of electromagnetic radiation share.

   _____

   _____

3. What does the word *frequency* mean when applied to radiation? What unit is used to measure it?

   _____

   _____

   _____

4. Explain the relationship between a wave's frequency and its energy.

   _____

   _____

5. If the length of a wave is doubled, what happens to its frequency?

   _____

   _____

6. Draw a line to match each word with its meaning.

   emitted   **a.** adjusted

   potentially   **b.** given out

   modulated   **c.** having the possibility of
                          doing or being something

CRITICAL THINKING

Circle the letter next to each correct answer.

1. Which wavelength has the greatest energy?

   a. 100,000 hertz   **b.** 1,000,000 hertz   **c.** 5,000,000 hertz   **d.** 50,000,000 hertz

2. Suppose you want to see if a sealed cardboard box contained a hard metal object. Which kind of radiation would you use?

   a. X-rays   **b.** visible light   **c.** radio waves   **d.** sound waves

3. Which kind of radiation does your body produce?

   a. visible light   **b.** infrared radiation   **c.** ultraviolet light   **d.** gamma rays

4. The frequency of a wave 2 meters long is 10,000 hertz. If the wave's frequency is reduced to 5,000 hertz, what is its wavelength?

    a. 1 meter   **b.** 2 meters   **c.** 3 meters   **d.** 4 meters

SKILL FOCUS: READING A DIAGRAM

Use Figure 1 to answer questions 1-4.

1. Briefly describe Figure 1 in your own words.

_____

_____

2. Visible light is at about the center of the electromagnetic spectrum. On which side of visible light are the types of radiation with the lower amounts of energy? _____

3. Which has a longer wavelength, visible light or gamma rays? _____

4. Which has more energy, visible light or radio waves? _____

5. Explain how X-rays are used to take X-ray pictures of the body.

_____

_____

6. Explain Figure 2 in your own words.

_____

_____

7. Explain Figure 3 in your own words.

_____

_____

8. Explain Figure 4 in your own words.

_____

_____

Reading-Writing Connection

On a separate sheet of paper, write a letter to a friend in which you explain what you do to protect yourself from ultraviolet light.

Skill: Word Problems

BACKGROUND INFORMATION

"Completing and Solving Word Problems" discusses the kind of mathematics that you come across in everyday life. In real life, the questions arise naturally from the situation. For example, if your bus leaves at 5:30 P.M., and it is now 3:00 P.M., you automatically figure out how long you must wait for the bus. Without realizing it, you have created and solved the math equation $X = B - T$, in which X is how long you must wait, B is the time the bus leaves, and T is the present time.

SKILL FOCUS: Word Problems

The following five steps will help you complete and solve **word problems**.

1. **Read the problem.** Sometimes the problem does not contain a question or a direction. In that case, you need to determine the problem yourself. To do this, you need to understand the information. Picture the information in your mind. Then read the problem again to be sure you know how the various facts are related.

2. **Decide on a question to ask about the facts, and decide how to answer the question.** To do this, you must look at the different pieces of information and decide what you need to find out to solve the problem. Write a sentence about each fact, and look for information that has not been given but that you can find by using the information that is given. Write a question about the missing information that logically connects the facts. Then decide which operation is necessary to answer your question. Write one or two equations that describe the operation.

3. **Estimate the answer.** This is one way to be sure that the question can be answered.

4. **Carry out the plan.** Solve the equation.

5. **Reread the problem and your question.** Is the answer logical? Is it close to your estimate?

▶ Find the answer to this real-life word problem. Explain your steps on the lines.

It is 7 P.M. when you call your cousin, but she says it is 5 P.M. You know that she lives to the west of you in a different time zone. If there is a one-hour difference in time from one time zone to the next moving west, how many time zones away from you does your cousin live?

_____

_____

_____

_____

WORD CLUES

The word problems in "Completing and Solving Word Problems" are about time zones. A *time zone* is a region in which all cities and towns operate on the same time standard. Before time zones were used, each city operated under its own time, based on the position of the sun in the sky. Now the Earth has 24 different time zones. Traveling from west to east, each time zone becomes later than the previous time zone.

> ### Strategy Tip
>
> In reading the problem situation in "Completing and Solving Word Problems," you need to picture a real-life situation in your mind and think of a logical question to answer. After you have decided on the question, you can solve the problem.

Completing and Solving Word Problems

As you travel across a country as large as the United States, you pass from one **time zone** to another. When you make a long-distance telephone call, you may also find that the person you are calling is in a different time zone. The change in time from one place to another across the globe results in many different problems.

When you read a set of information, you must first determine the fact that you want to find from the information given and then how to find it. In other words, you make up a question before you solve the problem. The answer to the problem gives you the missing fact.

Use the following five steps to complete a problem and to solve it.

1. Read the problem.
2. Decide on a question to ask about the facts, and decide how to find the answer.
3. Estimate the answer.
4. Carry out the plan.
5. Reread the problem and your question.

Read the Problem

Time zones are related to longitude. Each time zone is made up of a number of degrees of longitude. Longitude is measured from 0 degrees in Greenwich, England, to 180 degrees on the opposite side of the Earth. It is measured in both directions—east and west. It takes 24 hours for the Earth to complete one rotation.

Carefully read this information. Many practical problems concerning time zones are related to the basic facts in this description of longitude and the rotation of the Earth. One question that you could ask is what is the average number of degrees that the Earth rotates in one hour of time?

Decide on a Question to Ask and How to Find the Answer

You must decide what information to use and how to use it to get the answer. The problem gives

you information about longitude and about the number of hours that the Earth takes to rotate. It may help to write the facts that include numbers as individual sentences.

1. The Earth is divided into longitude lines that cover 180° east and 180° west.
2. There are 24 hours in one day.

You also know that each time zone contains a number of degrees of longitude, although no exact figures are given. Using the facts that are given, however, you can find out the number of degrees that the Earth rotates in one hour. Because there are 24 hours in a day, you must divide the total number of longitude degrees by 24.

This is actually a two-step problem. You first have to determine the total number of longitude degrees, *t*, for the entire globe by adding the number of degrees of east longitude and the number of degrees of west longitude. Then you can divide that figure by the number of hours in a day to find the average number of degrees rotated per hour, *a*.

$$180 + 180 = t$$
$$t \div 24 = a$$

Estimate the Answer

To estimate, round the numbers in each equation. For the first equation, you can round to hundreds. For the second equation, you can round to fives.

$$200 + 200 = 400$$
$$400 \div 25 = 16$$

Your estimate is that the Earth rotates an average of about 16 degrees of longitude in an hour of time. Notice that, because 180 was rounded *up* twice, the estimate of 400 is high, so the estimate for the quotient should be high. You might expect the answer to be less than the estimate of 16 degrees.

Carry Out the Plan

$$180 + 180 = 360$$
$$360 \div 24 = 15$$

MATHEMATICS

Reread the Problem and Your Question

After rereading the problem, write the complete answer to the question.

The Earth rotates an average of 15 degrees of longitude in one hour.

This answer is, as you expected, less than the estimate of 16 degrees.

Complete and solve the following word problem.

Read: *When Kathleen telephones you at 6 P.M., she tells you that it is 3 P.M. in Los Angeles, where she is. You need to telephone Kathleen the next day when it is 8 P.M. in Los Angeles.*

Make sure that you understand the problem. When it is 3 P.M. in Los Angeles, it is 6 P.M. local time. You need to call when it is 8 P.M. in Los Angeles.

Decide: What question does this information suggest? If you need to call Kathleen when it is 8 P.M. in Los Angeles, then you need to know what time it will be where you are (local time) when it is 8 P.M. in Los Angeles. A logical question would be: *To speak with Kathleen at 8 P.M. her time, at what local time should you place your call?*

You need to determine the difference, *d*, in time between your time zone, *t*, and that of Los Angeles, *l*. Then you need to use this information to find your local time, *t*, when it is 8 P.M. in Los Angeles.

These equations can be written

$$d = t - l \text{ or } d = 6 - 3$$
$$t = d + l \text{ or } t = d + 8$$

Estimate: Because all the numbers are small, rounding is not necessary. Instead, estimate by looking at the problem logically. When Kathleen made her first call, your local time was later than it was in Los Angeles. The answer, therefore, should be later than 8 P.M. local time.

Carry Out:

$$d = 6 - 3 \text{ or } d = 3$$
$$t = 3 + 8 \text{ or } t = 11$$

Reread: *You should call Kathleen at 11 P.M. local time.* Because this answer is later than 8 P.M. Los Angeles time, it matches your estimate.

The above problem was easy to figure out because both times were P.M. If both times were A.M., then you also wouldn't have to make a special conversion. However, if one time in a word problem is in A.M. and the other is in P.M., then you have to change one of the numbers.

The reason for doing so is that 1 A.M. and 1 P.M. cannot both be treated as the number 1, since 1 P.M. is 12 hours later than 1 A.M. For this reason, when you have a P.M. time, you must add 12 to that number, so 1 P.M. would be treated as $1 + 12$, or 13.

After you solve a word problem that deals with time as an answer, you know that the answer is P.M. if the number is greater than 12. However, the clock changes from A.M. to P.M. and from P.M. to A.M. every 12 hours. For instance, you would not say that a time is 14 P.M. To convert it back to the clock time, you must subtract 12 from 14. So the time is $14 - 12$, or 2 P.M.

COMPREHENSION

1. Before you can write the equations that describe a problem for a given problem situation, what must you do first?

   _____

2. Identify the city from which longitude is measured.

   _____

3. If the numbers in a problem are small, what should you do for Step 3, the estimate?

   _____

4. Describe the method used for measuring the Earth's surface in determining time zones.

_____

5. Explain why it is important to reread the problem and your question.

_____

CRITICAL THINKING

1. Time zones were not used until after the railroads were built over long distances. Why do you think they were not used earlier?

_____

_____

2. If you estimate a division problem by rounding up the divisor (the number by which another is divided), will the answer be less than or greater than the estimate?

_____

SKILL FOCUS: WORD PROBLEMS

For each of the following problem situations, write the question that you think should be asked. Then write the equations as a plan, make an estimate, carry out your plan, and state the answer to the question in a complete sentence.

1. Read: Time zones are about 15 degrees longitude apart. When it is 9:00 A.M. in Washington, D.C., it is 5:00 P.M. in Moscow, Russia.

Decide: _____

_____

Estimate: _____

Carry Out: _____

Reread: _____

2. Read: Time zones are about 15 degrees longitude apart. Buenos Aires, Argentina, is at 60 degrees west longitude, while Canberra, Australia, is 150 degrees east longitude.

Decide: _____

_____

Estimate: _____

Carry Out: _____

Reread: _____

3. **Read:** The 0 degree longitude line, called the prime meridian, passes through Greenwich, England, a suburb of London. You want to call Chicago, Illinois, from London at 4:00 P.M. London time. Chicago is at 90 degrees west longitude. As you travel west, the time becomes earlier.

Decide: _____

_____

Estimate: _____

Carry Out: _____

Reread: _____

4. **Read:** Los Angeles is at 120 degrees west longitude. You need to call Mogadishu, Somalia, which is about 45 degrees east longitude. It is 9:00 A.M. in Los Angeles.

Decide: _____

_____

Estimate: _____

Carry Out: _____

Reread: _____

5. **Read:** Someone in a town in Iceland that is about 15 degrees west longitude wants to call St. Petersburg, Russia. St. Petersburg is about 30 degrees east longitude. It is 6 A.M. in the town in Iceland.

Decide: _____

_____

Estimate: _____

Carry Out: _____

Reread: _____

Reading-Writing Connection

On a separate sheet of paper, write a letter to a younger student in which you pass along some tips for solving word problems. Try to make the letter as helpful as possible to someone who is having difficulty with word problems.

Skill: Suffixes

A **suffix** is a word part that is added to the end of a word to change its meaning. If the base word ends in *e*, its spelling may have to be changed.

love + able = lovable

When a word ends in *y* preceded by a consonant, change the *y* to *i* before adding a suffix. When the *y* is preceded by a vowel, do not make a spelling change.

rely + able = reliable   pay + able = payable

When a word ends in *e* and the suffix begins with a vowel, drop the final *e* before adding the suffix. When the suffix begins with a consonant, do not make a spelling change.

festive + al = festival   festive + ly = festively

Below are ten suffixes and their meanings. Study them carefully.

Suffix	Meaning	Suffix	Meaning
-able	that can be	-ful	full of
-al	of or like	-ive	having to do with
-ance	the act of	-ly	like in manner
-ant	a person or thing that	-ness	quality or state of
-ation	the condition of being	-ous	characterized by

A. Write the correct suffix after each word below. If the word needs a spelling change before the suffix can be added, cross out the final *e* or *y*. The first one is done for you.

1. desire __able__   that can be desired

2. fame _____   characterized by fame

3. ordinary _____   in an ordinary manner

4. occupy _____   a person who occupies

5. vary _____   the condition of being varied

6. territory _____   of territory

7. decorate _____   having to do with decoration

8. guide _____   the act of guiding

9. rude _____   the quality of being rude

10. grace _____   full of grace

B. Use the correct word above to complete each sentence below.

1. The Louisiana Purchase was a valuable _____ addition to the United States.

2. The library is _____ closed on Sundays.

3. The school clubs are under the _____ of teachers.

4. The _____ ice skater glided and twirled.

5. Wallpaper gives a _____ effect to the kitchen.

6. Being overworked was not an excuse for her _____.

7. The busy corner of Oak and Main is a _____ location for a clothing store.

Skill: Reading a Federal Income Tax Form

In late December or early January, the federal government makes available to all workers a **federal income tax form** to fill out. By February 1, employers must send employees a W-2 form, which tells how much money they earned in the previous year and how much tax was withheld from their earnings. Employees must then fill out their income tax form and mail it in, with any payments due, no later than April 15.

Study the front of the completed Form 1040 on page 59.

A. Circle the letter in front of the phrase that correctly completes each sentence.

1. The person filing the return checked "Head of Household" on line 4 because
    a. her two children live with her.
    b. she is not married.
    c. she is married but filing a separate return.
    d. she has no dependents.

2. You know that the person filing the return is in favor of public financing of presidential election campaigns because
    a. she filled in the amount of money she wished to contribute to the fund.
    b. she did not check the Presidential Election Campaign Fund box.
    c. she checked the Presidential Election Campaign Fund box.
    d. she subtracted $3 in figuring her adjusted income.

3. Adjusted gross income is the amount of money received on which you must pay tax. On line 37, the adjusted gross income of the person filing this return is less than her total income on line 22 because
    a. she doesn't work full-time.
    b. she claims three exemptions.
    c. she received unemployment compensation.
    d. she contributed money to an IRA (Individual Retirement Account).

B. Complete the following sentences.

1. The person filing this return checked "Head of Household" to identify her

    _____.

2. You can tell that the person filing the return was unemployed for part

    of the year because _____.

3. The person filing the return claimed three exemptions. They are for

    _____.

Form **1040**

Department of the Treasury—Internal Revenue Service
U.S. Individual Income Tax Return 2007

(99)   IRS Use Only—Do not write or staple in this space.

For the year Jan. 1–Dec. 31, 2007, or other tax year beginning ____, 2007, ending ____, 20 ____   OMB No. 1545-0074

Label
(See instructions on page 16.)

Use the IRS label. Otherwise, please print or type.

L A B E L   H E R E

Your first name and initial: **Lois C.**   Last name: **Robinson**   Your social security number: **555 55 5555**

If a joint return, spouse's first name and initial: Last name: Spouse's social security number:

Home address (number and street). If you have a P.O. box, see page 16.   **25 Hampton Lane**   Apt. no.

City, town or post office, state, and ZIP code. If you have a foreign address, see page 16.   **Athens, Ohio 45701**

▲ You **must** enter your SSN(s) above. ▲

Checking a box below will not change your tax or refund.

Presidential Election Campaign ► Check here if you, or your spouse if filing jointly, want $3 to go to this fund (see page 16) ► ☑ **You** ☐ **Spouse**

Filing Status

Check only one box.

1. ☐ Single
2. ☐ Married filing jointly (even if only one had income)
3. ☐ Married filing separately. Enter spouse's SSN above and full name here. ►
4. ☑ Head of household (with qualifying person). (See page 17.) If the qualifying person is a child but not your dependent, enter this child's name here. ►
5. ☐ Qualifying widow(er) with dependent child (see page 17)

Exemptions

6a ☑ **Yourself.** If someone can claim you as a dependent, **do not** check box 6a
b ☐ **Spouse**

c Dependents:		(2) Dependent's social security number	(3) Dependent's relationship to you	(4) ✓ if qualifying child for child tax credit (see page 19)
(1) First name	Last name			
Lisa	Robinson	401 83 7622	daughter	☑
Peter	Robinson	404 20 1504	son	☑
				☐
				☐

If more than four dependents, see page 19.

Boxes checked on 6a and 6b: **1**
No. of children on 6c who:
• lived with you: **2**
• did not live with you due to divorce or separation (see page 20):
Dependents on 6c not entered above:
Add numbers on lines above ► **3**

d Total number of exemptions claimed

Income

Attach Form(s) W-2 here. Also attach Forms W-2G and 1099-R if tax was withheld.

If you did not get a W-2, see page 23.

Enclose, but do not attach, any payment. Also, please use **Form 1040-V.**

7	Wages, salaries, tips, etc. Attach Form(s) W-2	7	38742 00
8a	**Taxable** interest. Attach Schedule B if required	8a	155 00
b	**Tax-exempt** interest. **Do not** include on line 8a 8b		
9a	Ordinary dividends. Attach Schedule B if required	9a	
b	Qualified dividends (see page 23) 9b		
10	Taxable refunds, credits, or offsets of state and local income taxes (see page 24)	10	
11	Alimony received	11	
12	Business income or (loss). Attach Schedule C or C-EZ	12	
13	Capital gain or (loss). Attach Schedule D if required. If not required, check here ► ☐	13	
14	Other gains or (losses). Attach Form 4797	14	
15a	IRA distributions 15a b Taxable amount (see page 25)	15b	
16a	Pensions and annuities 16a b Taxable amount (see page 26)	16b	
17	Rental real estate, royalties, partnerships, S corporations, trusts, etc. Attach Schedule E	17	
18	Farm income or (loss). Attach Schedule F	18	
19	Unemployment compensation	19	1582 00
20a	Social security benefits 20a b Taxable amount (see page 27)	20b	
21	Other income. List type and amount (see page 29) _____	21	
22	Add the amounts in the far right column for lines 7 through 21. This is your **total income** ►	22	40479 00

Adjusted Gross Income

23	Archer MSA deduction. Attach Form 8853 23		
24	Certain business expenses of reservists, performing artists, and fee-basis government officials. Attach Form 2106 or 2106-EZ 24		
25	Health savings account deduction. Attach Form 8889 25		
26	Moving expenses. Attach Form 3903 26		
27	One-half of self-employment tax. Attach Schedule SE 27		
28	Self-employed SEP, SIMPLE, and qualified plans 28		
29	Self-employed health insurance deduction (see page 29) 29		
30	Penalty on early withdrawal of savings 30		
31a	Alimony paid b Recipient's SSN ► _____ 31a		
32	IRA deduction (see page 31) 32 2000 00		
33	Student loan interest deduction (see page 33) 33		
34	Jury duty pay you gave to your employer 34		
35	Domestic production activities deduction. Attach Form 8903 35		
36	Add lines 23 through 31a and 32 through 35	36	2000 00
37	Subtract line 36 from line 22. This is your **adjusted gross income** ►	37	38479 00

For Disclosure, Privacy Act, and Paperwork Reduction Act Notice, see page 80.   Cat. No. 11320B   Form **1040** (2007)

Freedom and Responsibility

Skill: Conflict and Resolution

BACKGROUND INFORMATION

In "New Car, New Image," a driver with a new car must learn for himself the importance of defensive and responsible driving. In most states, drivers receive a learner's permit before their license. With a learner's permit, the person can only drive with an adult licensed driver in the car.

SKILL FOCUS: Conflict and Resolution

In literature, the main character facing a conflict is called the **protagonist.** Often the protagonist is opposed by a rival, who is the **antagonist.**

A protagonist has a goal to achieve or a problem to solve. The struggle to achieve the goal or solve the problem is called **conflict.** By the end of a story, the protagonist succeeds in resolving the conflict. The way a conflict is settled is called the **resolution.**

A character can face three main types of conflict.

1. **Conflict with self** The character struggles with emotions or feelings. This is an internal conflict.

2. **Conflict with another character** The character struggles against another person. This is an external conflict.

3. **Conflict with an outside force** The character struggles against nature, society, technology, or some other force. This is also an external conflict.

▶ Read the paragraph below. Then fill in the Story Map in the next column. Provide your own resolution.

Jack didn't really want to race, but he felt he had no choice. The stranger had been daring him to prove what a skillful driver he was. Besides, Jack reasoned, it would look good in front of his friends if he could win. Still, deep down, Jack knew someone could get hurt. Was it really worth it?

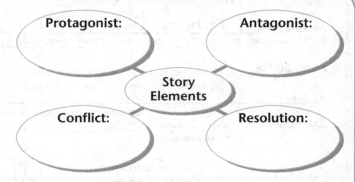

Protagonist:

Antagonist:

Story Elements

Conflict:

Resolution:

CONTEXT CLUES: Antonyms

Antonyms are words that have opposite meanings. Sometimes an antonym appears near a new word in a paragraph to make the meaning of that word clear. Read the sentence below. Look for antonym context clues that help explain the underlined word.

He looked conceited, Curt thought, and __egotistical__, too. He certainly wasn't modest.

If you are unfamiliar with the word *egotistical,* the phrase *wasn't modest* can help you. *Egotistical* and *modest* are antonyms. *Egotistical* means "not modest."

▶ Read the sentences below. Circle the antonym of the underlined word.

On a racetrack, all the drivers know what they're doing. They're __competent__ and in control. That's not true on the highway. There are all sorts of incapable drivers on the road.

In "New Car, New Image," the words *nonentity, seething,* and *elude* are underlined. Look for the nearby antonyms to figure out the words' meanings.

> **Strategy Tip**
>
> As you read "New Car, New Image," look for the conflicts that the protagonist faces.

New Car, New Image

Curt gave the sleek, green fender one last swipe with the chamois cloth before he opened the door on the driver's side and jumped into the car. As Curt pressed on the accelerator, the engine responded with a roar. Curt then looked into the rearview mirror. Was he imagining it, or did he somehow look more mature, more experienced, more sophisticated?

Heading for the beach, Curt couldn't wait to see Carmen's face. The car would have to impress her, and she wouldn't ignore him now.

Curt roared into the beach parking lot and came to an abrupt halt. He saw Carmen and her friends clustered around a new guy. They didn't turn around to check out Curt's car or Curt.

Curt was extremely upset that no one had seen him drive up. Who was that guy, soaking up all the attention and taking the spotlight away from him? He looked conceited, Curt thought, and egotistical, too. He sure wasn't modest.

"Hi, Curt," someone said, as he joined the group. "This is Darrell Jackson. He's a race-car driver."

Ordinarily Curt would have been thrilled to meet a race-car driver, but now he felt angry—cheated of his moment of glory. He felt like a <u>nonentity</u> again, instead of a somebody.

"I have my own car," Curt offered loudly, so Carmen would definitely have to hear. "Fixed it up myself."

"That's fantastic!" responded Darrell heartily. Curt thought that he sounded false and patronizing. "That's how I started, too."

"Darrell was just telling us about a defensive-driving course that he's teaching," Carmen said.

"Since you have a car, you should take the course, Curt," said Darrell.

Curt bridled. "I know how to drive. I have my license and my own car."

"Sure," said Darrell, "but you can never learn too much about driving, especially defensive driving. An automobile is the most dangerous instrument in everyday use. Every time you drive, you're taking a chance."

"Most worthwhile things involve risk," Curt argued. "You're a race-car driver. That's risky."

"Yes, but I understand the risk that I'm taking, and I know what to do in case of an emergency. Most drivers don't. Anyway, ordinary driving is far more dangerous than race-car driving."

"Yeah? Why?"

"Because of the other drivers. On a racetrack, all

the drivers know what they're doing. They're competent and completely in control. That's not necessarily true on the highway. There are all sorts of irresponsible drivers on the road—people who are drunk, careless, or out to prove something."

"Prove something?" Carmen interrupted. "You mean people who always have to be the fastest?"

Darrell gave Carmen his brightest smile.

What an operator this guy is, Curt thought.

Darrell answered Carmen. "Right. People like that are bad drivers who let themselves be manipulated by others and by their own emotions, instead of controlling the situation themselves. Good drivers don't need to prove they're good. They know that a car is a convenience and a pleasure, but also a potential danger."

"I'm a good driver," Curt grumbled. "I don't see any reason to take a defensive-driving course." Curt was no longer calm. In fact, he was <u>seething</u>. Not only was this Darrell a racer, he was smart and self-confident. Look at the way he was talking to Carmen—so easily, so casually.

Curt was beginning to realize that just having a car wasn't going to turn him into Mr. Personality overnight. The realization hurt. Watching Darrell, he wondered how he could possibly compete. Again he felt like a nonentity.

Darrell was directing all his attention to Carmen. "Defensive driving is essential, so that if an emergency comes up, you'll know exactly what to do. In an emergency, most drivers just press on the brake and brace their arms on the steering wheel—usually the worst things to do."

Carmen was listening raptly to Darrell's every syllable. Curt was disgusted. "I've got to get going," he muttered.

"Here's my card," said Darrell. "Give me a call if you decide to take the course."

Curt dragged himself back to his car. He was furious. No one had even noticed his sparkling new car! His big moment—and that Darrell Jackson had spoiled it. Once inside his car, he instantly felt better, more in control. He felt important.

"Curt!" It was Carmen, asking for a ride home. She slid in beside him.

"Wouldn't your friend Darrell give you a ride?" he inquired casually.

"Oh, him…," said Carmen. "He was nice, wasn't he—for an older man, anyway?"

Suddenly Curt's heart soared. Here he was in his own car, with Carmen beside him! He turned the key, and the motor caught with a quick surge of power. Curt pulled out of the parking lot, driving quickly, surely. This was his chance to prove he was as good as that hotshot Darrell!

At the stoplight, a car pulled up alongside them, the driver gunning the motor. It was a green compact, almost the twin of his own. Curt glanced at

the two boys in it, and they grinned back mockingly. Here was his chance to prove himself. Success with Carmen wouldn't <u>elude</u> him now. He would capture it and keep it within his grasp in one masterful move!

The light changed. Curt's foot came down hard on the accelerator. The car shot forward with a roar, tires screeching. They were off!

The other car moved with him, wheel to wheel. Curt was nosing ahead of the other car when they came to a bend. He pressed hard on the accelerator as he swept into the turn. The car wobbled under him. He wrestled with the wheel, almost losing control.

"Are you crazy?" Carmen screamed, "Stop!"

"I can beat him," Curt said through clenched teeth.

"So what? What are you trying to prove?"

Suddenly Darrell's words came into Curt's mind: "Good drivers don't need to prove they're good." He lifted his foot from the accelerator, and the other car thundered past him and disappeared.

"Let's go get something to eat," Curt suggested, as casually as he could.

Two hours later, after taking Carmen home, Curt pulled up at his own house. He was thinking about Carmen. She was going out with him tomorrow!

"Thank goodness!" his mother greeted him. "It wasn't you!"

"What are you talking about?" Curt was jogged out of his daydreaming.

"It was broadcast on the radio. Two cars collided. Four teenagers were killed instantly in the accident. Apparently one of the cars was a green compact like yours—and I was terrified…."

A green compact? Was it the one he had raced? Suddenly Curt realized that he and Carmen could have been the victims.

He dug into his windbreaker and pulled out a card.

"Where are you going?" his mother asked.

"I've got to make a phone call," Curt replied.

COMPREHENSION

1. Why didn't Carmen and her friends notice Curt's new car?

   _____

   _____

   _____

2. According to Darrell, why is race-car driving safer than everyday driving?

   _____

   _____

   _____

3. Darrell says that many drivers make two mistakes in an emergency. What are they?

   _____

   _____

   _____

   _____

4. A story's climax marks the turning point in the plot. After the climax, the reader can predict the story's ending. Circle the letter next to the statement below that describes the climax in this story.

   a. Curt begins to race the other car, wheel to wheel.

   b. Darrell takes the spotlight away from Curt in the beach parking lot.

   c. Curt lifts his foot from the accelerator and lets the other car pass him.

   d. Carmen decides to go out with Curt.

5. Complete each sentence with the correct word.

   elude   seething   nonentity

   a. Before being discovered, the dancer was a(n)

      _____ in the chorus line.

   b. The rabbit tried to _____ its pursuers.

   c. The coach was _____ because the team's carelessness cost them the game.

1. Tell why Curt felt so different when he was in his car.

   _____

   _____

2. **a.** Contrast Curt and Darrell.

   _____

   _____

   b. Describe how they are alike.

   _____

   _____

3. Explain how Curt hopes to become popular.

   _____

   _____

4. At first, Curt assumes that Carmen is not interested in him. Is he correct? Explain.

   _____

   _____

5. What happens that draws Curt and Carmen together?

   _____

   _____

6. From her reaction to Curt's reckless driving, what kind of driver do you think Carmen would be?

   _____

   _____

7. Do you think Curt will take the defensive-driving course? Explain.

   _____

   _____

8. Suppose Curt ignored Carmen's outburst and decided to prove that he could outrace the other car. How might the story have ended?

   _____

   _____

Think about the protagonist and the major and minor conflicts in this story. Use the information in the story to answer the following questions.

1. Who is the protagonist, the chief or leading character, in this story? _____

2. **a.** What internal conflict does the protagonist face?

    _____

    _____

    b. How is this conflict resolved?

    _____

    _____

3. The protagonist also faces two external conflicts.

    a. Underline the statements that best describe these conflicts.

    Should Curt race the two boys in the green compact?

    How can Curt persuade Darrell that he doesn't need a defensive-driving course?

    How can Curt impress Carmen?

    b. Identify the antagonist in each of the two conflicts above, and tell how each conflict is resolved.

    _____

    _____

    _____

    _____

4. How does the protagonist's internal conflict cause the external conflicts?

    _____

    _____

5. Think about the protagonist's feelings and actions. Is the protagonist a static or dynamic character? Discuss.

    _____

    _____

Reading-Writing Connection

To increase road safety in your county or state, what new driving law would you like to see enacted? Write a letter to the editor of a newspaper on a separate sheet of paper to explain your views.

Skill: Reading a Map

BACKGROUND INFORMATION

"Coping With an Energy Crisis" deals with the skyrocketing cost of natural resources in California, including natural gas, coal, and oil. California has the largest population in the United States and, therefore, uses the most energy. Due to a combination of factors, California faced the very real threat of an energy crisis in 2001.

SKILL FOCUS: Reading a Map

A map often provides more than a picture of a geographic area. There are many kinds of maps. A **resource map**, for example, can show the location of different types of resources, such as power plants. When studying a resource map, you can determine which type of power plant is used most frequently, as well as where the highest concentration of power plants is located.

The following questions will help you read resource maps.

- What is the title of the map?
- What symbols and colors are used in the map key? What do the symbols and colors show?
- What geographic areas does the map show?
- What conclusion can you draw from the information on the map?

▶ Look at the resource map at the top of the next column. Then answer the questions below.

1. How much of California's petroleum comes from Alaskan power plants? _____

2. What percentage of California's electricity is imported from foreign countries? _____

3. What percentage of California's natural gas comes from inside the state? _____

4. California produces the greatest percent of what kind of energy in-state? _____

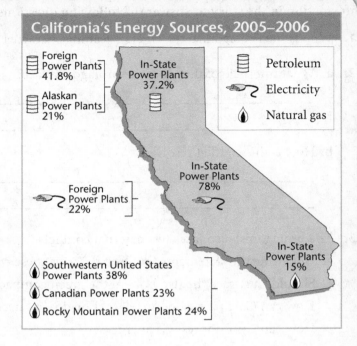

California's Energy Sources, 2005–2006

Foreign Power Plants 41.8%
In-State Power Plants 37.2%
Alaskan Power Plants 21%
Petroleum
Electricity
Natural gas
Foreign Power Plants 22%
In-State Power Plants 78%
In-State Power Plants 15%
Southwestern United States Power Plants 38%
Canadian Power Plants 23%
Rocky Mountain Power Plants 24%

CONTEXT CLUES: Synonyms

When you read a word that you don't know, look for **synonyms** in the next sentence to make its meaning clear. Synonyms are words that mean the same thing or almost the same thing. Read the sentences below.

*California has looked for **aid** from other states. However, this help is not enough.*

If you don't know the meaning of the word *aid*, the word *help* in the second sentence can help you. These words are synonyms.

▶ Read the sentences below. Circle the synonym that helps you figure out the meaning of the underlined word.

*Some sources of energy are **regenerated**. They are recreated, so they are available again and again.*

In "Coping With an Energy Crisis," look for synonyms for the underlined words *crisis, consumption,* and *menacing* as you read.

Strategy Tip

In the selection, use the maps to broaden your understanding of the energy crisis.

Coping With an Energy Crisis

We turn on a light. We watch TV. We heat food in a microwave oven. We boot up our computers. We take this for granted until one day we can't turn them on.

That is what happens when the electricity goes out, or we experience a power failure. Power failures can occur for several reasons. They can happen because something caused a major power line to break, disrupting the electric current. Storms can knock down power lines or cause **power plants** themselves to lose power.

Power outages have also been the result of **rolling blackouts**. These occur when the power company decides that the power plant is working too hard, and that too much electricity is being used. The power company shuts down different sectors, causing some homes and businesses to be without power for several hours. During the summer of 1999, the state of New Jersey had rolling blackouts.

In 2001, faced with the problem of an energy crisis, California raised the threat of possible rolling blackouts. Energy problems can be the result of several factors: continually increasing demand for power, natural weather forces, and **deregulation** of power companies. Deregulation means that a state no longer controls the power companies.

To understand how a state could simply run out of energy, it helps to look at what is meant by energy and how it is produced.

Energy Sources

In its simplest form, **energy** gives something the ability to work. Food is energy for people, allowing us to move and work and function. Gasoline is energy that powers cars. Similarly, electricity is energy that powers machines.

Energy that creates electricity can come in two forms. Some energy is renewable—it doesn't run out, but is always being regenerated. Solar energy, or energy from the sun, is a renewable power source. Other power sources include wind, water, and geothermal energy—heat deep inside the Earth.

The biggest concern to power companies and the energy industry is the overuse of nonrenewable energies, such as **fossil fuels**, which is what most power plants use. Natural gas, oil, and coal are all fossil fuels. They were formed inside the Earth millions of years ago. People must dig and mine and drill to get these fossil fuels.

Unlike wind or water or heat from the sun, fossil fuels cannot be regenerated. Once they are pulled from the ground and used, they are gone.

Power Plants

Energy sources such as fossil fuels are used by power plants to produce electricity. For example, coal is burned to make steam. The steam causes a turbine to spin, which in turn spins a shaft leading to a generator. In the generator, the shaft spins a large magnet, and the spinning of the magnet creates the electricity. Electricity then flows through power lines and transformers to the places that require electricity. Today's power plants depend heavily on fossil fuels. The resource map of California's power plants on the next page shows the distribution of power plants throughout the state of California. Although all kinds of energy are used, the most common kinds of energy are fossil fuels.

California Up Close

California's energy crisis was unique, but it could happen in other states. With an estimated 36 million people living in California in 2006 and another 4 million projected to live there by 2015, California is the most heavily populated state in the country. The energy needed to power the homes and businesses of 30 million people is extraordinary.

In addition, people are relying more and more on electricity. Electricity powers computers and video games and cordless phones. Most of these items were not commonly found in homes 20 years ago. According to the U.S. Department of Energy,

California's Power Plants, 2003

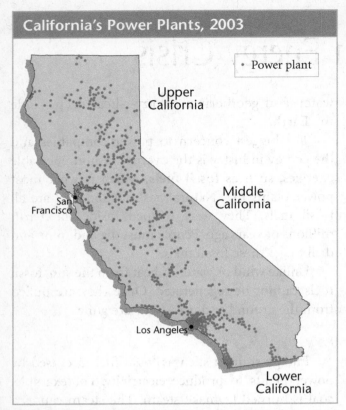

· Power plant

Upper California

Middle California

San Francisco

Los Angeles

Lower California

The highest concentration of power plants is in the San Francisco and Los Angeles areas.

California's electricity usage increased 15 percent from 1995 to 2000—a rate that nearly doubled the average rate of growth since 1980.

The resource map of population growth and electricity usage at the bottom of the second column shows the increase in population and annual electricity <u>consumption</u> in the western states of the United States. The rate of annual electricity usage is increasing along with the growth of the population. Although these numbers might not look <u>menacing</u> when compared to the states around them, the numbers are troubling because the population and electricity usage are already so large.

Deregulation

Perhaps the biggest cause of the California energy crisis has been deregulation. Until 1996, plants that generated power were owned by utility companies. These companies determined the prices that consumers paid for electricity, and those prices were regulated, or controlled, by the state. In 1996, however, the California Assembly voted unanimously to deregulate the pricing structure. This meant that power would no longer be generated and delivered by only one company.

The California Power Exchange, a private organization, held an auction. They auctioned off to various companies the right to supply power and to set prices for that power.

In addition, the utilities had owned all the power lines. Now they only owned the lines that supplied power directly into homes and businesses. After deregulation, the transmission lines—power lines that transmit electricity over long distances—were managed by a private company, the California Independent System Operator.

Because energy prices were no longer regulated, utility companies had to buy energy, just as you would buy a pair of sneakers. The more the products are in demand, the higher the prices will go.

These economic factors were only part of the energy picture. In January 2001, the state of

Western United States Population Growth and Annual Increase in Electricity Use, 2000–2006

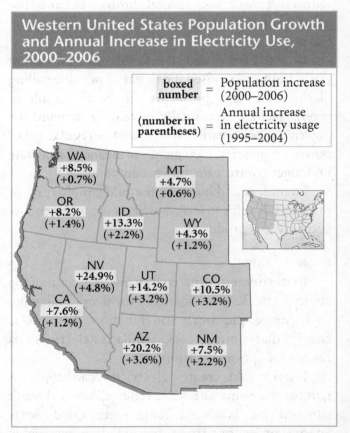

| **boxed number** | = | Population increase (2000–2006) |
| (**number in parentheses**) | = | Annual increase in electricity usage (1995–2004) |

WA +8.5% (+0.7%)

MT +4.7% (+0.6%)

OR +8.2% (+1.4%)

ID +13.3% (+2.2%)

WY +4.3% (+1.2%)

NV +24.9% (+4.8%)

UT +14.2% (+3.2%)

CO +10.5% (+3.2%)

CA +7.6% (+1.2%)

AZ +20.2% (+3.6%)

NM +7.5% (+2.2%)

As the population of any state grows, so does its consumption of electricity.

California went into a Stage Three alert, which meant that the state's power grid had less than 1.5 percent power in reserve. A powerful storm contributed to the problem. Not only did it knock out power for thousands of people, but also one of the most important power plants had to reduce output by 80 percent. Like many power plants along the coast, the Diablo Canyon nuclear power plant in San Luis Obispo sucks in cold ocean water to keep its systems cool. High surf from the storm brought in kelp and other ocean debris, forcing the plant to close.

California looked for aid from other states, which have been granted permission to sell electricity to California. However, this help was not enough. To add to the problem, Pacific Gas and Electric and SoCal Edison, the two major utility companies, claimed to be on the brink of bankruptcy. If the power companies went out of business, 25 million people would have no utility companies to service their homes and businesses. States around the country have their eyes on California. The California energy crisis is a problem that could have ramifications for the whole country.

COMPREHENSION

1. What kind of energy is each resource below? Write *renewable* or *nonrenewable*.

   a. Solar energy _____

   b. Coal _____

   c. Oil _____

2. Identify three causes that led to the California energy crisis.

   a. _____

   b. _____

   c. _____

3. Number the steps below to show the correct order in the process for creating electricity.

   _____ **a.** Steam causes a turbine to spin.

   _____ **b.** A spinning magnet inside a generator makes electricity.

   _____ **c.** Coal is burned.

   _____ **d.** The turbine is attached to a shaft, which is attached to a generator.

4. Draw lines to match the synonyms.

   crisis   **a.** troubling

   consumption   **b.** problem

   menacing   **c.** usage

CRITICAL THINKING

1. Identify each of the following statements as fact or opinion. Write *F* or *O* on the line.

   _____ **a.** Deregulation has forced California's utility companies to buy energy.

   _____ **b.** Deregulation of power companies has never been a good idea.

   _____ **c.** Coal should never be used for energy because it is a fossil fuel.

   _____ **d.** Coal is a fossil fuel that is nonrenewable.

2. Read the paragraph with a ✔. Write the main idea of the paragraph on the lines below.

   _____

   _____

3. Write a generalization based on the facts in the following paragraph.

> *Unlike wind or water or heat from the sun, fossil fuels cannot be regenerated. Once they are pulled from the ground and used, they are gone. It took millions of years for fossil fuels to be created, but they can be depleted much more quickly.*

_____

_____

4. Explain why power plants should try to use more renewable forms of energy than fossil fuels.

_____

_____

5. Describe how people experiencing rolling blackouts might react.

_____

_____

6. Look at the map on page 66. Compare the type of energy used in the western part of California with the energy used in the eastern part of the state. What inferences can you make?

_____

_____

SKILL FOCUS: READING A MAP

A. Use the the maps on page 68 to answer the following questions.

    1. What are the titles of the two maps?

        a. _____

        b. _____

    2. What state appears on both maps? _____

    3. How are the maps related? _____

B. Draw conclusions about the two maps to answer the questions below.

California's Power Plants, 2003

    1. Are there more power plants north or south of San Francisco?

_____

_____

2. Where is the highest concentration of power plants?

_____

_____

3. What can you infer about the location of power plants in California?

_____

_____

4. What conclusions can you draw based on this map?

_____

_____

Western United States Population Growth and Annual Increase in Electricity Use, 2000–2006

1. What information is shown on this map?

_____

_____

2. Which years are represented on the map?

_____

_____

3. What can you infer about California from this map?

_____

_____

4. What conclusions can you draw from this map?

_____

_____

Reading-Writing Connection

On a separate sheet of paper, write a letter to the editor of a newspaper summarizing what you have learned and what you think could be done to avoid a future energy crisis.

Skill: Main Idea and Supporting Details

BACKGROUND INFORMATION

"Improving on Genetics" highlights the contributions that Gregor Mendel made to the science of genetics. Mendel was an Austrian monk who taught science to high school students. He was the first person to trace the traits of a living thing from one generation to the next. The account of his work, "Experiments With Plant Hybrids," written in 1866, became one of the most influential publications in the history of science.

SKILL FOCUS: Main Idea and Supporting Details

To understand how ideas in a section of text are related and which ideas are important, you need to look for the **main idea** and **supporting details.**

When you read a section that contains a lot of information, use the following steps.

1. Use the heading of each section as the main idea.

2. Within each section, find at least two major details that develop or support the main idea.

3. Look for minor details that give more information about the major details.

4. Organize the major and minor details to show how they are related.

▸ Read the heading and paragraph below. Fill in the main idea and supporting details on the chart at the top of the next column.

Reproduction in Pea Plants

The flower of each garden pea plant used by Mendel contained both male and female parts. The female parts include the stigma, the style, and the ovary. The egg is produced in the ovary. The style connects the ovary to the stigma. The male parts of the flower are called the anthers. Anthers produce pollen, which contains sperm. Before the pea flower opens, pollen is transferred to the stigma. Then the sperm travels through the stigma and style, and finally reaches the ovary.

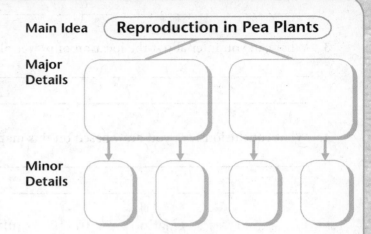

CONTEXT CLUES: Appositive Phrases

Sometimes the meaning of a new word is made clear by a phrase that follows it. This is called an **appositive phrase.** It is usually set apart by commas and may start with the word *or.* Read the sentence below. Look for an appositive phrase that helps explain the underlined word.

The study of __heredity__, or the passing along of characteristics from one generation to another, is a relatively new science.

The appositive phrase *or the passing along of characteristics from one generation to another* explains what the word *heredity* means.

▸ Read the sentence below. Circle the appositive phrase that explains the meaning of the underlined word.

All __organisms__, or living things, possess certain characteristics that they pass on from one generation to the next.

In "Improving on Genetics," the words *factors, hypotheses,* and *environment* are underlined. Look for appositive phrases that explain what these words mean.

Strategy Tip

As you read "Improving on Genetics," look for major and minor details. Remember that minor details support the major details.

Improving on Genetics

Scientists have long known that offspring resemble, or look like, their parents. This resemblance applies to the several million different kinds of plants and animals living today. All organisms, or living things, possess certain characteristics that they pass on from one generation to the next. The passing on of traits from parents to offspring is called **heredity.**

The study of heredity is a relatively new science. For centuries, people applied the principles of heredity to improve their animals and plants, but they did not understand the patterns and processes involved. Not until the work of Gregor Mendel, an Austrian monk, was recognized in the early 1900s did **genetics,** the study of heredity, begin.

Mendel's Experiments

Mendel's interest in the mechanism of **inheritance,** or the passing on of traits from one generation to the next, led him to conduct experiments with pea plants. He chose pea plants because they grow rapidly, produce many seeds, and have contrasting traits that are easy to observe. His experiments involved over 10,000 pea plants.

Mendel chose several plant characteristics to study, including seed shape, seed color, and stem length. The traits occurred in contrasting pairs. For example, seeds were either round or wrinkled and either green or yellow; plants were either tall or short.

Mendel's first step was to grow **purebred** plants by allowing them to self-pollinate. Self-pollination occurs when the male and female reproductive organs are on the same plant. The seeds of such plants always produce other plants with identical traits, generation after generation. For example, a purebred tall plant produces tall offspring. Purebred plants with yellow seeds produce offspring with yellow seeds.

Mendel wondered what would happen if two purebred plants with contrasting traits were cross-pollinated. Cross-pollination occurs when the male and female reproductive organs are on different plants. If a purebred tall plant and a purebred short plant were cross-pollinated, would a plant of medium height result?

Calling the two plants with contrasting traits the **parental generation,** or P_1, Mendel crossbred for all observable traits. The offspring of these crosses were designated, or referred to, as the **first filial generation,** or F_1. In all the crosses, the F_1 generation showed only one of the two traits of the P_1 generation. For instance, a tall plant and a short plant produced only tall offspring. It seemed that the traits of one parent had disappeared in the F_1 generation.

Next Mendel allowed the plants of the F_1 generation to self-pollinate and produce a **second filial generation,** or F_2. To his surprise, some of the offspring showed the "lost" trait. Among the offspring of the tall plants, there were about three times as many tall plants as short plants. See Figure 1.

Mendel believed that hereditary factors, or units, carried the traits that he was studying. A pair of factors was responsible for each trait. Because the offspring of contrasting purebred parents exhibited only one trait, that trait must be stronger than the other. Mendel called this trait the **dominant** trait. He called the trait that seemed to disappear the **recessive** trait.

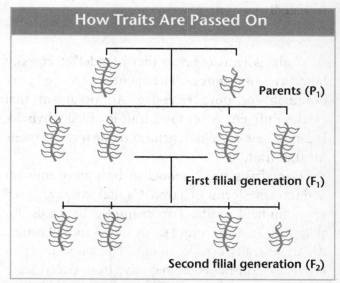

How Traits Are Passed On

Parents (P_1)

First filial generation (F_1)

Second filial generation (F_2)

FIGURE 1. The F_1 generation shows only the trait of one parent. Some of the F_2 generation show the "lost" trait.

Mendel's Laws of Heredity

Mendel conducted the same experiments repeatedly, each time obtaining the same results. He tried to explain his observations by developing <u>hypotheses</u>, or logical explanations, for what he saw. For nearly 35 years, Mendel's work was ignored. Finally, supported by the results of other experiments, Mendel's conclusions were accepted as laws.

The **Law of Dominance** states that, of two contrasting traits, one trait is dominant over the other. The dominant trait appears in the offspring; the recessive trait does not appear. In pea plants, tallness is dominant over shortness; round seed shape is dominant over wrinkled seed shape.

The **Law of Segregation** states that hereditary factors occur in pairs. These pairs are segregated, or separated, during the formation of reproductive cells. A parent hands down only one factor of every pair to each of its offspring.

The **Law of Independent Assortment** states that each pair of hereditary factors is inherited independently of the other pairs. For example, a tall pea plant can have round or wrinkled seeds. This law is not always followed in nature.

Since Mendel's time, scientists have discovered exceptions to Mendel's laws. For example, some traits are determined not by one pair of hereditary factors but by several pairs in combination. However, Mendel's theories in general have been repeatedly proven.

Concepts of Heredity

Today scientists know that Mendel's factors of heredity are **genes**. The genes can be pure dominant or pure recessive. An organism that carries different genes for a trait is called a **hybrid**. It carries one dominant gene and one recessive gene for that trait.

Geneticists use symbols to indicate dominant and recessive forms of a trait. Capital letters are used for dominant traits. For example, Y stands for yellow seeds, R for round seeds, and T for tall plants. All these traits are dominant. The same letter in lowercase represents the recessive trait. Green seeds are represented by y, wrinkled seeds by r, and short plants by t. For a purebred tall plant that has two dominant genes, the genetic symbol is TT. For a purebred short plant with two recessive genes, the symbol is tt. For a plant with one dominant and one recessive gene, the symbol is Tt.

Geneticists use Mendel's laws and the principles of probability to predict possible offspring types. They also use a special chart, called a **Punnett square**, to show the possible combinations resulting from a cross of two organisms. The two genes of one parent are identified at the top of the square. The genes of the other parent are identified on the left side of the square. Each box within the square represents the possible combination of genes that one offspring could have. See Figure 2.

Some gene pairs contain neither a dominant nor a recessive gene. In such cases, the offspring exhibit a blending of the traits of the parents. The genes are said to exhibit **incomplete dominance**. For example, when red four o'clock flowers are crossed with white four o'clock flowers, the offspring are pink.

Inherited Traits

Traits that an organism inherits from its parents can be both physical and mental. In pea plants, seed color, seed shape, and plant height are physical traits. Some common physical traits in humans are eye color, hair color and texture, skin color, general body shape and size, and blood type. Many abnormal conditions and diseases are inherited, including hemophilia, muscular dystrophy, color blindness, and sickle cell anemia.

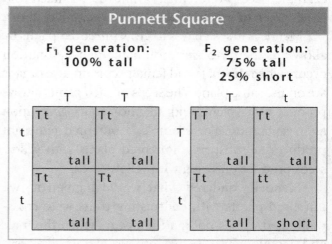

FIGURE 2. **The Punnett square shows possible genetic combinations.**

Mental traits include general intelligence—a basic mental ability that influences the capacity to learn—and aptitudes in art, music, mathematics, languages, and other fields. Obviously, people are born with certain mental traits. However, scientists do not agree on whether such traits are entirely inherited or are partly the result of other factors that we do not yet understand.

Inherited physical and mental traits alone do not determine what an organism becomes. A person's environment, or surroundings, affects his or her hereditary traits, strongly influencing whether and how these traits develop. For example, research has shown that mental stimulation can raise a child's intelligence level. So, despite genetics, we still have some ability to influence what we will become.

COMPREHENSION

1. If two purebred plants with contrasting traits were crossed, what would the first generation offspring be like?

   _____

   _____

   _____

2. Explain the Law of Dominance.

   _____

   _____

   _____

3. Explain the existence of tall pea plants with smooth seeds and tall pea plants with wrinkled seeds.

   _____

   _____

   _____

4. A tall pea plant is crossed with a short pea plant. About half of the offspring are short. What is probably true of the tall parent plant?

   _____

   _____

   _____

5. In addition to inherited physical and mental traits, what other factor influences how an organism develops?

   _____

   _____

   _____

6. Draw a line to match each word with its explanation.

   hypotheses   a. units

   factors   b. logical explanations

   environment   c. surroundings

CRITICAL THINKING

Circle the letter of the answer choice that best completes each sentence.

1. Incomplete dominance occurs in shorthorn cattle. If red shorthorn cattle are crossed with brown shorthorn cattle, the offspring are

   a. red.   c. roan, or reddish brown.

   b. white.   d. none of the above

2. If a purebred tall pea plant (TT) is crossed with a purebred short pea plant (tt), the first generation offspring are

   a. all tall purebred.

   b. half tall purebred, half short purebred.

   c. all short hybrid.

   d. all tall hybrid.

3. Farmers could use the laws of heredity to improve their animals by

   a. cross-breeding animals that have the traits they want.

   b. feeding animals the kind of food that makes them grow larger.

   c. knowing in advance how many offspring an animal will have.

   d. none of the above

SKILL FOCUS: MAIN IDEA AND SUPPORTING DETAILS

The Main Idea and Supporting Details map below shows how the major and minor details are related in the section on Mendel's experiments. Using this model, complete the diagram on the next page for two of the remaining three sections in the selection. For each diagram, write the heading of the section in the *Main Idea* box. Then reread the paragraphs in each section. Write a sentence in each of the three *Major Details* boxes. To complete the diagram for each section, write at least two minor details, using phrases instead of sentences.

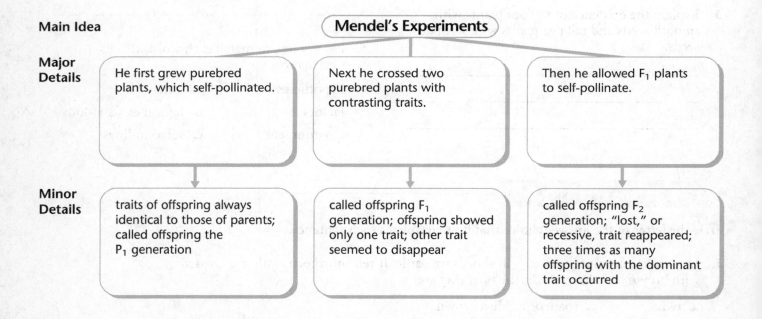

Main Idea — Mendel's Experiments

Major Details

- He first grew purebred plants, which self-pollinated.
- Next he crossed two purebred plants with contrasting traits.
- Then he allowed F_1 plants to self-pollinate.

Minor Details

- traits of offspring always identical to those of parents; called offspring the P_1 generation
- called offspring F_1 generation; offspring showed only one trait; other trait seemed to disappear
- called offspring F_2 generation; "lost," or recessive, trait reappeared; three times as many offspring with the dominant trait occurred

Main Idea

Major Details

Minor Details

Main Idea

Major Details

Minor Details

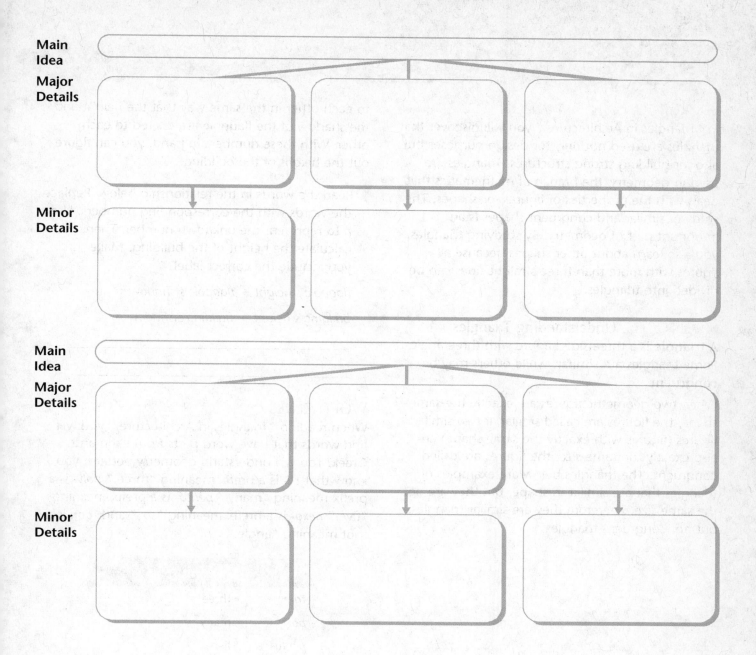

Skill: Understanding Triangles

BACKGROUND INFORMATION

In "Triangles in Architecture," you will discover that triangles are used not only for design purposes but also for building strong structures. Triangles are used in geometry, the branch of mathematics that deals with the properties of figures, or shapes. The study of similar and congruent shapes is an important part of geometry. By studying triangles, you also learn about other shapes because all figures with more than three straight sides can be divided into triangles.

SKILL FOCUS: Understanding Triangles

A **triangle** is a three-sided figure with three angles. Some triangles are **similar**, while others may be **congruent.**

When two geometric figures are exactly the same shape, the figures are called similar. If two similar figures (figures with exactly the same shape) are also exactly the same size, the figures are called congruent. The triangles below are examples of triangles that are similar in shape, but they are not the same size. Therefore they are similar triangles, but not congruent triangles.

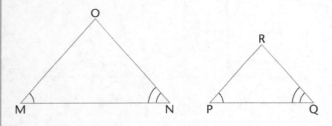

The relationships between similar figures can be used to find the measurements of an object that is too tall or too distant to measure. For example, suppose you need to find out the height of a building. You know that the height of a nearby flagpole is 18 feet. You measure its shadow and find that the shadow is 12 feet. It is easier to measure the shadow of the building than the building itself. The shadow of the building measures 48 feet. The height and the shadow of the building are related

to each other in the same way that the height and the shadow of the flagpole are related to each other. With these numbers in hand, you can figure out the height of the building.

▶ Read the words in the relationship below. Replace the words with the corresponding numbers. Use *n* to represent the unknown number. Then calculate the height of the building. Make sure you include the correct label.

flagpole's height ÷ flagpole's shadow =

building's height ÷ building's shadow

_____ =

_____

WORD CLUES

When reading "Triangles in Architecture," you will find words that have word parts from Latin and Greek. You will understand geometry better if you know that *tri-* is a prefix meaning "three," *poly-* is a prefix meaning "many," *penta-* is a prefix meaning "five," *hexa-* is a prefix meaning "six," and *-gon* is a root meaning "angle."

Prefix	Meaning
tri-	three
poly-	many
penta-	five
hexa-	six

Strategy Tip

As you read "Triangles in Architecture," look for examples of similar and congruent triangles. Check all descriptions against the figures to make sure that you understand the text.

TRIANGLES IN ARCHITECTURE

Architecture is the art and science of designing and constructing buildings. When architects design buildings, they use a variety of shapes to make their buildings not only functional but also pleasing to the eye.

As you view a building, your mind identifies the shapes you see. For example, the building known as the Capitol, in Washington, D.C., has a round dome. The Sears Tower in Chicago is a very long, very tall rectangle. The rooftops of many houses are rectangular in shape. Many sports stadiums and arenas are oval.

Geometry plays a large part in the actual design of a building. Geometric figures of various kinds appear in different combinations to make up the shape of a building. When two geometric figures are exactly the same shape, they are said to be **similar**. When two similar figures (figures having exactly the same shape) are also exactly the same size, the figures are said to be **congruent**.

Figure 1 shows a basic outline for what is known as the Carpenter Gothic house. In geometric terms, this shape is a **polygon**. A polygon is a closed figure whose sides are all straight line segments that meet, but do not cross. A polygon with five straight sides and five angles is called a **pentagon**.

Carpenter Gothic House Basic Outline

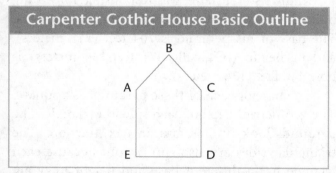

FIGURE 1. A polygon is a many-sided figure. This polygon is a pentagon. A pentagon has five sides and five angles.

The five sides of the shape in Figure 1 can be labeled: *AB*, *BC*, *CD*, *DE*, and *EA*. The sides are named by the points at the ends of each line segment. The five angles are *A*, *B*, *C*, *D*, and *E*. An angle is named by the point where the two sides meet, called the **vertex** of the angle. Angles can also be named by using three letters. The vertex of the angle is the middle letter of the three-letter name, while the other two letters are the names of points on the sides. For example, angle *A* could also be called angle *EAB*. Angle *B* could also be called angle *ABC*.

The shape in Figure 1 can be split into two other shapes. See Figure 2 below. If a line segment is drawn connecting points *A* and *C*, the top half of the shape becomes a triangle, and the bottom half is a rectangle. A triangle is a polygon with three sides, and a rectangle is a polygon with four sides. Here you can see the beginnings of a house design, with a rectangular base and a triangular roof.

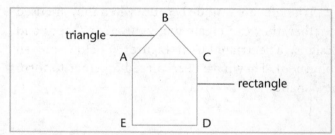

FIGURE 2. Architects can use a base like this and add other details to design the exterior of a house.

Types of Triangles

A regular triangle, or a triangle that has equal sides and angles, is also called an **equilateral triangle**. An **isosceles** (eye SAHS ə leez) **triangle** has two equal sides. A **scalene** (skay LEEN) **triangle** has no equal sides. A **right triangle** has one angle equal to 90 degrees, called a **right angle**.

Compare the roofs of numerous buildings, and you can see many triangles. Although these triangles may be similar, they are probably not congruent. The rules for showing that two triangles are congruent can be used for showing that other polygons are congruent. Following are four of those rules. Notice that all the rules for congruence have abbreviations.

MATHEMATICS

1. **SSS (side, side, side):** Two triangles are congruent if all three sides of one have the same lengths as all three sides of the other.

2. **SAS (side, angle, side):** Two triangles are congruent if two sides of one have the same lengths as two sides of the other, and the angle between the matching sides is the same size in both triangles.

3. **ASA (angle, side, angle):** Two triangles are congruent if two angles of one are the same sizes as two angles of the other, and the side between these matching angles has the same length in both triangles.

4. **HL (hypotenuse, leg):** Two right triangles are congruent if the longest side of each triangle has the same length and a shorter side of each has the same length.

The abbreviation *HL* may not be clear. The longest side of a right triangle is called the **hypotenuse** (*H*) (hy PAHT ən yoos). The shorter sides are called **legs** (*L*). The abbreviation *HL* stands for hypotenuse-leg.

Triangles are unique because when they are used together, they can create many different shapes and designs. The triangles in Figure 3, below, are all congruent. They have been pieced together to form new shapes.

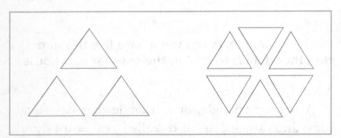

FIGURE 3. The first set of triangles creates a larger triangle. The second set of triangles creates a hexagon—a six-sided polygon.

Building With Triangles

Triangles are used extensively in building because they are very stable and have great strength. One of the ways triangles are used in building is to provide reinforcement in trusses. A **truss** is a lightweight beam with triangular shapes inside that provide support, as shown in Figure 4. The triangles fit within the long rectangular shape of

the beam. In this truss, not only are the triangles congruent, but they are also right triangles. Trusses are used extensively to provide support for roofs and floors.

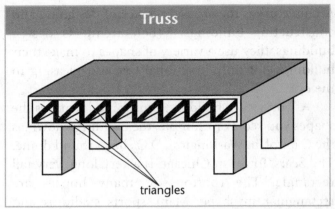

Truss

triangles

FIGURE 4. Triangular shapes can be found inside trusses. The triangles make the trusses lightweight, sturdy, and strong.

Perhaps the most well-known examples of triangles in architecture are the pyramids of Egypt. Although the ancient Egyptians built a number of pyramids of various sizes, the largest and most impressive were built at Giza. The pharaoh Khufu, who was also known as Cheops, is known as the father of pyramid building at Giza. The base of his Great Pyramid measures 754 feet (230 meters), and its height is 449 feet (137 meters). See Figure 5 on page 81. Originally it was 481 feet (147 meters) tall, but over the centuries, it has lost some of its paving stones.

Khufu's son, Khafre, was responsible for having built the second-largest pyramid complex at Giza. The base of his pyramid is 704 feet (215 meters), and its height (originally 471 feet/144 meters) is now 446 feet (136 meters).

The base of each of these pyramids is a square. The geometric shape of each side is a triangle. The pyramids look similar, and, in fact, they are. The triangular sides are also similar, but because each triangle has a different base and height, they are not congruent.

Although it may be easy to figure out the design of the pyramids, their actual construction still remains open to debate among scientists. This is mostly due to the immense size and weight of the stones used in their construction.

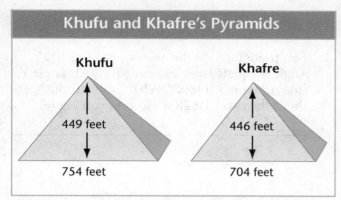

Khufu and Khafre's Pyramids

Khufu

449 feet

754 feet

Khafre

446 feet

704 feet

FIGURE 5. Khufu's pyramid has a base of 754 feet and a height of 449 feet. The pyramid of his son, Khafre, has a base of 704 feet and a height of 446 feet.

Through the centuries, different architectural designs have come and gone. Perhaps one of the most dramatic changes in architecture was the skyscraper. In the past, stone and wood were the main building components. The taller the building, the thicker the walls had to be in order to support such weight.

That changed when architects and engineers began using iron, which was not as thick, but just as strong. An even greater advancement was steel, which proved to be not only lighter than iron, but also stronger.

Skyscrapers

The first skyscraper was the Empire State Building in New York City. It was built in an amazingly short amount of time for such a large structure—averaging about four and a half floors a week. When it was completed, it was the tallest building in the world, with over 100 floors towering above New York City. The building opened on May 1, 1931.

However, constructing any building comes with responsibility. Photographs of the Empire State Building under construction show daring workers hundreds of feet in the air with no safety equipment. Today safety is required—not only for workers but also for the building itself. Safety inspectors check a new building to make sure it is safe for the people who will live and work in it. A building may look attractive on the outside with its geometric shapes and patterns, but it must also be safe.

Triangles Everywhere

From triangular rooftops to triangular-shaped windows, the triangle is a shape that can be found everywhere you look. You can even find triangles in the profile of bridges that span wide rivers. The Sidney Lanier Bridge in Brunswick, Georgia, is an example. Because it is a cable-stayed bridge, its silhouette takes the shape of a number of triangles. The base of each triangle is the deck of the bridge. The height of each triangle is formed by one of two huge towers. The stay cables themselves—which stretch from the tower and support the deck of the bridge—form the third side of the triangle. When you look at the bridge, you may see four right triangles; or you may see two or more isosceles triangles. It all depends on your point of view.

COMPREHENSION

1. Explain what makes two figures similar.

_____

_____

2. Explain what makes two figures congruent.

_____

_____

3. Identify the longer side of a right triangle.

_____

_____

4. Are the triangular sides of the pyramids of Khufu and Khafre similar or congruent? How do you know?

_____

_____

_____

MATHEMATICS

1. Circle the letter of the correct statement below.

    a. All congruent polygons are similar.

    b. All similar polygons are congruent.

2. How many sides would you expect to find on a polygon with seven angles?

    _____

3. Two triangles have the points *ABC* and *XYZ*. Angle *A* equals angle *X*. Angle *B* equals angle *Y*. Side *AB* equals side *XY*. What can you conclude about the two triangles? How do you know?

    _____

SKILL FOCUS: UNDERSTANDING TRIANGLES

1. **Look at each shape below. On the lines, write the letters that identify each triangle, and tell if they are similar, congruent, or neither.**

    a.

    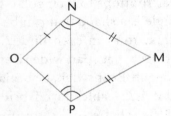

    _____

    _____

    b.

    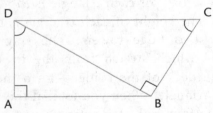

    _____

    _____

2. **a.** An architect measures a triangle as having two sides of 250 meters each, with the angle between them being 60 degrees. The third side of the triangle measures 300 meters. The architect then lays out another triangle that has two sides of 250 meters each, with the angle between the sides being 60 degrees. What is the length of the third side of the second triangle? Why?

    _____

    b. In triangles *FGH* and *IJK*, sides *FH* and *IK* are equal. Angle *F* equals angle *I*. Angle *H* equals angle *K*. Does angle *G* equal angle *J*? Why or why not?

    _____

Reading-Writing Connection

Find a photograph of a building that uses a triangular shape as part of its design. On a separate sheet of paper, write a paragraph about the building, describing the use of triangles, as well as a brief history of the building. Include the photograph with your paragraph.

Skill: Multiple-Meaning Words

Some words have entirely different meanings when used in different subject areas. Examples of such words are listed below.

cone	date	force	organ	plant
current	figure	note	plane	scale

Read the two definitions for each word below. Notice the subject areas that they come from. Then write the word from the list that fits both definitions on the line above the first definition.

1. _____

   Music: a large wind instrument consisting of various sets of pipes

   Science: a body part made up of specialized tissues and having a special purpose

2. _____

   Science: a living organism that cannot move from place to place by itself and can make its own food

   Social Studies: the buildings, machinery, and other fixtures of a factory

3. _____

   Mathematics: a solid with a circular base and a curved surface tapering evenly to a point

   Science: the seed-containing fruit of some evergreen trees

4. _____

   Art: the outline or shape of something

   Mathematics: the symbol for a number

5. _____

   Mathematics: a regularly spaced series of marks along a line, used for measuring

   Science: any of the thin, flat, hard plates forming the outer covering of many fish and reptiles

6. _____

   Social Studies: now in progress; now going on

   Science: a flow of liquid or gas in a specific direction

7. _____

   Science: a push or a pull on an object

   Social Studies: fighting strength or military organization of a nation

8. _____

   Literature: a statement added to a book at the back or at the bottom of a page, to explain something or to give more information

   Music: a tone of definite pitch; also, a symbol for a tone indicating pitch and duration

9. _____

   Social Studies: the time at which a thing happens or is done

   Science: the sweet, fleshy fruit of a cultivated palm

10. _____

   Mathematics: a surface that wholly contains every straight line joining any two points lying on it

   Science: to rise partly out of the water while moving at a high speed

Skill: Main Idea and Supporting Details

Many paragraphs that you read are packed with information. Knowing how to find the main ideas and the supporting details will help you understand the information in a paragraph. The **main idea** expresses the subject of a paragraph. A **major detail** is a supporting idea that is an important example or a fact about the main idea.

The major details of a paragraph help develop or complete the thought expressed by the main idea. The main idea and major details work together as a unit to support one another. You could say that the main idea depends on major details.

Not all details in a paragraph are major details. Paragraphs often contain details that are not important to the main idea. They are called **minor details**, and they explain or tell more about the major details. While the minor details may add interest to the main idea, the main idea does not depend on them.

The following selection is about the training of Seeing Eye guide dogs at Seeing Eye Headquarters in Morristown, New Jersey. As you read, look first for the main idea. Then try to determine which of the details are major and which are minor.

The Seeing Eye Team

1. Before being given to a sightless person as a Seeing Eye guide, a dog goes through a special process. After the puppy comes to the Seeing Eye Headquarters from an independent breeder or the Seeing Eye breeding station, it goes to live with a 4-H family for 14 months. The dog stays in this loving home and is taught basic obedience. The children in the family might take their puppy on buses, on trains, or into stores, introducing it to situations that it will meet as a guide dog. Next the dog spends a month in a holding kennel. There strenuous physical exams show if the dog could serve a sightless master well. Then the dog is assigned with nine other dogs to a qualified instructor for three months of rigorous training.

2. The training period with the instructor is the most important and demanding. During training, the instructor walks many miles a day with the eager dog. The dog thus encounters typical outdoor situations of the average American town. Then while blindfolded, the instructor takes the dog out for obedience exercises and traffic tests. With the instructor holding the harness, the dog must avoid such hazards as traffic and low-hanging tree branches. In this way, the instructor acts as a stand-in for the sightless member of the future Seeing Eye team.

3. The ultimate meeting of the two team members is well planned and emotional. The dog has been vigorously trained to be a faithful, responsible, and hard-working companion. The sightless person has answered many questions about his or her lifestyle and home environment. When the sightless person reaches out to his or her new friend, a stirring relationship of interdependence begins. He or she will always know a new kind of freedom. The dog will always know a new kind of responsibility. They both will learn a new kind of love.

For each paragraph above, complete the chart on page 85. In the box labeled *Main Idea,* write the sentence from the paragraph that states the main idea. When filling in the boxes labeled *Major Details* and *Minor Details,* use your own words. Use the completed boxes to guide you.

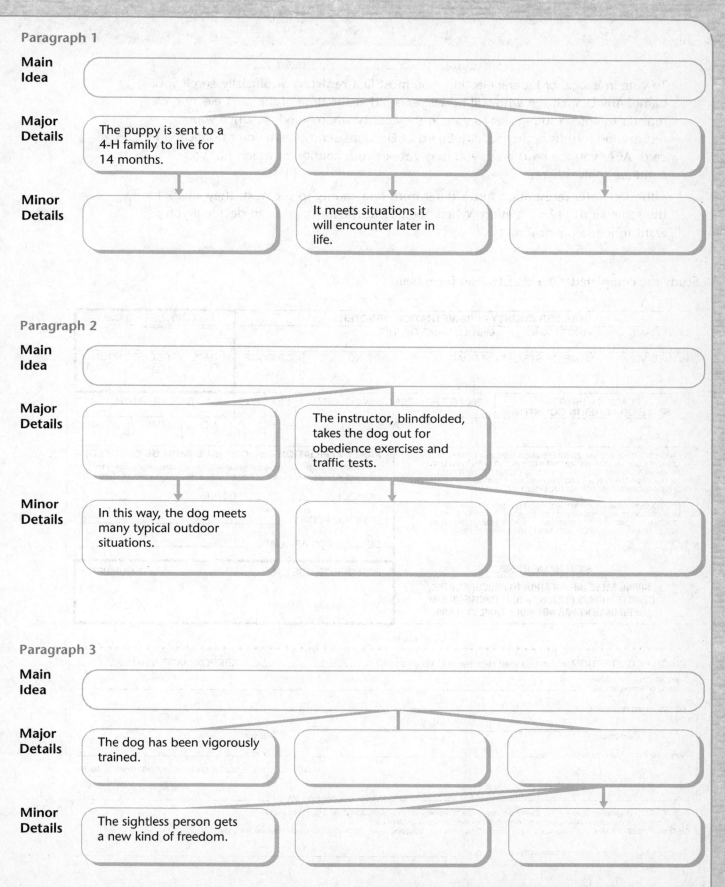

Paragraph 1

Main Idea

Major Details

The puppy is sent to a 4-H family to live for 14 months.

Minor Details

It meets situations it will encounter later in life.

Paragraph 2

Main Idea

Major Details

The instructor, blindfolded, takes the dog out for obedience exercises and traffic tests.

Minor Details

In this way, the dog meets many typical outdoor situations.

Paragraph 3

Main Idea

Major Details

The dog has been vigorously trained.

Minor Details

The sightless person gets a new kind of freedom.

Skill: Reading a Voter Registration Form

To vote in a local or federal election, you must first **register**, or officially enroll your name. Any U.S. citizen who will be 18 years old at the time of the next election can register to vote. You register to vote in the county where you live. Once your registration form is approved, the Board of Elections sends you a voter notification card. After you are registered, you may vote in your county for as long as you continue to live there.

Although voter registration forms differ from one county to the next, they all ask for the same kinds of information. When you fill out the form, you can decide if you want to join a political party.

Study the completed voter registration form below.

BOULDER COUNTY — REGISTRATION OF VOTERS				FOR OFFICE USE ONLY		
LAST NAME	FIRST NAME	MIDDLE NAME OR INITIAL		DIST.	PREC.	AFFIL.
Torres	Marcos	Juan				
HOUSE NO.	NAME OF STREET OR ROAD	APT. NO.	ZIP CODE	DATE OF REGISTRATION		
				MO.	DAY	YEAR
503	39th Street	3B	80302			

PLACE OF BIRTH— STATE OR FOREIGN COUNTRY	TERM OF RESIDENCE IN COLORADO	SEX	AGE	DATE OF BIRTH		
	YEARS			MO.	DAY	YEAR
Mexico	1	M	21	2	20	87

I AM A CITIZEN OF THE UNITED STATES AND A RESIDENT OF BOULDER COUNTY, COLORADO. I HAVE NOT BEEN CONVICTED MORE THAN ONCE OF AN INFAMOUS CRIME NOR AM I CURRENTLY UNDER THE SENTENCE IMPOSED PURSUANT TO A CONVICTION OF AN INFAMOUS CRIME. I AM NOT UNDER GUARDIANSHIP FOR MENTAL DISABILITY.

I DO SOLEMNLY SWEAR (OR AFFIRM) THAT THE INFORMATION SET FORTH HEREON ABOUT MY PLACE OF RESIDENCE, NAME, PLACE OF BIRTH, CRIMINAL OFFENSES, QUALIFICATIONS AS A VOTER AND MY RIGHT TO REGISTER AND VOTE UNDER THE LAWS OF THIS STATE IS TRUE.

☞ *Marcos Juan Torres*

SIGN NAME IN FULL

GIVING FALSE INFORMATION TO PROCURE VOTER REGISTRATION IS PERJURY AND IS PUNISHABLE BY IMPRISONMENT FOR NOT MORE THAN 10 YEARS.

PARTY AFFILIATION CHOICE   (ONE MUST BE CHECKED)

PARTY AFFILIATION. Only voters affiliated with the Democratic or Republican Party vote in the primary election of their party. All voters vote in a general election.

DEMOCRAT _____   REPUBLICAN _____

OTHER (SPECIFY) _____

DECLINES TO AFFILIATE _____✔_____

FOR OFFICE USE ONLY   I.D. NUMBER

- - - - - - - - - - - - - - - - - - Fold here for mailing - - - - - - - - - - - - - - - - - -

PRIOR REGISTRATION Have you ever registered to vote before? ____*yes*____   APPROXIMATE YEAR __*2005*__

If yes, complete the following:
Name on last registration *Marcos Juan Torres* _____

Address on last registration *9 Mulberry Avenue* _____

Las Cruces	*Doña Ana*	*New Mexico*	*88001*
(Post Office)	(County)	(State)	(Zip)

Party affiliation on last registration _____ Date of Birth __*2/20/87*__

SIGN YOUR NAME BELOW AND AFTER HAND SYMBOL ABOVE

Marcos Juan Torres

Date __*9/20/08*__ Signature of Voter __*Marcos Juan Torres*__

RESIDENCE: Registering to vote in this county is a declaration of residence in this county and state, and authorization to cancel any prior registration in another Colorado locality or another state.
DISQUALIFYING CRIME: Contact Boulder County Board of Supervisors of Elections, 494-3161, if you have been convicted of a crime.

Telephone Number (In the event we need clarifying information) *555-2282*

Answer each question by underlining the correct phrase or sentence.

1. What is the name of the person registering to vote?
   a. Torres Marcos Juan
   c. Juan Marcos Torres
   b. Marcos Juan Torres
   d. Marcos Torres Juan

2. How is it determined where this applicant is supposed to register?
   a. He is registering in the state in which he was born.
   b. He may register in any county as long as he registers in the state in which he lives.
   c. He may register in any state in the United States.
   d. He is registering in the county where he lives.

3. What could be the result if the applicant did not fill out the voter registration form honestly?
   a. He could have to pay a costly fine.
   c. He could be jailed for up to ten years.
   b. He could lose his party affiliation.
   d. He could never vote in an election.

4. The two major parties are required to choose their candidates for a general election by holding a primary election. Would this applicant be allowed to vote in a primary election?
   a. Yes, he is affiliated with the Democratic party.
   b. Yes, he is affiliated with the Republican party.
   c. No, he is not affiliated with any political party.
   d. No, he would not be at least 18 years old at the time of the election.

5. Once each party chooses its candidate, a general election is held. According to this application, who is permitted to vote in general elections?
   a. all voters, regardless of party affiliation
   c. voters affiliated with the Universal party
   b. voters with no party affiliations
   d. voters who have voted before

6. How do you know that the applicant has registered to vote before?
   a. He is over 18 years old, and an 18-year-old can register to vote.
   b. This application is only for applicants who have registered before.
   c. He completed the "Prior Registration" section of the application.
   d. He has lived in Boulder for only one year, so he probably voted elsewhere in the last election.

7. What is the result of registering to vote in one county or state?
   a. You can vote in any other state in the country.
   c. You can vote in any county in the state.
   b. You cannot vote in another county or state.
   d. You must register there again next year.

8. When was this voter registration form filled out?
   a. February 20, 1987
   c. February 20, 2005
   b. February 20, 2007
   d. September 20, 2008

Careers

LESSON 23

Skill: Theme

BACKGROUND INFORMATION

In the play "Other Times, Other Customs," a young woman from Elizabethan times in the year 1598 suddenly appears before a modern young woman. Elizabethan dress was very elaborate, reflecting the prosperity of the times. The Elizabethan era was one of the greatest periods of English literature.

SKILL FOCUS: Theme

A writer usually does not directly state the **theme**, or message. Instead the reader must infer the message of a story or play from clues in the plot, setting, dialogue, and title of the work. In a play, the stage directions also signal the characters' attitudes and feelings. The following questions may help you infer the theme.

- What words, especially in the stage directions, suggest each character's feelings and attitude?

- How does your attitude toward the subject compare with each character's attitude?

- How do the characters' attitudes help you infer the theme?

▸ Read the following paragraphs. On the line at the top of the next column, write what you think the theme might be.

Shannon finished reading about King Arthur's court, and she thought how wonderful it would be to live at that time. Suddenly the room filled with mist, and when the air was clear, Shannon realized that she was inside a castle.

"Yuck!" Shannon thought to herself. Wasps and bees flew in through the window openings and dozens of flies buzzed overhead or landed briefly on the cold stone floor.

No screens, no electric lights, no bathroom— King Arthur's time isn't that great after all!

CONTEXT CLUES: Footnotes

When you read, you may come across **footnotes** for words that are unusual or that are used in an unusual way. Read the sentence and footnote below.

Arabella is 18 and dressed in the stylish Elizabethan upper-class fashion of 1598—a starched ruff, a farthingale,[1] an undergown, and an overgown.

[1] farthingale (FAR thin gayl): a hoop or series of hoops worn beneath a woman's skirt in the 16th and 17th centuries.

The raised number after the word *farthingale* is a signal to look at the bottom of the page for a footnote with the same number. The footnote gives a brief explanation of the word *farthingale*.

▸ The same sentence appears below, except that the word *ruff* is footnoted. Look up the word in a dictionary. On the lines below, write the definition of the word as a footnote.

Arabella is 18 and dressed in the stylish Elizabethan upper-class fashion of 1598—a starched ruff,[1] a farthingale, an undergown, and an overgown.

_____

_____

As you read, use the footnotes as clues to find the meanings of the numbered words *pomander, ciphers, elixirs, nostrums, dulcimer,* and *autres temps, autres moeurs.*

Strategy Tip

As you read "Other Times, Other Customs," notice how the stage directions help to suggest the characters' feelings and attitudes.

Other Times, Other Customs

Cast

Kate, 17, a high school senior
Lady Arabella, 18, a noblewoman of
    Elizabethan times

The Scene

The open, airy library of Cornelia Seton High School. It has glass window-walls, modern upholstered seating, and carpeting. Kate is sitting at a desk in an alcove, preparing an assignment for English IV.

Kate (*reading*): "Studies serve for delight, for ornament, and for ability. Their chief use for delight is in privateness and retiring; for ornament, is in discourse; and for ability, is in the judgment and disposition of business." (*to herself, skeptically*) Yes, that's great, Sir Francis Bacon, but in your day men took care of all the business. So what did young women study? Tell me that.

Lady Arabella appears suddenly beside Kate. Arabella is 18 and dressed in the stylish Elizabethan upper-class fashion of 1598—a starched ruff, a farthingale,[1] an undergown, and an overgown. She is also wearing a gold <u>pomander</u>[2] on a chain around her neck. Her blonde hair is frizzed, and her face painted.

Arabella: Why, we had to attend to our own business, to be sure. You have a chair for me, of course?

Kate reluctantly gets out of her chair and offers it to Arabella with an ironic, sweeping gesture.

Kate (*challenging*): Who are you, anyway? Lady Macbeth? The Lady of the Lake?

Arabella (*with great dignity*): I am Lady Arabella Mayne, and my business is to manage my husband's household, which I can assure you is a considerable task.

Kate: I don't see why. Anybody can keep house.

---

[1] farthingale (FAR thin gayl): a hoop or series of hoops worn beneath a woman's skirt in the 16th and 17th centuries.

[2] pomander (PAH man der): an apple-shaped case or box containing perfume, spices, and other aromatic substances; worn as a protection against odor and infection.

Arabella: Perhaps you have married too young, my dear, and have come to rely too heavily on your housekeeper. Believe me, that is a serious mistake.

Kate: I'm not married.

Arabella (*sympathetically*): Not married! Oh, my poor dear!

Kate: Nowadays women don't have to get married; they can have careers. Even if I marry, I'll still have a career. (*proudly*) I'm going to be a veterinarian. (*Arabella looks puzzled.*) A veterinarian, you know, an animal doctor.

Arabella (*disapprovingly*): Will, our groom, does that. (*graciously*) Yet, of course, a lady must know how to make medicines.

Kate: Is that what you learned at school?

Arabella: Oh, my dear, I wouldn't go to school. That would hardly be suitable for a woman of my station. I was taught at home by a governess. (*sentimentally*) Dear Dame Willoughby! She taught me to read and write.

I can also do the household <u>ciphers</u>[3] (*noticing that Kate is not impressed*), but then I see that you can read, too. (*patronizingly*) Can you write?

Kate (*insulted*): Of course! Have you taken leave of your senses, m'lady? (*Kate is beginning to take on some of Arabella's condescending airs as if to put her down a bit.*)

Arabella (*not even hearing Kate's remarks*): It was Mother who taught me to make medicine. Why, Sir Barnaby never would have married me if I hadn't known how to make <u>elixirs</u>[4] or other helpful <u>nostrums</u>.[5] After all, I have to keep the servants—all 28 of them—healthy. (*sighs importantly*) If that were the worst of it, I'd be grateful. But, no, I have to oversee all their labors—spinning, baking, tending cattle, and so forth. Of course, I must discipline the maids and servants too. So that is my business, and I studied hard to learn it. Fortunately Mother was an excellent teacher. (*sighs again, importantly*) Having so many maids and servants is such a responsibility, isn't it?

Kate (*irritated*): How do you imagine I would know? Do you believe we're millionaires? My father's a carpenter, and my mother sells shoes.

Arabella (*amazed*): A carpenter! (*severely*) Why should a carpenter's daughter want to be educated? And your mother sells…

Kate: Naturally, they work, and so will I. Today social class does not limit someone's potential. Education is a great equalizer. Everyone goes to school nowadays.

Arabella: Why?

Kate: Well…

Arabella (*disapprovingly*): What do you learn in your school?

Kate: In economics we're learning about marketing in developing countries; in physics we're studying nuclear technology; and last year in biochemistry we studied genetics.

Arabella: Who manages your households?

[3] ciphers (SY fərz): numbers used in accounting or budgeting.
[4] elixirs (i LIK sərz): a medicinal solution thought to have curative or restorative powers.
[5] nostrums (NAHS trəmz): household remedies.

Kate: (*with a grimace*): Fortunately that doesn't take up much time nowadays. (*lightly*) We have machines to do the work—dishwashers, vacuum cleaners, refrigerators, microwave ovens, home computers…

Arabella (*firmly*): These things mean nothing to me, and your education sounds very peculiar. It seems to be all about things you will never see and places where you are not likely to go.

Kate (*huffily*): Well, your education sounds pretty peculiar to me. Wouldn't you rather learn something besides how to keep house?

Arabella (*with great pride*): But oh, my dear, I did. I play the dulcimer[6] and lute. I sing. I dance. I am fluent in French—my Norman heritage, of course. I speak some Italian and German. My business—is that what you mean by career? My career, then, is to be Sir Barnaby's capable wife. Your career, well, that is different. Each of us has been educated for the life she expects to lead. Forgive me if I prefer my own.

Kate (*earnestly*): Wouldn't you really rather be in my shoes if you could?

Arabella (*amused*): Absolutely not! (*as if to a child or an underling*) Permit me to explain: Your life, my dear, sounds just a little bit dull— dull and not very responsible. Sincerely, now, don't you envy me?

Kate (*firmly*): Not a whit, m'lady!

Arabella (*shrugging elegantly*): Well, <u>autres temps, autres moeurs</u>.[7] I must go now. This has all been most educational. (*She vanishes.*)

Kate: I'll say. (*She picks up her book again but sits contemplating for a moment before she opens it. She then speaks thoughtfully.*) Well, there's no accounting for tastes. (*She opens her book and proceeds to read.*) "Studies serve…"

Curtain

---

6 dulcimer (DUL sə mer): a musical instrument with wire strings stretched over a sound box, played with two padded hammers or by plucking.

7 *autres temps, autres moeurs:* A French saying meaning "other times, other customs."

COMPREHENSION

1. What is the full name of Kate's visitor?

_____

_____

_____

2. What is the actual setting of this play?

_____

_____

_____

3. **a.** How are Kate and Arabella alike?

_____

_____

_____

b. How are they different?

_____

_____

_____

_____

4. a. How is Arabella's education different from Kate's?

_____

_____

_____

b. Why does Arabella say that Kate's education sounds peculiar to her?

_____

_____

_____

_____

5. Draw a line to match each word or phrase with its explanation.

pomander   **a.** numbers used in accounting or budgeting

elixirs   **b.** household remedies

ciphers   **c.** a medicinal solution thought to have curative or restorative powers

nostrums   **d.** an apple-shaped box containing spices and other aromatic substances

dulcimer   **e.** a French saying meaning "other times, other cultures"

autre temps, autres moeurs   **f.** a musical instrument with wire strings

CRITICAL THINKING

1. There is an implied setting in the play as well as the actual one. Describe the implied setting.

_____

_____

2. In what ways do Arabella's manner and attitude reflect her time?

_____

_____

3. Why does Arabella say Kate's life is irresponsible compared to hers?

_____

_____

4. Kate says, "Everyone goes to school nowadays," and Arabella asks, "Why?" How would you answer Arabella?

_____

_____

5. Explain how the purpose of education in the 1590s was different from the purpose of education today.

_____

_____

6. In the England of Arabella's day, only about 30 percent of all adults could read and write. Most of these were men. Explain how these two facts would have made the lives of Elizabethan men and women different from yours.

_____

_____

SKILL FOCUS: THEME

1. Kate and Arabella share the same opinion about education.

   a. Circle the word below that best describes their opinion.

     comic   sentimental   ironic   serious

   b. Explain your choice.

_____

_____

2. **a.** Underline the two words below that best identify Kate's attitude.

     earnest   bitter   sincere   cautious   sad

   b. Go back to the play. Underline the words and phrases in the stage directions and dialogue that reveal Kate's attitude.

3. **a.** Circle the three words that best identify Arabella's attitude.

     bitter   boastful   arrogant   dignified   carefree

   b. Go back to the play. Circle the words and phrases in the stage directions and dialogue that reveal Arabella's attitude.

4. What does Kate learn from her encounter with Arabella?

_____

_____

5. Despite the differences in the two women's tones of voice, the author's attitude about the education of women is clear, and it can be expressed as the theme of the play. In a few lines, write what you believe to be the theme of the play.

_____

_____

Reading-Writing Connection

In your opinion, what is the biggest change in education since the late 1500s? Write a short essay on a separate sheet of paper.

Skill: Comparing and Contrasting

BACKGROUND INFORMATION

"Work—Past and Present" explores the shift in the kinds of jobs people in the United States have had over the past 200 years. For most people, work is part of life. People must have jobs in order to earn money, which enables them to buy the things they need, such as food, clothing, and shelter, as well as the things they want, such as cars, recreation equipment, and hobby items. However, the way people have earned their money has changed since the founding of this country.

SKILL FOCUS: Comparing and Contrasting

When reading, you often need to compare and contrast information about people, places, and trends. To **compare**, you need to look for similarities. To **contrast**, you need to look for differences.

One way to compare and contrast information about two or more topics is to put the information into visual form. For example, statistics, or numerical facts, are sometimes presented in the form of graphs and tables.

The steps below will help you compare and contrast using information from graphs and tables within a selection.

1. Preview the graphs and tables before reading.
2. Read the selection carefully to understand the topics being compared and contrasted.
3. Identify the type of statistical information given on the graph or table.
4. Study the graph to find numerical relationships.
5. Use the statistical similarities and differences to draw conclusions about trends.

▶ Look at the table below. Answer the questions about it at the top of the next column.

1. What does the graph compare?

_____

_____

2. Which age group has decreased the most?

_____

3. Which age group has increased the most?

_____

CONTEXT CLUES: Appositive Phrases

Sometimes the meaning of a new word is made clear by an **appositive phrase**. It is usually set apart by commas and may start with the word *or*. Read the sentence below. Look for an appositive phrase that helps explain the underlined word.

Most of the jobs at the time were of an **agricultural**, *or farming, nature.*

If you do not know the meaning of the word *agricultural*, the phrase *or farming*, can help you.

▶ Read the following sentence. Circle the appositive phrase that explains the underlined word.

Workers received little or no satisfaction from doing the same **repetitious**, *or tiresomely repeated, task day after day.*

In "Work—Past and Present," find the appositive phrases for the underlined words *mass produce*, *consumers*, and *self-employed* to explain the meanings of these words.

> ### Strategy Tip
>
> Before reading "Work—Past and Present," preview the graphs. As you read, compare and contrast the information in the text with the statistics in the graphs.

Age Distribution in Workforce					
Year	Age 16–24	Age 25–34	Age 35–45	Age 46–54	Age 55 and over
1992	16%	28%	27%	18%	12%
2006	17%	21%	24%	24%	16%

Work—Past and Present

When you imagine the world of 200 years ago, many differences from today's world probably come to mind. A large number of those differences are most likely of a technological nature. For example, today we have appliances that run on electricity and machines that didn't even exist in the 1800s. Other changes include the growth and diversity of the population of the United States, as well as changes in politics and governments around the world.

One of the areas in which the greatest changes have occurred is employment. The ways in which people work at their jobs, and often the very jobs they do, have undergone change. Comparing and contrasting the jobs of the past and the present is both a lesson in history and a reflection of how the United States has changed over time.

Farm-Based Jobs

As a newly settled country, the United States was a land of opportunity. Carpenters were needed to build homes and other buildings. Farmers were needed to grow food and tend the land. If someone was willing to work, a job could be found.

Most of the jobs at the time were of an agricultural, or farming, nature. There were no industries that manufactured goods in factories yet. In fact, 95 percent of the population at the time worked on farms. Of the remaining 5 percent, 60 percent were skilled craftspeople, and the other 40 percent were unskilled laborers.

The pie charts in Figure 1 compare the kinds of workers before the Industrial Revolution in the United States with the kinds of workers after the Industrial Revolution. Over a period of 150 years, the ratio of farm workers to non-farm workers reversed completely.

The non-farm workers usually specialized in one or two skills. They might have been blacksmiths or shoemakers. The height of a craftsperson's career was to own his or her own shop. A craftsperson usually owned his or her home, as well.

The road to this goal was often long. Aspiring craftspersons needed to start out as unpaid apprentices, gradually moving up and becoming paid. Finally they would have obtained enough skill, experience, and money to venture out on their own. They usually owned their own tools and equipment.

Unskilled laborers also had a niche in the work force, if a less appreciated one. Their work required little training. For example, they might take on work digging ditches or loading cargo onto ships. They were paid barely enough to afford food and shelter.

For the most part, however, workers at this time were self-sufficient, relying on their own lands and skills to earn a living and to live a comfortable life.

Factory-Based Work

The Industrial Revolution is the term applied to the era when products began to be manufactured in large quantities in factories, rather than in small quantities by individual craftspeople. For example, instead of one person in a town making and selling shoes, a factory full of people would <u>mass produce</u>, or make large quantities of, shoes in a much shorter period of time. The result was that as mass production increased, the need for the skilled craftsperson decreased, and before long, they were no longer needed.

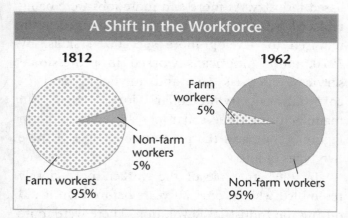

A Shift in the Workforce

1812   1962

Farm workers 5%

Non-farm workers 5%

Farm workers 95%

Non-farm workers 95%

FIGURE 1. Prior to the Industrial Revolution, most Americans worked in the agricultural field in farm-based jobs.

It is difficult to pinpoint the exact date that the Industrial Revolution began in the United States. It first occurred in Britain at the end of the 1700s, but it soon caught on and spread around the world.

The Industrial Revolution emerged as a science that began to combine with practical knowledge. New systems for production were invented, both labor-based and technology-based, which proved to be more efficient than traditional handmade production. For example, by using an assembly line, it was possible to make goods in a single factory centered in a metropolitan area, rather than in many small shops spread out among several towns. Factories became big business—bigger than the sum of all the individual craftspersons they replaced.

✔ Although mass production might have seemed good for <u>consumers</u>, or people who bought the products, it was not good for the worker. One of the biggest complaints from factory workers was that their jobs were boring. Workers received little or no satisfaction from doing the same repetitious, or tiresomely repeated, task day after day. Workers no longer owned their own tools, or even saw the finished product. As a result, the pride workers once took in a job well done began to disappear.

Conditions in many workplaces were also unappealing. Employees worked from dawn to dusk six days a week. Most received only four days off each year, for which they did not receive pay. There were no sick days or personal days. If a worker did not work, he or she was not paid. Moreover, since factory work was unskilled work, the pay rate was low. Consequently, many people who worked in factories were barely able to support their families.

Post-Industrial Revolution (mid-1900s to Present)

The 1940s saw a boom in industrialized America, chiefly because of World War II. Conditions in factories had improved over the years, as had hours and wages. To help their country in the war effort, workers flocked to the factories, motivated to build ships, planes, and tanks as quickly as possible. The bar graph in Figure 2 shows the number of workers building airplanes in 1939—

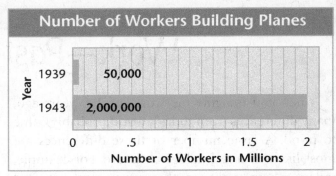

FIGURE 2. **In a four-year period, the number of workers building planes in factories increased dramatically.**

before American involvement in World War II—and in 1943—during American involvement in World War II.

After World War II, the United States saw a period of economic prosperity. Due to the demand for workers, many Americans had steady paychecks. However, because many products were hard to find during the war, Americans were not spending their money. For example, factories were not making family cars while they were building tanks. Americans, therefore, had a surplus of cash to spend after the war.

Factory production also changed. Many inventions, such as the transistor, were developed during the war years. The tiny size of the transistor, which replaced much larger tubes, led to the production of small radios, televisions, and even computers.

This, of course, led to a whole new technology-based industry. As more and more jobs were being replaced by machines, workers were once again required to develop more specialized skills. By 1970, more Americans worked in professional services, such as law and medicine, and in corporations (white-collar jobs), than in manufacturing (blue-collar jobs). The bar graph in Figure 3 compares the percentage change in these two types of jobs.

In 2003, the role of the worker more closely resembled what it did 200 years before than it did during the Industrial Revolution. There were more people who were <u>self-employed</u>, or had their own

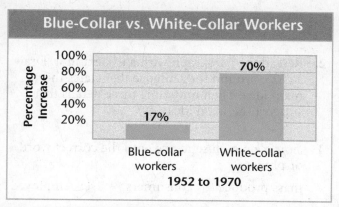

FIGURE 3. **After World War II, the percentage increase of workers in white-collar professions rose more dramatically than the percentage increase of workers in blue-collar professions.**

businesses, than there were large corporations or partnerships. Of course, most larger companies have many employees working for them. Still the number of people earning money in one-person businesses shows this trend back toward self-employment. Figure 4 compares the numbers and percentages of business types, based on the income tax returns and data collected by the U.S. Census Bureau.

Although jobs for American workers have changed dramatically over the course of the past 200 years, in some ways it seems as if workers' roles have returned to where they came from. Many people are once again relying on their own skills and working for themselves rather than earning a living by working for a large company or factory. Although the traditional jobs of craftspeople may have disappeared, technology has created new possibilities for the self-employed.

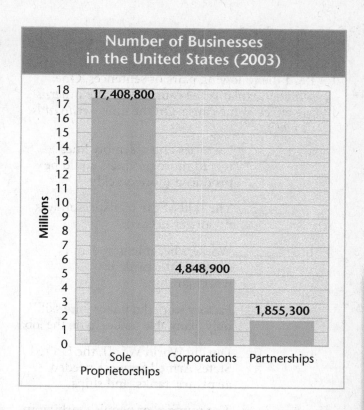

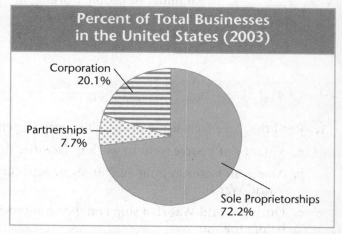

FIGURE 4. **The bar graph and pie chart above show that in 2003, the number of businesses owned and operated by a sole proprietor was over three times the number of big corporations.**

SOCIAL STUDIES

1. Read the following pairs of sentences. One sentence explains the cause, while the other is the effect of the cause. On the lines, write *cause* or *effect*.

   a. _____ Factories and assembly lines meant more products could be produced more quickly.

   _____ The skill of the craftsperson was no longer needed.

   b. _____ Workers became bored and showed little pride in workmanship.

   _____ Factory work did not require skill, only many able bodies to do the job.

   c. _____ During World War II, the United States Armed Services needed airplanes, tanks, and ships.

   _____ The number of people working in factories during World War II skyrocketed.

2. Reread the paragraph with a ✔ next to it. Draw a circle around the sentence that states the main idea. Then underline three details that support the main idea.

3. Complete each sentence with the correct word or phrase.

   mass produce   consumers   self-employed

   a. The sole proprietor of a business is said to be _____.

   b. Businesses view the people who buy products as _____.

   c. Factories _____ large quantities of products.

CRITICAL THINKING

1. Read the three facts listed below. Then write a generalization based on these facts.

   a. Millions of people went to work in factories during World War II.

   b. American factories built 12,000 ships, 300,000 planes, and 87,000 tanks during World War II.

   c. During World War II, a ship could be built in 56 days, compared to nearly a year before the war.

   _____

   _____

2. Explain why so many people went to work in factories during World War II.

   _____

   _____

3. Write the effect for the following cause.

   Cause: Workers are replaced by machines.

   Effect: _____

   _____

Use the information in the selection and the graphs to answer the following questions.

1. **a.** What do the sections on the pie chart in Figure 1 compare?

   _____

   _____

   b. What do the bars on the bar graph in Figure 2 compare?

   _____

   _____

   c. What do the bars on the bar graph in Figure 3 compare?

   _____

   _____

   d. What do the bars on the bar graph in Figure 4 compare?

   _____

   _____

2. **a.** Use Figure 1 to describe the change in the percentage of workers from the era before the Industrial Revolution to the era after the Industrial Revolution.

   _____

   _____

   b. Use Figure 2 to draw a conclusion from the statistics.

   _____

   _____

   c. Use Figure 3 to draw a conclusion from the statistics.

   _____

   _____

   d. Use Figure 4 to determine which type of business equals more than half of the businesses reported in 2003. How can you tell?

   _____

   _____

Reading-Writing Connection

People have always worked for themselves or worked for other companies. Which do you think you would like to do? On a separate sheet of paper, write a paragraph that explains your ideas. Include the job or career you might see for yourself.

Skill: Classifying

BACKGROUND INFORMATION

"Careers in the Sciences" describes a variety of science careers in different areas of science. The education required for a career in science varies depending on the particular career chosen. For example, to become a physician, an individual must first complete four years of college and then attend medical school. A landscape architect, who plans large-scale gardens, generally must have a college degree in the field. A landscape gardener may have received only on-the-job training.

SKILL FOCUS: Classifying

Sometimes information is organized by **classifying** similar objects or ideas into groups. Classifying makes it easier to see similarities and differences among the groups. People who work with a great number of objects, as scientists do, group them according to their characteristics. When scientists classify plants or animals, for example, the members of each group are similar in some way.

Scientists also classify the branches of scientific study. Three major categories are the life sciences, the earth sciences, and the physical sciences. Many different types of scientists work in each category.

To read a selection that describes many groups, ask yourself these questions.

- What characteristics do the members in the same group share?
- How are the members of one group different from those of another?

▶ The chart below classifies nine animals into three groups, based on characteristics they share. Study the chart, and then add one more animal to each group.

CONTEXT CLUES: Definition

When reading about science, you will come across words that you do not know. Sometimes the **definition** of a word appears as a context clue. It explains what the word means.

Read the following sentences. Look for a definition that explains the underlined word.

When people think of careers in science, they often picture a person dressed in a white coat doing <u>esoteric</u> experiments in a laboratory. Something that is esoteric is understood by very few people.

The second sentence contains the definition of the word *esoteric*. It means "something that very few people understand."

▶ Read the following sentences. Circle the definition that explains the meaning of the underlined word.

Paleontologists study <u>fossils</u> to reconstruct Earth's history. Fossils are the remains or a trace of an animal or plant of a past geologic age embedded in Earth's crust.

As you read the next selection, look for definitions that explain the meanings of the underlined words *imperative*, *transmitted*, and *ascertain*.

Strategy Tip

As you read "Careers in the Sciences," think about how careers in science are classified.

	Mammals	Insects	Fish
Characteristics	warm-blooded have hair breathe air young born alive	cold-blooded have exoskeleton 6 legs; 3 body parts young hatch from eggs	cold-blooded usually have scales breathe underwater young can hatch from eggs
Examples	bear, human, dog	bee, ant, grasshopper	flounder, tuna, catfish

Careers in the Sciences

When people think of careers in science, they often picture a person dressed in a white coat doing esoteric experiments in a laboratory. Something that is esoteric is understood by very few people. Another science career that people are familiar with is medicine, which includes doctors, nurses, technicians, and medical aides. In many other professions, often not identified as science careers, a strong background in one or more of the sciences is <u>imperative</u>. Something that is imperative is absolutely necessary. The following paragraphs describe some of the many careers in science, the requirements for these careers, and some of the specialists who work in science professions.

The Life Sciences

Careers in the life sciences can be divided into two major groups: the biology professions and the health professions. The professions in biology include many kinds of specialists who are involved in research and teaching. In general, entrance into these careers requires many years of college training plus original research.

Most biologists who study animals specialize in one group. For example, scientists called ichthyologists (ik thee AHL ə jists) study fish, entomologists (en tə MAHL ə jists) study insects, and herpetologists (her pə TAHL ə jists) study reptiles and amphibians. Anatomists and physiologists (fiz ee AHL ə jists) study the structure of living organisms and the functioning of their bodies. Cytologists (sy TAHL ə jists) are biologists who study cells.

Plant biologists, or botanists, may also specialize. Bryologists (bry AHL ə jists) study mosses, while lichenologists (ly kə NAHL ə jists) specialize in the study of lichens. Some botanists specialize in plant pathology, the study of plant diseases. Others specialize in plant genetics, the study of how plant characteristics are <u>transmitted</u> from one generation to the next. The word *transmitted* means "passed along."

(*left*) An entomologist specializes in the study of insects. This entomologist is studying insects from Costa Rica to understand more about the country's living things. (*above*) This herpetologist —a scientist who studies reptiles—is studying king cobra snake eggs.

SCIENCE

Many other careers depend on a knowledge of plants or animals but require less formal education. Landscapers, for example, know which plants grow best under specific conditions, and they select and artistically arrange plants around a home or building. Animal keepers in a zoo must have a knowledge of the animals under their care in order to keep them healthy. Certain technicians in sewage treatment plants use their knowledge of microscopic organisms to monitor the safe, effective operation of this essential community facility. Such careers require on-the-job training or one- or two-year specialized college courses or training programs.

While doctors and nurses treat people who are ill, there are many other challenging career opportunities in the health field. Physical therapists work with people who have various physical problems and help them regain or improve their ability to move. Speech and language pathologists help people who have lost their ability to speak or understand speech due to an accident or illness, or who have other speech and language problems. Laboratory technicians perform the numerous tests used to <u>ascertain</u> if a person is healthy. The word *ascertain* means "to find out." Genetic counselors provide information to people who have a family history of an inherited disease or disorder. All these careers require college training.

The Earth Sciences

People who work in the earth sciences are often fascinated with the way the oceans move, with the unpredictability of weather, or with the mysteries of outer space. Earth scientists include meteorologists, who monitor weather patterns and predict future weather conditions, and astronomers, who study the objects and events in space. Seismologists (syz MAHL ə jists) study earthquakes. Geologists study the rocks of the Earth, using them as clues to the Earth's past. Paleontologists (pay lee ahn TAHL ə jists) study fossils to reconstruct the Earth's history. These careers require college preparation and original research.

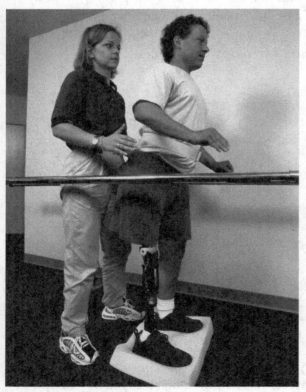

(*above*) A physical therapist works with people who have physical problems to help them regain or improve their ability to move.

(*right*) A paleontologist studies fossils to learn about pre-historic times.

Even though gem cutters and stonemasons are not scientists, they must have a knowledge of the composition of stones to cut and shape them with precision. Surveyors take precise measurements of the size, shape, and elevation of parts of the Earth's surface, and cartographers, or map makers, use these measurements to make accurate drawings of part or all of Earth. Many of these careers are learned through apprenticeships and on-the-job training.

The Physical Sciences

The physical sciences deal with the study of the chemical and physical properties of matter in the universe, and they can be roughly divided into two areas: chemistry and physics.

Careers in chemistry include organic chemistry, which is the study of chemical compounds made primarily of carbon, such as gasoline and plastics. Research chemists analyze existing substances and create new ones for a variety of uses. Assayers (as SAY ərz) analyze the composition of ores and scrap metal and determine their value. Pharmacologists (far mə KAHL ə jists) understand the chemistry of medicines and study the effects of drugs. Some criminologists are chemists, too; they chemically analyze evidence from a crime scene, such as drugs, explosives, and paints. Their findings can help in the apprehension of criminals.

The field of physics includes many professions. Nuclear physicists (FIZ ə sists) study the structure and behavior of atoms. Astrophysicists study the chemical and physical properties of objects in space. Knowledge of the physical sciences is important to aeronautical (er ə NAW tic əl) engineers, as well as to nautical engineers. Structural engineers understand the properties of construction materials and the forces that act on a completed structure. These careers require four or more years of college education.

Other careers in the physical sciences require less formal education. Computer repair technicians must have a knowledge of electronics. Opticians grind and polish lenses for eyeglasses according to prescription requirements. Automotive engineers apply their knowledge of physical principles to the design and manufacture of safe, efficient, and comfortable vehicles.

(*above*) A surveyor measures the size, shape, and elevation of a section of land for a construction site.

(*left*) A pharmacologist understands the chemistry of medicines and studies the effects of drugs.

1. What does a plant pathologist do?

   _____

   _____

2. Name a specialist who helps people with physical problems regain or improve their ability to move.

   _____

   _____

3. What does a meteorologist do?

   _____

   _____

4. Identify two careers in earth science that usually require on-the-job training rather than a college education.

   _____

   _____

5. Explain what a pharmacologist does.

   _____

   _____

6. What does an optician do?

   _____

   _____

7. Why does a structural engineer need to understand physics?

   _____

   _____

8. Draw a line to match each word with its explanation.

   imperative   a. find out

   transmitted   b. absolutely necessary

   ascertain   c. passed along

CRITICAL THINKING

1. Both families of a couple have a history of diabetes. Who should the couple consult to find out the chances that a child of theirs will have diabetes?
   a. a genetic counselor
   b. a speech/language pathologist
   c. a paleontologist
   d. biologist

2. What career might a person with an interest in rocks and mining find enjoyable?
   a. entomologist
   b. seismologist
   c. botanist
   d. geologist

3. A _____ would analyze samples of soil and fibers left behind by a burglar.
   a. criminologist
   b. meteorologist
   c. lichenologist
   d. ichthyologist

4. To do their work accurately, cartographers depend on the work of _____.
   a. astrophysicists
   b. oceanographers
   c. surveyors
   d. assayers

Complete the following chart with information about careers in sciences.

Careers in Science				
		Specialty	**Description**	**Education**
Life Sciences	**Biology**			
	Health			
Earth Sciences				
Physical Sciences	**Chemistry**			
	Physics			

Reading-Writing Connection

Which field of science appeals to you most—the life sciences, the earth sciences, or the physical sciences? On a separate sheet of paper, write a paragraph in which you explain your choice.

Skill: Understanding Probability

BACKGROUND INFORMATION

"Probability" explains the concept of probability—the chance that some event will happen or will not happen. Almost every day people think and talk about probability. People ask each other "what the odds are" that something will happen—that a favorite team will win, that a certain actor will receive an award, or that they will get a good grade or do well on a test. Each of these questions involves probability.

SKILL FOCUS: Understanding Probability

Sometimes a mathematical problem states that two or more different things must be combined according to a given set of rules. The problem then asks how many different results can occur from the combination. One way to solve such a problem is to make a chart and fill it with every possible combination according to the rules, and then count the number of different results. For example, if you wanted to know how many different ways the numbers 2 and 5 and 7 can be arranged, you could list 2, 5, 7 and 2, 7, 5; you could list 5, 2, 7 and 5, 7, 2; and you could list 7, 2, 5 and 7, 5, 2. By counting, you can see that there are only six ways in which these numbers can be arranged.

Sometimes the number of possibilities to be counted can be very large. Mathematicians have developed rules for arriving at the different kinds of possible arrangements without counting. A basic rule of **probability** tells you how to find the number of possibilities without counting. Suppose that one thing can happen two ways, another can happen three ways, and still a third can happen four ways. You do not have to make a list and count the possibilities. The number of possibilities is simply the product of $2 \times 3 \times 4$.

▌ How many different ways can you arrange 3 colors into groups of 2? The colors are red, white and blue. Write your answer on the lines below.

_____

_____

WORD CLUES

Knowing the meanings of the following words will help you to get the most out of "Understanding Probability." *Chance* is any measure of the likelihood that something will happen or not happen; *possibility* is anything that could happen; *probability* is a mathematical measure of chance.

Strategy Tip

As you read "Probability," study the diagrams. Think about how they relate to the mathematical ideas presented in the paragraphs.

Probability

Probability is the chance that some event will happen or will not happen. To find out the chance that a particular arrangement of objects or events will or will not happen, you can use methods of computing probability. Determining the possible arrangements of objects or events involves special techniques because the number of possible arrangements of even a few things can be very high.

Read the following problem.

Sara is planning her college program. In addition to her required courses, she can take two other courses. One must be a humanities course (H), and the other must be a science course (S). She has decided that she will take two of the following courses: Music Appreciation (H), European History (H), Introduction to Physics (S), Advanced Algebra (S), or Computer Programming (S). How many different combinations of courses can Sara take?

If Sara chooses one of the humanities courses, she cannot choose the other one. For example, suppose Sara decides to take the course in Music Appreciation. Then she cannot take European History as the other course. However, she still has three courses from which to choose, since she can take any one of the three science courses.

You can show this arrangement in the following **tree diagram.**

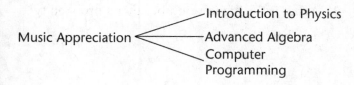

The number of possibilities, or "branches," represented in this tree diagram is three. If Sara had not decided on Music Appreciation and was still considering European History, she would have more possibilities. In that case, another tree would start with European History and branch to the three science courses. The total number of possibilities would be six.

The Multiplication Rule

There is another way to look at this problem. Picking one of the science courses first is one possibility that can happen two ways: It can be paired with one of the two humanities courses. The other possibility, picking a humanities course first, can happen three ways: It can be matched with one of the three science courses. Either way, the total number of ways is therefore 2 × 3, or 6. This method, called the multiplication rule, is easier to use with large numbers than is using a tree diagram.

The multiplication rule can also be used when several different things are being combined. For example, an automobile company might offer a car in six different colors, in four different body styles, and with either an automatic or standard transmission. One part of the tree diagram for this problem follows.

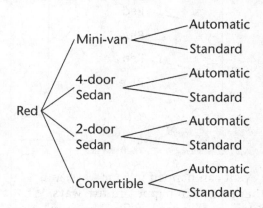

To arrive at the total number of possibilities, it would be necessary to do a total of six such diagrams—one for each color. It is easier, however, to use the multiplication rule.

6 (colors) × 4 (body styles) × 2 (transmission types) = 48

You get the same answer with either the multiplication rule or the tree diagram. In the part of the tree diagram shown for this problem, there are eight possibilities. This diagram, however, represents the possibilities for just one color. For all six colors, there are 6 × 8 = 48 of the smallest branches, or possibilities.

MATHEMATICS

One way to think about probability problems is to picture a number of marbles in a bag. Think of a bag that contains four marbles—a red, a green, a white, and a blue one. If you were to take one marble from the bag without seeing its color, there would be a probability of 1 out of 4 that the marble would be red. The same probability applies to the other three marbles. Mathematically, this probability is expressed as $\frac{1}{4}$. The fraction indicates the chance that something will happen.

A probability is always expressed as a fraction between 0 (no choice) and 1 (certainty). For example, if all four marbles in the bag were red and you were to take one of them, the probability that it would be red is 1. The probability of red is a certainty. The probability of a green marble is 0—no chance.

Now consider a bag with two red and two blue marbles. If you were to remove one marble from the bag, what is the probability that it would be red? What is the probability that it would be blue? There are equal chances of getting either a red or a blue marble.

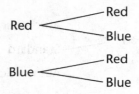

Suppose you replaced the first marble and picked again from the four marbles. The chance of getting one marble of each color would be 2 out of 4, or $\frac{2}{4} = \frac{1}{2}$.

A probability does not guarantee that an event will actually occur. It only indicates the chance that something will occur. For example, suppose that you were to draw a marble from the bag, replace it, and repeat the experiment several times. The chance that you would get a red marble is $\frac{1}{2}$ for each repetition. In actuality, you might draw the blue marble much more often than the red, or vice versa. For a very large number of repetitions, however, you would draw the red about half the time and the blue about half the time.

There is a connection between counting and probability. If you can count the total number of equally likely events, then you can use that number to find the probability. As an example, consider the problem about the different kinds of automobiles. The chance of selling any one color, body style, or transmission is the same. For any particular car, such as a red convertible with automatic transmission, the probability of selling that combination is therefore $\frac{1}{48}$.

COMPREHENSION

1. One event can happen in four ways, and another event can happen in five ways. What operation can be used to find the number of ways that both events can happen?

   _____

2. What is the lowest number that a probability can be? _____

3. What is the highest number that a probability can be? _____

CRITICAL THINKING

1. In the first problem in the selection, Sara must choose one humanities course and one science course. If she could take any two of the five courses she wanted, would the number of possibilities go up, go down, or stay the same? Why?

   _____

   _____

2. If you have two red marbles and three blue marbles in a bag, is the probability of drawing one red marble $\frac{1}{5}$? Why or why not?

_____

_____

SKILL FOCUS: UNDERSTANDING PROBABILITY

A. For each problem below, write the number of possible arrangements on the line. You may draw tree diagrams on another sheet of paper.

1. To mix batter, a cook can use a mixer with two bowl sizes and six speeds. _____

2. To install a faucet, a plumber can use one of three wrenches and one of five fixtures. _____

3. An airline inspector is going to make a round trip between two cities. She wants to be on different airlines going and returning. She has a choice of four different airlines. _____

B. A bag contains one red, one blue, and one green marble. You draw a marble from the bag, replace it, and draw another for a total of three draws. The tree diagram below shows the different arrangements possible. Use the diagram to solve each of the following problems.

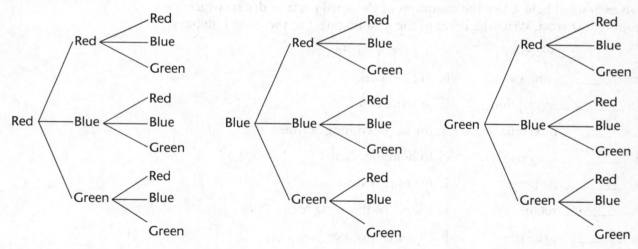

1. What is the probability of drawing one red marble each time in the three draws? _____

2. What is the probability of getting a red marble on the second draw? _____

3. What is the probability of getting a red, a blue, and a green marble in the three draws in that order? _____

Reading-Writing Connection

On a separate sheet of paper, create your own probability problem about the options available on a product that you would like to buy.

Skill: Word Parts

When you are trying to figure out the meaning of an unknown word, it helps to know the meanings of the word's parts. Roots, prefixes, and suffixes are **word parts**. Many of the words you know are made up of roots with prefixes and suffixes added to them.

The word *interject* is formed by combining the prefix *inter-* and the root *ject*. The prefix *inter-* means "between," and the root *ject* means "to throw." If you know these meanings, you can figure out that *interject* means "to throw between or to insert."

Look at the following prefixes, roots, suffix, and their meanings. Notice that some of the roots have more than one spelling.

Roots		Prefixes		Suffix	
ject	to throw	con-	with, together	-ion	the act of
scrib (script)	to write	in-	in, into, on		
tain	to hold	inter-	between		
ven (vent)	to come	pre-	before		
		re-	back		

A. Read each word below. Use the meanings of the word parts to decide which meaning is correct. Write the letter of the meaning next to the word it defines.

1. _____ rejection   **a.** the act of writing on

2. _____ contain   **b.** to hold back

3. _____ inscription   **c.** to write before

4. _____ intervene   **d.** the act of coming between

5. _____ intervention   **e.** to hold together

6. _____ convene   **f.** to come between

7. _____ retain   **g.** the act of throwing back

8. _____ prescribe   **h.** to come together

B. Use one of the words above to complete each sentence below.

1. The blue pitcher will _____ a quart of milk.

2. The meeting will _____ promptly at 4:00.

3. The weakened dam could not _____ the water.

4. The _____ of the faulty parts was due to an engineer's mistake.

5. The president was asked to _____ in the dispute between the two countries.

6. The _____ on his class ring included the date of his graduation.

Skill: Syllables

When dividing words of three or more **syllables,** you use the same rules that you use with two-syllable words. The only difference is that you have to use two or more rules. For example, in dividing the word *recovery* you use three rules.

- Divide between the prefix and the rest of the word: re covery.
- In words with one consonant between two sounded vowels with the first vowel short, divide after the consonant: re cov ery.
- Divide between the rest of the word and the suffix: re cov er y.

Here is a summary of rules to help you divide words into syllables.

RULE 1 In a compound word, divide between the two smaller words.

RULE 2 In words with double consonants, divide between the double consonants.

RULE 3 In words with a prefix or suffix, divide between a root word and its prefix or suffix.

RULE 4 In words with two consonants between two sounded vowels, divide between the two consonants.

RULE 5a In words with one consonant between two sounded vowels with the first vowel long, you usually divide before the consonant.

RULE 5b In words with one consonant between two sounded vowels with the first vowel short, you usually divide after the consonant.

RULE 6 Do not divide between a consonant blend or consonant and -*le*.

Divide each of the words below into syllables. Write the syllables separately on the line to the right of the word. Then write the numbers of the rules you used on the line to the left of the word. The first word is done for you.

1. __3, 2__ disapprove ____dis ap prove____
2. _____ Bermuda _____
3. _____ cylinder _____
4. _____ astringent _____
5. _____ culturist _____
6. _____ acceptance _____
7. _____ limitedness _____
8. _____ tapestry _____
9. _____ uncertain _____
10. _____ buttermilk _____
11. _____ frolicsome _____
12. _____ legalize _____
13. _____ romantic _____
14. _____ Kentucky _____
15. _____ fingerprint _____
16. _____ Philippine _____
17. _____ tornado _____
18. _____ unbridle _____
19. _____ syllable _____
20. _____ singular _____

Skill: Outlining

A good way to understand and remember something you read is to make an **outline**. A good outline shows how the main idea and supporting details in a selection are organized.

In a paragraph, the most important idea is the **main idea**. In an outline of a selection or a chapter, the main idea of each paragraph is restated in a few words and written next to a Roman numeral: I, II, III, and so on.

The details that give important supporting information about the main idea are the **major details**. The major details are written next to capital letters: A, B, C, and so on. These letters are indented, or moved a little to the right, below the Roman numerals. By positioning them this way, you can see how the main idea and major details are related.

The details that give information about the major details are **minor details**. The minor details are written next to numbers: 1, 2, 3, and so on. These numbers are indented below the capital letters. This positioning shows you how the minor details are related to the major details.

Read the first paragraph from an article about the Gray Panthers. Then look at the outline to the right of the paragraph.

The Gray Panthers

The story of the Gray Panthers is an interesting one. The group was founded by Margaret E. (Maggie) Kuhn and a few of her friends in 1970 when they were forced to retire from their jobs. From the beginning, Maggie and her friends organized for educational and charitable purposes. The Gray Panthers' members are people of all ages, dedicated to the cause of equal rights for all, regardless of age. The actual name of the group was given to it by the producer of a television talk show.

The Gray Panthers
I. Background
    A. Founded by Maggie Kuhn and friends
        1. In 1970
        2. Forced to retire from jobs
    B. Organized for educational and charitable purposes
    C. Made up of people of all ages
    D. Dedicated to equal rights, regardless of age
    E. TV producer gave group name

Notice that *Background*, the main idea of the paragraph, is written next to Roman numeral I. *Founded by Maggie Kuhn and friends*, written next to capital letter A, is the first major detail about the group. *In 1970,* written next to number 1, tells a minor detail about when the group was founded. Notice the outline uses only words and phrases instead of full sentences.

Several other things are important to know about outlining. Every outline needs a title. An outline should always include at least two main ideas; it can never have a Roman numeral I without a II. There should be at least two major details under each main idea and at least two minor details under each major detail.

Read the next two paragraphs about the Gray Panthers. Use the information in them to complete the outline.

The Gray Panthers have been very active since their beginning. They work on the "network principle" to get things done. Gray Panther chapters are in communities all over the country. There are more than 20,000 members in 60 local groups. The groups are involved directly with local issues. They are also involved in national concerns. The Gray Panthers have used three major methods to achieve their goals. Advocacy, education, and projects to help changes happen have all been effective. The Panthers have brought several issues to the people's attention. They have published findings of an investigation of unfair practices in the hearing aid industry. They were the first to organize for nursing home reform. They've lobbied for an end to mandatory retirement. They've addressed the special problems of older women and the minority aged.

Although Maggie Kuhn died in 1995, the future looks bright for the Gray Panthers. They have a number of short-term goals. They want "patients' rights" for people living in nursing homes. They want the media to show older people in a more realistic, less negative way. The Panthers' long-term goals are less specific. They want the rigid separations between youth, adulthood, and old age to be broken down. They want workday alternatives that will let more people be productive for a longer time. They want learning to be a lifelong process. Finally, they believe first-rate healthcare should be available to all.

II. _____

  A. _____

    1. _____

    2. _____

    3. _____

  B. _____

    1. _____

    2. _____

    3. _____

  C. _____

    1. _____

    2. _____

    3. _____

    4. _____

III. _____

  A. _____

    1. _____

    2. _____

  B. _____

    1. _____

    2. _____

    3. _____

    4. _____

The word *résumé* (REZ oo may) means "summary" in French. A **résumé** is a summary of your job qualifications. It contains a brief but complete account of your job objective, or goal, personal history, education, job experience, and hobbies. An interesting and well-prepared résumé can help you stand out from other applicants in the eyes of a possible employer. A résumé should be neatly typed and should contain no spelling errors.

Read the sample résumé on the next page.

A. Match each part of a résumé listed below to its description in the right column. Write the letter of each correct description on the line.

1. _____ Job Objective   **a.** people who know about you and your abilities

2. _____ Education   **b.** what kind of work you want to do

3. _____ References   **c.** things you do after school hours

4. _____ Employment   **d.** schools you went to and graduated from

5. _____ Personal Data   **e.** work you have done that paid a salary

6. _____ Extracurricular Activities   **f.** name, address, and telephone number

B. Answer the following questions using the information on the sample résumé.

1. To whom does this résumé belong? _____

2. What is her current address? _____

3. Why did she write this résumé? _____

4. From what high school did she graduate? _____

5. What school team was she captain of? _____

6. What club relates to her interest in plants? _____

7. In what two sports does Sharon participate? _____

8. How do you know that she excelled in gymnastics? _____

9. Notice that Sharon's places of employment are listed with her last job first. This is the correct way to list job experience on a résumé. Where was Sharon's first job? _____

10. How can you tell that she did not work full-time at her first job? Give two reasons.

_____

Sharon Waskiewicz

92401 Woodley Street • Fresno, California • 93711
(209) 555-9371

JOB OBJECTIVE

Summer job with plant store or greenhouse, growing and caring for plants, with potential for returning each summer

EDUCATION

Fresno Senior High School
Received academic diploma – June 2007   B+ average
Plan to major in horticulture in college

EXTRACURRICULAR ACTIVITIES

Sports: volleyball team (2005–2007, captain), gymnastics club
School Organizations: glee club, Spanish club, yearbook editor
Honors: National Honor Society, City Gymnastic Award (2007)
Special Interests: plants, swimming, dancing, writing poetry
Civic Organizations: Fresno Garden Club, church choir, library volunteer

EMPLOYMENT

1/07 – 6/07   California State University, Department of Horticulture
(after school) *5011 E. Calby, Fresno, California*
                Assistant to Professor Timothy Lee. Grew and cared for
                ornamental plants in greenhouse.

6/06 – 8/06   Camp Wonderwood
                1099 E. Greenstone, Fresno, California
                Counselor. Led nature walks and taught tumbling classes.

12/05 – 6/06   The Plant Shed
(Saturdays)   *4234 E. Rogers, Fresno, California*
                Stockperson. Cared for ornamental plants and flowers.
                Sold merchandise, operated cash register.

REFERENCES

Prof. Timothy Lee
Department of Horticulture
California State University at Fresno
5011 E. Calby
Fresno, California   93740
(209) 555-2107

Lorna Alvarez, M.D.
4645 W. Hawthorne
Fresno, California 93740
(209) 555-6200

Ms. Janet Lord
Director
Camp Wonderwood
1099 E. Greenstone
Fresno, California 93711
(209) 555-1349

Mr. Brandon Lowell
Principal
Fresno Senior High School
4000 E. Dunbar
Fresno, California 93740
(209) 555-0100

Laws: Written and Unwritten

LESSON 31

Skill: Point of View

BACKGROUND INFORMATION

In "The Chance of a Lifetime," Rafael feels like an outsider in his new school until a group of students known as the Club invite him to join them—but for a price. People have always had to make such choices. Each person must balance the need for friendship against the need to retain one's personal integrity.

SKILL FOCUS: Point of View

Before writing, an author must decide who is going to narrate the story. If the author wants the narrator to reveal the thoughts and feelings of all the characters in the story, the author must use an omniscient, or all-knowing, narrator. In a story told from a third-person omniscient **point of view**, the narrator is not identified. The omniscient narrator can reveal as much or as little about the characters as is necessary for the story's development.

When you examine the point of view in a story, think about the following questions.

- Is the narrator an outsider or a participant in the events?
- Does the narrator reveal what one or all of the characters in the story are thinking or feeling?
- Why might the author have chosen this point of view?

▶ Read the following two paragraphs. Circle the one that tells the story from the third-person omniscient point of view.

1. *Katherine was enraged. She could hardly speak. Rachel, on the other hand, was delighted with events and could hardly conceal her joy. Donna, caught between two friends, wisely did not betray her emotions.*

2. *I was so angry! I couldn't believe what had happened. To make it worse, it was obvious that Rachel was delighted by the turn of events. I*

could see her smiling but trying not to. I have to give Donna credit, though. I couldn't tell how she was feeling.

CONTEXT CLUES: Dictionary

When you read a word that you do not know, look for context clues to help you understand it. If there are no clues in the context, you may have to use a **dictionary** to find out what the word means. Read the following sentence from the story.

*Every time he walked the length of the hallway between classes, he felt as if he were running the **gauntlet**.*

There are no context clues to help you clearly understand the meaning of *gauntlet*. A dictionary can help. You may find it convenient to finish what you are reading before looking up the word.

▶ Read the sentences below. Look up the underlined word in a dictionary. On the line below, write the meaning of the word as it is used in the sentence.

*Rick nodded. "We've got a **proposition** for you. If you agree to it, you'll have it made."*

_____

_____

In "The Chance of a Lifetime," the words *overtly*, *nonchalantly*, and *candor* are underlined. Look up their meanings in a dictionary to help you understand what you read.

Strategy Tip

As you read "The Chance of a Lifetime," notice how the author uses the narrator to give clues to the personality of the characters by revealing their thoughts and feelings.

The Chance of a Lifetime

Rafael gazed down the long corridor toward his locker. Every time he walked the length of the hallway between classes, he felt as if he were running the gauntlet.

It wasn't that people were <u>overtly</u> nasty. In fact, no one had been unpleasant in the two months since he had transferred to Seneca High. It was just that no one had particularly welcomed him, either. So Rafael couldn't help feeling that the absence of a warm welcome was actively excluding him, too.

Rafael was something of a computer whiz, but he was shy and not at ease communicating with others. He was at his best when he was tinkering with a program or playing a computer game.

As Rafael walked down the hall, he noted anxiously that Rick and a couple of other guys were clustered around his locker. Rafael admired them— the easy way they stood, the way they dressed, the laughing, casual way they had with everyone. They were the Club, and Rafael thought they must be the most popular group in school.

Since arriving at Seneca High, Rafael had done his utmost to impress Rick and the rest of the Club. He attempted to be funny and acted as though he was not too serious about his classes. He didn't think, however, that his act was working. Until this moment, he hadn't believed that the Club even knew he existed. Now it seemed they were waiting for him. Rafael tried to remain calm; he tried not to fumble with the lock on his locker.

Rick was watching every move Rafael made— sizing him up and estimating his chances of success. He decided Rafael was just the person they needed. He sidled over to Rafael. "What's up? Are you getting adjusted to the new school, or what?"

Rafael turned abruptly, surprised at the friendly overture from Rick. "Uh, things are okay. I'm getting along…"

Rick nodded. "We've heard you know a lot about computers. Maybe you could help us. We've got a proposition for you. If you agree to the proposition, you'll have it made. You'll be a member of the Club— we might even make you an officer or something."

Rafael couldn't believe he was being offered an opportunity to join the Club. It seemed too good to be true.

"What do you say?" Rick asked.

To hide his excitement, Rafael turned and opened his locker. "Sure," he said, as <u>nonchalantly</u> as possible. "What do you want me to do?"

Rick leaned closer, lowering his voice. "We want you to get a copy of the chemistry exam out of the school computer for us. Your aunt works in the

office. It should be simple for you to strike up a conversation with her and then dawdle around until you can check out this week's password into the computer system. Then you could log onto the school computer with your own terminal and get us a copy of next week's exam. Can you do it?"

Rafael began slowly, "I can do it. The only question is…"

"Don't worry," Rick said reassuringly and with an edge of challenge, "nobody will suspect you. They'll never know! Besides, you're not even taking chemistry."

With a grin and a wave, Rick and his pals sauntered off. Rick was delighted. He thought that Rafael would never really fit in, but if he could get the job done, they might make him a sort of unofficial member of the Club—keep him happy until they needed him again.

Rafael stared after them, stunned. He felt slightly nauseous. All morning, Rafael was oblivious to everybody around him. Rick's words kept echoing in his mind. I could never do it, he thought; I'd be too terrified.

Rafael was completely aware, however, that Rick was correct. No one would ever suspect him—least of all his aunt, who trusted him implicitly. She probably kept the password near her terminal. It would be a simple matter to tap into the school computer and get a printout of the exam. No one would ever know, and he would have the friends he so desperately wanted.

The only problem was that it was outright theft. A voice continuously nagged Rafael: "You don't want to do this. You know it's wrong." He attempted not to listen to that voice, but it wouldn't go away.

By lunchtime, his temples were throbbing. The last thing he wanted was his tuna sandwich. Unable to eat, Rafael opened his notebook and began to write. Writing down his thoughts often helped him to sort them out.

"What do you do," he wrote, "if you have to choose between friendship and honesty? Aren't friends the most important thing? Why does integrity have to rear its righteous head and get in the way? What good is it to be right but alone?"

Rafael wrote through lunchtime. When he closed his notebook, he knew what had to be done. Suddenly famished, he gulped down his sandwich on the way to English class, but when he walked into the room, his stomach knotted again. He had forgotten to complete the essay that was due today. There was only one thing to do. Rafael scrawled his name on the notes he had composed during lunch and handed them in.

Rafael put the whole thing out of his mind until English class the next day. Ms. Grady started the class by saying, "I'd like to read one extraordinary essay."

To his dismay, Rafael recognized his paper. How awful to have his innermost thoughts on display for everyone! The class would definitely disdain him. For sure they'd think he was a loser.

The class stirred restlessly as Ms. Grady began, but the room was absolutely still by the time she read Rafael's last paragraph: "There is something more important than having friends. You can't have friends until you have self-respect."

Silence hung over the room for a long moment before students began to applaud. Ms. Grady felt relieved. The students had responded to Rafael's essay as positively as she had envisioned. A wave of relief swept over Rafael, too. They had not laughed; they had understood. Indeed many of the students were relieved that someone had spoken up for honesty.

Rafael was particularly pleased when Emily approached him after class. She had never spoken to him before. "What a terrific essay!" she said warmly. "It was so honest." Emily was surprised at Rafael's candor and courage; she had thought him to be a lot different. She had the wrong impression because she had noticed he was around the Club.

Rafael responded with a smile; he had always liked her, but he had thought he would have no chance unless he was a member of the Club.

"I guess this is the first time I ever let anyone know my real feelings," he said.

Suddenly, Rick interrupted them. His face made it evident that he had not appreciated Rafael's essay. He was enraged—in fact, furious. He felt completely betrayed. "So," he sneered, "you're not going to do it!"

"No, I'm not," Rafael agreed.

"I thought you had guts! I sure had you figured wrong."

"I guess you did," responded Rafael. I never really respected Rick at all, Rafael realized. He pivoted abruptly on his heel and addressed Emily: "You know, I was so ecstatic about becoming a member of the Club that I was willing to abandon my own integrity. But that's really not what I wanted at all. I realize now what I really wanted was to be respected, not because I belonged to a certain exclusive clique, but because of my own worth."

"I imagine that's what we all want," Emily said, "but it takes forever for the majority of us to realize it."

They walked down the corridor together. Rafael felt Rick's eyes boring into him, but he was no longer concerned with Rick's opinion of him.

COMPREHENSION

1. State why no one would suspect Rafael of stealing the chemistry exam.

   _____

   _____

2. Explain why Rafael became anxious and ill at ease during morning classes.

   _____

   _____

3. What conflict does Rafael face? How does he resolve it?

   _____

   _____

4. A story's climax marks the turning point in the plot. After the climax, the reader is able to predict how the story will end. Circle the statement that describes the turning point in this story.

   a. Rafael decides to turn in his notes.

   b. The class responds to Ms. Grady's reading of Rafael's essay.

   c. Rafael realizes that he could get away with stealing the chemistry exam.

5. Write the letter of the correct meaning on the line next to each word.

   _____ overtly   a. casually, indifferent

   _____ nonchalantly   b. outwardly, in the open

   _____ candor   c. sincerity, frankness

1. Explain how Rick learned that Rafael wouldn't steal the chemistry exam.

   _____

   _____

2. **a.** Tell why Emily assumed that Rafael was like Rick.

   _____

   _____

   b. Explain how Emily feels about Rick.

   _____

   _____

3. At the beginning of the story, Rafael believes that Rick and the rest of the Club must be the most popular group in the school. Is he correct? Support your answer.

   _____

   _____

4. **a.** Is Rafael a static or dynamic character? Explain.

   _____

   _____

   b. Is Rick a static or dynamic character? Explain.

   _____

   _____

   _____

5. Was Rafael really given "the chance of a lifetime"? Explain.

   _____

   _____

6. Circle the statement that best describes the story's theme, or message.
   a. Friendship must come first.
   b. The principle of honesty must be upheld, no matter how difficult it is to do so.
   c. If you are honest, everyone will respect you.

SKILL FOCUS: POINT OF VIEW

1. **a.** Does the author of the story tell you who the narrator is? _____

   b. Is the narrator an outsider or a participant in the story? _____

   c. Whose thoughts and feelings does the narrator reveal?

   _____

2. Go back to the story and do the following.

    a. Circle phrases and sentences that reveal Rafael's thoughts and feelings about the Club and about Emily.

    b. Underline phrases and sentences that reveal Rick's thoughts and feelings about Rafael.

    c. Put brackets around phrases and sentences that reveal Emily's thoughts and feelings about Rafael.

    d. Put parentheses around phrases and sentences that reveal Ms. Grady's thoughts about reading Rafael's essay aloud to the class.

3. Does the narrator look into the mind of Rafael's aunt? Explain.

_____

_____

_____

4. Why is the omniscient point of view suitable for this story?

_____

_____

_____

5. Read the following paragraph. It does not reveal the thoughts and feelings of any of the characters.

> *The toddler grinned, looked around, and pushed his cup over the edge of the high chair. Immediately, his mother leaped up, grabbed a sponge, and began mopping up the mess. Alison, his seven-year-old sister, began chanting, "Billy made a mess! Billy made a mess!"*

    a. Rewrite the paragraph using the omniscient point of view.

_____

_____

_____

_____

    b. Circle phrases or sentences in your paragraph above that reveal the mother's thoughts and feelings.

    c. Underline phrases or sentences that reveal Alison's thoughts and feelings.

    d. Put brackets around phrases or sentences that reveal Billy's thoughts and feelings.

Reading-Writing Connection

What would you do if you saw your best friend cheating on an exam? On a separate sheet of paper, write a paragraph describing your response. Give reasons for this response.

Skill: Reading a Flowchart

BACKGROUND INFORMATION

"How a Bill Becomes a Law" traces the steps in the process of creating laws in the United States. In order to protect the interests of U.S. citizens, no single person can make a law. Instead the legislative branch of the government (the Congress) writes and approves any bills designed to change the law. The bills are then forwarded to the President before they can become law.

SKILL FOCUS: Reading a Flowchart

A **flowchart** shows the important stages, or steps, in a process. Information that explains these stages is presented in boxes. Arrows or lines connect the boxes to show the flow or movement from one stage to another.

When reading a flowchart, first become familiar with the information inside the boxes. Be sure you know the meanings of all the words. Then read the flowchart by following the arrows. Sometimes color is used to show different parts of the same process.

▶ The flowchart below shows three of the stages in the process by which a bill becomes a law. Study the flowchart. Then answer the questions that follow.

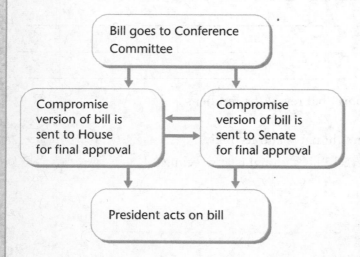

1. How many steps are presented in this flowchart?

   _____

2. Where does the first step take place?

   _____

3. What is the last step?

   _____

4. What do the arrows joining the middle boxes mean?

   _____

CONTEXT CLUES: Definition

Sometimes the meaning of a word is made clear by a **definition** that is provided in the next sentence. Read the sentences below. Look for the definition context clue that explains the underlined word.

In the House, a representative drops the proposed bill into the __hopper__. The hopper is a large box hanging at the edge of the clerk's desk.

If you do not know the meaning of the word *hopper* in the first sentence, read on. The word *hopper* is defined in the next sentence.

▶ Read the following sentences. Circle the words that provide a definition for the underlined word.

Congress processes over 20,000 __bills__ during one Congressional session. Each bill is a proposed law for the United States.

In "How a Bill Becomes a Law," the words *pigeonholed*, *subcommittee*, and *veto* are underlined. Look in the text for definitions that explain what they mean.

Strategy Tip

As you read "How a Bill Becomes a Law," refer to the flowchart on page 124, which traces the lawmaking process in a visual form.

How a Bill Becomes a Law

Citizens of the United States are governed and protected by the laws set forth in the Constitution. Congress, the legislative, or lawmaking, branch of the federal government, processes over 20,000 bills, or proposed laws, during one Congressional session. Of this huge number of bills, fewer than 10 percent actually become laws. Where do these bills originate? How does Congress decide which bills should be passed into laws? What steps are involved in the process? The legislative procedure is an intricate one filled with rules, regulations, and human drama.

To understand how a bill becomes a law, we will follow a fictional bill through Congress. The bill is titled Jobs for Young Americans. If passed into law, it would provide full-time or part-time employment opportunities and job-training programs for citizens between the ages of 16 and 18.

The Introduction of a Bill

The idea for a bill may come from various sources—a member of Congress, the executive branch of the government, an interest group, or even a private citizen.

✗ However, only an official member of the House of Representatives or the Senate may formally introduce a bill. In the House, a representative drops the proposed bill into the hopper, a large box hanging at the edge of the clerk's desk. In the Senate, a senator formally presents a proposed bill to the members of the Senate.

Our Jobs for Young Americans bill is introduced in the House of Representatives. It is assigned a number and a title, and it is entered in the *House Journal* and the *Congressional Record*.

House Committee Action

Both houses of Congress have a number of standing committees with responsibility for bills on certain subjects. After a bill is introduced, the Speaker of the House assigns it to the appropriate committee. The Jobs for Young Americans bill is handed over to the House Committee on Employment Opportunities. It is at this stage that most bills die. Members of the House Committee decide if the bill has merit and if it is politically acceptable.

If the committee majority decides against a bill, it is pigeonholed. Pigeonholed means put aside to be forgotten. If the bill survives, the chair of the House Committee on Employment Opportunities assigns it to a subcommittee. A subcommittee is a committee within a committee. During this stage, the subcommittee conducts public hearings, at which testimonies are given for and against passage of the bill.

Finally the members of the subcommittee "mark up" the bill. That is, they go through it line by line, making changes that they believe are necessary. The subcommittee recommends to the full committee that the "marked-up" version of the bill be approved.

The Committee on Employment Opportunities can decide either to kill the bill by not acting on it or to report it to the House floor. During the committee stage, the procedure for handling a bill introduced in the Senate is similar.

The House Rules Committee

In the next stage, a House bill is sent to the House Rules Committee, sometimes referred to as the "traffic cop of the House." Members of this committee hold a hearing to decide how and when to schedule a bill for action on the floor of the House. By majority vote, the Rules Committee can handle the bill in several ways. It can prevent a bill from reaching the floor for political reasons, rush it through for immediate consideration, or schedule it on one of the House calendars. A Senate bill does not go through this stage; instead, it goes directly from the appropriate committee to floor action at the discretion of the floor Majority Leader.

The Rules Committee decides by a majority vote to report the Jobs for Young Americans bill to the House. The Speaker of the House and the Majority Leader confer with influential House members about scheduling the bill for debate.

Floor Action

On the House floor, the bill is read to the representatives so that they can propose and vote on amendments. Once it is in its final form, the bill is opened up for House debate. Because the House is such a large body, strict regulations limit the time allowed for debating a bill.

Finally our Jobs for Young Americans bill is put to a vote in the House. In the past, this was done by a time-consuming roll call; today, a computer-operated electronic voting system is used. A personal computer card identifies each representative's vote.

If the bill is defeated by the floor vote, the process has to begin all over again. However, most bills that come this far pass at this stage. Our House bill, Jobs for Young Americans, is sent to the Senate for consideration.

Senate Action

To become a law, a bill must be passed by a majority vote in both houses of Congress and presented to the president for approval or disapproval. Our Jobs for Young Americans bill was introduced in the House and passed; it now goes on to the Senate. If the bill had been introduced and passed in the Senate, it would then proceed to the House.

The Senate follows the same basic steps as the House except that the Senate does not have a Rules Committee. When a floor debate is finished on a

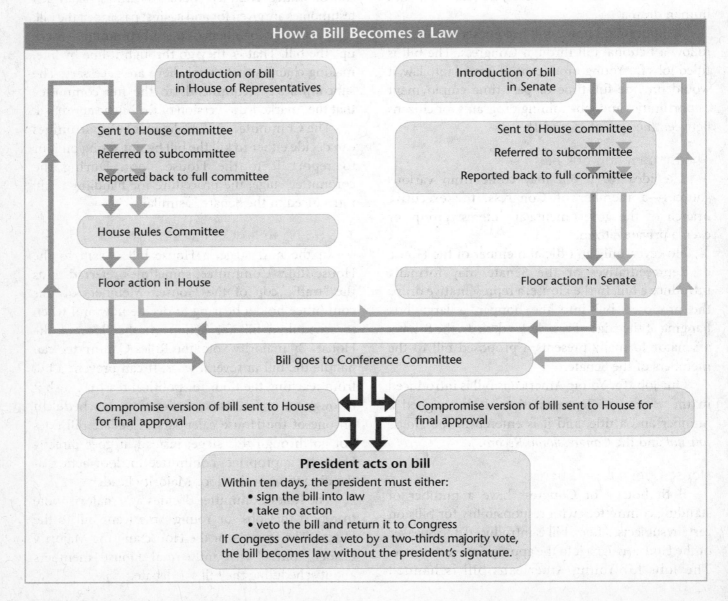

How a Bill Becomes a Law

Introduction of bill in House of Representatives

Introduction of bill in Senate

Sent to House committee
Referred to subcommittee
Reported back to full committee

Sent to House committee
Referred to subcommittee
Reported back to full committee

House Rules Committee

Floor action in House

Floor action in Senate

Bill goes to Conference Committee

Compromise version of bill sent to House for final approval

Compromise version of bill sent to House for final approval

President acts on bill
Within ten days, the president must either:
- sign the bill into law
- take no action
- veto the bill and return it to Congress

If Congress overrides a veto by a two-thirds majority vote, the bill becomes law without the president's signature.

bill, senators vote on it using the traditional roll-call system. The Senate passes our Jobs for Young Americans bill, but in a slightly altered form. As a result of the debate, some wording changes may have to be made before a majority will pass a bill.

The Conference Committee

✔ Before the Jobs for Young Americans bill is sent to the president, the House and the Senate must agree on a single version of it. The Conference Committee, the next group that the bill must pass through, arrives at this version. The party leadership of each house appoints a few members to the committee. In arriving at an agreeable version of the bill, the members of this committee do some of the toughest bargaining in Congress. The members work out a compromise, which is then considered by the whole Congress.

Finally majorities in both the House and the Senate agree upon our Jobs for Young Americans bill. It has successfully passed through the legislative branch of the government, but it is not yet a law.

Presidential Action

For a bill to become law, it must be presented to the president of the United States. This final stage of the lawmaking process can be a dramatic one. The president may <u>veto</u> the bill. To veto a bill is to give a negative response to it. Then the bill is returned to the house in which it originated. In some cases, the Congress may choose to override the presidential veto by a two-thirds vote in each house. If the president supports the bill, he or she will sign it into law. The president may also choose not to act on the bill and let it become law without the presidential signature. This occurs ten days after he or she has received it from Congress, as long as Congress is in session. If Congress adjourns before the ten days are up, the president's lack of action on a bill becomes a pocket veto.

With the president's approval, our fictional Jobs for Young Americans bill becomes a law of the United States. The American democratic system of government serves the idea of law expressed long ago by the Latin poet Ovid:

For this reason the laws are made: that the strong shall not have power to do all that they please.

COMPREHENSION

1. Number in the correct order the steps that a bill in the House goes through to become a law.

    _____ **a.** Floor action

    _____ **b.** Conference Committee

    _____ **c.** Introduction of a bill in House

    _____ **d.** Senate action

    _____ **e.** Rules Committee

    _____ **f.** President acts on bill

    _____ **g.** Committee stage

    _____ **h.** Congressional vote on compromise bill

2. On the lines provided, write the cause for the effect below.

    Cause: _____

    _____

    Effect: The bill must pass through the Conference Committee.

3. **a.** In which house of Congress is debate limited in time by strict rules and regulations?

    _____

    _____

    b. In which house of Congress is debate freer and less limited in time?

    _____

    _____

4. Reread the two paragraphs that are marked with ✘. In each paragraph, underline the sentence that best states its main idea. Then circle two details that support the main idea.

5. Complete each sentence with the correct word.

pigeonholed   subcommittee   veto

a. There were enough votes in Congress to

override the president's _____.

b. A group was chosen from the committee to

serve on a _____ discussing

endangered animals.

c. The unpopular bill was rejected by the

House Committee and _____

without further consideration.

CRITICAL THINKING

1. Explain why the president would choose to let a bill become a law without
his or her signature.

_____

_____

2. The House of Representatives uses a computer voting system because _____.

In contrast, the Senate still uses a roll-call vote because _____.

3. On the line provided, write the effect for the cause below.

Cause: The United States Constitution set up a system of checks and balances
among the various branches of the government.

Effect: _____

4. Why would a political party like to have the most power in the
House Rules Committee?

_____

_____

5. Reread the paragraph with a ✔ next to it. Write a sentence describing its main idea.

_____

_____

6. Identify each of the following generalizations as true or false. Write *true* or *false* on the
lines.

_____ a. The president plays the most important role in the lawmaking process.

_____ b. The House Committee or Senate Committee stage is the most difficult period
for a bill to survive.

_____ c. The president's decision on a bill is final.

To answer the questions below, use the selection and the flowchart on page 124.

1. What process does the flowchart describe? _____

2. **a.** Identify the two different starting points on the flowchart.

   _____

   b. How are they distinguished on the flowchart? _____

   c. What is the last stage shown on the flowchart? _____

3. What three major areas of the government are represented on the flowchart?

   _____

4. How does the flowchart show the order and movement of the stages in the process?

   _____

5. **a.** If a bill is introduced in the House, where does it go after its passage there?

   _____

   b. If a bill is introduced in the Senate, where does it go after its passage there?

   _____

   c. At what point do the two different paths of the flowchart come together?

   _____

6. **a.** Explain how the events on the flowchart are related to each other.

   _____

   b. For a bill introduced in the House, what stage must it go through between
   committee consideration and floor action?

   _____

   c. The Conference Committee consists of members from which two groups?

   _____

Reading-Writing Connection

Think of a process that takes place in stages over time, such as applying to get into a college
or going through a training program. On a separate sheet of paper, explain how a flowchart
might make the process easier to understand.

Skill: Following Directions

BACKGROUND INFORMATION

"Laws of Motion" discusses speed, velocity, acceleration, and Newton's Laws of Motion. Throughout history, scientists have attempted to explain the concept of motion. During the time of ancient Greece, Aristotle and Archimedes tried to unlock motion's mysteries. Much later, Isaac Newton developed his Laws of Motion, which are still valid today.

SKILL FOCUS: Following Directions

Following directions is an important skill, whether in the kitchen, on the highway, or in the classroom. To carry out an experiment in a science textbook, you must follow directions precisely. Here are the five parts of an experiment.

1. **Problem:** the question you should be able to answer at the end of the experiment

2. **Aim:** what will be done in the experiment

3. **Materials:** objects or equipment needed for the experiment

4. **Procedure:** the steps that must be carried out to complete the experiment

5. **Observations or Conclusions:** conclusions to draw about the outcome of the experiment

▶ Look at the chart below and read the directions at the top of the next column for performing the experiment. Identify which part of the experiment the chart might be used for. Write its name on the line.

Item	Force	Distance
Cap		
Rock		
Wooden block		

Problem: How does friction affect movement?

Aim: In this experiment, several different objects will slide down the same surface. Each object has a different texture, so each will have a different amount of friction as it slides.

Materials: You will need: a smooth board, a bottle cap, a rock, and a wooden block.

Procedure: Follow these steps: 1) Line up the objects on one end of the board. 2) Raise that end of the board, tilting it until the objects begin to slide. 3) Observe and record which objects slide most quickly.

Observations or Conclusions: Objects with smoother surfaces move more quickly down the tilted surface. They have less friction. Therefore, friction affects movement.

CONTEXT CLUES: Diagrams

Sometimes special science words are explained in a paragraph and also shown in a **diagram**. In this case, study both the text and the diagram to help you understand the words.

▶ Read the following sentence and look at the diagram on page 130. On the lines below, explain what the underlined word refers to.

*Place the meter stick on the table and attach the **spring trigger** to the edge of the table, as shown in Figure 3.*

_____

_____

In "Laws of Motion," the words *speed*, *velocity*, and *acceleration* are underlined. Find these words in the diagrams to help understand their meanings.

> **Strategy Tip**
>
> After reading "Laws of Motion," carefully study the directions for the experiment.

Laws of Motion

Did you know that when you move, you do work? Work is defined as **force**—a push or pull—acting over a distance. The phrase *acting over a distance* means that something is moving, or in **motion**. So whenever you move, you are doing work. Scientists have developed definitions and laws to describe the Laws of Motion.

Speed, Velocity, and Acceleration

Speed is defined as the distance covered in a specific amount of time, usually a second, minute, or hour. Speed-limit signs tell drivers the maximum speed at which they may travel. These signs express speed in miles per hour (mph) or in kilometers per hour (kph). Speed can be calculated using the following formula.

$$\text{speed} = \frac{\text{distance}}{\text{time}} = \frac{\text{kilometers}}{\text{hour}}$$

By knowing any two of the three variables in the formula, you can find the third.

A second concept that is related to motion is velocity, which is closely related to speed. Velocity is the speed of an object in a specific direction. For example, 6 m/s is the speed of an automobile, while 6 m/s due east is its velocity. (See Figure 1.)

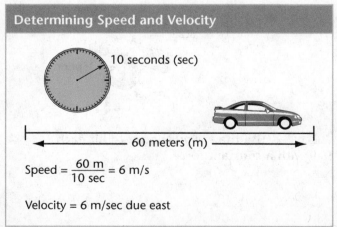

Determining Speed and Velocity

10 seconds (sec)

60 meters (m)

Speed $= \dfrac{60 \text{ m}}{10 \text{ sec}} = 6$ m/s

Velocity = 6 m/sec due east

FIGURE 1. If you know an object's velocity, you have more information than if you know its speed.

Any change in velocity is called underline{acceleration}. Acceleration occurs when velocity increases or decreases. Although people commonly call decreasing velocity deceleration, scientists do not use this term. (See Figure 2.)

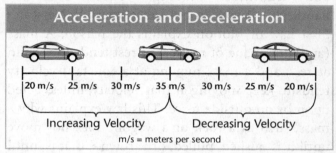

Acceleration and Deceleration

20 m/s   25 m/s   30 m/s   35 m/s   30 m/s   25 m/s   20 m/s

Increasing Velocity   Decreasing Velocity

m/s = meters per second

FIGURE 2. Acceleration indicates either an increase or a decrease in an object's velocity.

The formula below shows how acceleration is calculated.

$$a = \frac{v_2 - v_1}{t}$$

a = acceleration
v_1 = beginning velocity
v_2 = ending velocity
t = time

If a car is going north at 20 m/sec, and 5 seconds later it is going 25 m/sec, the acceleration can be figured as follows.

$$a = \frac{25 \text{ m/sec} - 20 \text{ m/sec}}{5 \text{ sec}}$$

$$= \frac{5 \text{ m/sec}}{5 \text{ sec}} = 1 \text{ m/s/s}$$

Acceleration always indicates a change in velocity per unit of time. Since velocity is always expressed as distance covered per unit of time, acceleration can be expressed in terms of distance per unit of time per unit of time.

In this example, the answer is in meters per second per second. An answer might also be in kilometers per hour per hour or any other distance unit per unit of time per unit of time.

SCIENCE

Newton's Laws of Motion

Force and motion are related in specific ways. In the late 1600s, after studying the relationships between force and motion, English mathematician Isaac Newton developed three laws describing these relationships.

The first law is illustrated by the following example: If you are riding a bicycle and suddenly put on your brakes, the bicycle stops, but your body continues moving forward over the handlebars if you do not brace yourself. Newton's First Law of Motion explains the reason: A mass (anything made of matter) at rest tends to remain at rest, and a mass moving at a constant velocity tends to keep moving at that velocity, unless acted upon by an outside force. This law explains why a mass, such as a rock or a wagon, does not move until it is pushed, pulled, or thrown—that is, until a force is applied. This law also explains the bicycle example. When you put the brakes on a bicycle, you apply a force that changes the velocity of the bicycle, but your body continues to move forward unless you brace yourself.

Newton's first law is also called the law of **inertia** (in ER shə). Inertia is the tendency of a mass to resist having its motion changed. The greater an object's mass is, the greater is its inertia. Unless acted upon by an outside force, a mass at rest tends to remain at rest, and a mass moving at a constant velocity tends to keep moving at that velocity.

Newton's Second Law of Motion describes the relationship between force, mass, and acceleration. The law states that the acceleration of an object depends on the object's mass and on the amount of force applied to the object. The law is expressed in the following formula.

EXPERIMENT

PROBLEM
When the same force is applied to objects with different masses, how does it affect the acceleration of each object?

AIM
In this experiment, the same force will be applied to balls of different masses. The acceleration of each ball will be approximated by measuring the distance it moves.

MATERIALS
You will need a smooth, flat tabletop, a spring trigger, three balls of the same size but of different masses (one solid wood, one solid steel, one solid styrofoam), masking tape or chalk, and a meter stick.

PROCEDURE
1. Place a piece of masking tape or a chalk dot near the edge of the table. Each ball will be placed on this marker before force is applied.
2. Place the meter stick on the table and attach the spring trigger to the edge of the table, as shown in Figure 3.

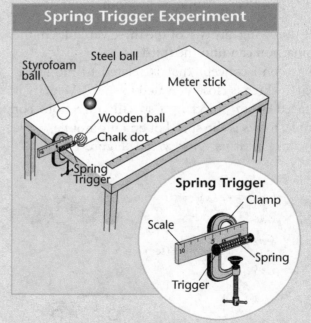

FIGURE 3. **Use the spring trigger to hit each ball with a constant force.**

3. Place the wooden ball on the marker.

4. Line up the trigger on the spring trigger with the wooden ball. Pull the spring back to number 5 on the scale. This is your constant force.

5. Release the trigger, and let it hit the wooden ball. Record the distance that the ball moves in the following chart.

6. Repeat steps 3–5 with the steel ball and again with the styrofoam ball.

Ball	Force	Distance
Wooden	5	
Steel	5	
Styrofoam	5	

OBSERVATIONS OR CONCLUSIONS

With the constant force, the steel ball moves the shortest distance and the styrofoam ball moves the longest distance; the distance moved by the wooden ball is between the other two. The conclusion is that when a constant force is applied, an object with less mass moves farther (is accelerated more) than an object with great mass.

$$F = m \times a$$

F = force applied to an object

m = mass of the object

a = acceleration of the object

Newton's Third Law of Motion states that for every action, there is an equal and opposite reaction. A rocket taking off is a dramatic example of this law. However, a rocket is not the only example. Every time you lean against a wall, the wall pushes back against you. When you throw a ball against the sidewalk, the ball bounces back.

The concepts of speed, velocity, and acceleration, plus Newton's Laws of Motion, help scientists to predict the performance of moving objects.

The beginning experiment on page 130 will help you to explore the relationship between mass and acceleration described in Newton's Second Law.

COMPREHENSION

1. What is force?

_____

_____

2. What does the phrase *acting over a distance* mean?

_____

_____

3. What is speed?

_____

_____

4. How is velocity different from speed?

_____

_____

5. What is Newton's First Law of Motion?

_____

_____

_____

6. Explain Newton's Second Law of Motion.

_____

_____

7. Explain Newton's Third Law of Motion.

_____

_____

8. Draw a line to match each word with its definition.

velocity   **a.** increase or decrease in velocity

speed   **b.** speed of an object in a certain direction

acceleration   **c.** distance covered per unit of time

CRITICAL THINKING

Circle the letter next to each correct answer.

1. If a car's speed is 60 km/hr and it travels for 6 hours, the distance it travels is _____.

    a. 10 km   **b.** 66 km   **c.** 300 km   **d.** 360 km

2. If a rocket is going 30 km/sec and accelerates 2 km/s/s, its velocity after 10 seconds is _____.

    a. 20 km/sec   **b.** 50 km/sec   **c.** 60 km/sec   **d.** 70 km/sec

3. One object has a mass of 10 grams, and another object has a mass of 20 grams. If the same force is applied to both objects, the acceleration of the lighter object is _____.

    a. twice that of the heavy object

    b. half that of the heavy object

    c. the same as that of the heavy object

    d. four times that of the heavy object

4. When amusement-park rides start, the riders are often pushed backward in their seats. When the rides stop, the riders are often thrown forward in their seats. These two reactions illustrate Newton's _____.

    a. First Law   **b.** Second Law   **c.** Third Law   **d.** Fourth Law

5. When you bounce on a diving board, your downward push produces an upward push or springing-back in the diving board, which lifts you into the air. When you throw a ball against a wall, it bounces back toward you. These two reactions illustrate Newton's _____.

    a. First Law   **b.** Second Law   **c.** Third Law   **d.** Fourth Law

A. In your own words, summarize the experiment on pages 130–131. When you finish, check your summary by rereading the experiment, and make any corrections that are necessary.

_____

_____

B. The experiment that you will write below shows how force must increase or decrease, relatively speaking, to accelerate three balls of different masses by the same amount. The distance that a ball moves is used to indicate the amount of its acceleration. Use the same materials as in the experiment on pages 130–131. Also using that experiment as a model, write the directions for this experiment on the lines provided. Be sure to number the steps in the procedure. Fill in the chart with the information you collect.

EXPERIMENT

PROBLEM

_____

_____

_____

AIM

_____

_____

_____

MATERIALS

_____

_____

_____

PROCEDURE

_____

_____

_____

_____

_____

_____

_____

OBSERVATIONS OR CONCLUSIONS

_____

_____

_____

Item	Force	Distance
Wooden		
Steel		
Styrofoam		

Reading-Writing Connection

Find an experiment in a science textbook. On a separate sheet of paper, write a paragraph that summarizes the five parts of the experiment.

Skill: Interpreting Statistics

BACKGROUND INFORMATION

In "Statistics," you will discover how to analyze groups of numbers and how to draw conclusions from them. Statistics can be found in many areas of everyday life. For example, baseball statistics enable you to quickly find out a player's hits, runs, errors, and batting average. When reading statistics tables, use a ruler to make sure you focus on the correct column or row.

SKILL FOCUS: Interpreting Statistics

There are several ways to analyze **statistics**, or numerical data. One way is to find the **average** of the numbers by dividing the total of all the figures in a group by the total number of figures in that group. The result is a single number, or average, that represents the entire group of numbers. For example, if five children are ages 2, 2, 3, 4, and 9, their average age is 4. (The sum of their ages, 20, divided by 5 children.)

A second way to analyze numerical data is to find the **median**, or the middle of the set of numbers. Finding the median is easy when the set of numbers is odd: It is simply the middle number. In the example above, the median age of the children is 3, because there are equal numbers of children older and younger than 3.

A third way to analyze numerical data is to find the **mode**, or the number that occurs the most. In the example above, the mode is 2.

▶ Study the statistics in the following paragraph. Then look at the three numbers below. Identify each as the average, the median, or the mode.

Leslie's bowling trophy is 6 inches tall. Her soccer trophy is 7 inches tall. Her baseball trophy is 6 inches tall. Her track trophy is 9 inches tall. Her spelling bee trophy is 8 inches tall. Her basketball trophy is 15 inches tall, and her field hockey trophy is 5 inches tall.

6 _____

7 _____

8 _____

WORD CLUES

The words *statistics, mean, median,* and *mode* all have their origin in Latin or Greek, but their meanings have changed over time. *Statistics* originally meant the study of the state or nation; even today, much of the data that is analyzed concerns the populations, costs, and taxes of nations. Both *mean* and *median* come from the Latin word for *middle.* Both a *mean* and a *median* are averages. The word *mode* is from the Latin for *measure.* In statistics, the mode is most often useful when something is being measured or counted.

Strategy Tip

As you read "Statistics," you will learn how to find three kinds of averages: the mean, the median, and the mode. Study the examples carefully to be sure that you understand how these different averages are used.

Statistics

Statistics is the mathematical method for extracting information from sets of numbers so as to better understand their meaning. One of the most important skills in interpreting statistics is finding a single number that in some way represents an entire set of numbers. One such number is commonly called an **average**. Different kinds of averages are used in statistics. The different kinds of averages are called **measures of central tendency**.

Mean

The most familiar measure of central tendency is the **mean**. The mean is found by adding the members of a set and dividing the sum by the number of members. The mean is especially useful if the average is to be later used in a computation.

For example, a small business employs ten part-time workers. Here is a list of the hours they work each week.

Ada Blanco	11	Frank DeLucca	20
Bill Martin	20	Keesha Miller	17
Cathy Donahue	20	Harold Smith	12
Don Sheng	2	Inge Pederson	18
Emily Goldberg	37	José Vazquez	20

To find the mean number of hours worked, add the number of hours for all ten workers and divide by 10. The sum is 177, so the mean number of hours is 17.7. You can use the mean instead of using the original set of numbers, or **data**.

One use of the mean would be to compare two different weeks. If you wanted to know whether the part-time workers were working more or less than they did the previous week, the mean would be an appropriate measure to use because it reflects the total. If the number of workers changes from week to week, the mean would still indicate the average amount that each worked, even though the total amount of work done would be different.

Median

A different measure of central tendency would better express how many hours the average person worked. This measure is the **median**, or the middle of the set. It shows that half the workers worked more than that amount, while the other half worked less. Notice that the mean is usually different from the median. In the example given, six workers worked more than 17.7 hours, while only four workers worked fewer than 17.7 hours.

There are two different ways to find the median, depending on whether the set of data has an even or an odd number of members. If the number of members is odd, the median is simply the middle number of the set. For example, suppose the set is 2, 9, 4, 1, 8, which has five members (an odd number). To find the middle number, arrange the set from least to greatest (or vice versa), and count to find the third member. From least to greatest, the set is 1, 2, 4, 8, 9, so the median is 4.

When the number of members is even, there is no middle number in the set. To identify the median as a single number, *the mean of the two middle numbers* is used. For example, suppose the set is 2, 9, 4, 1, 8, 5, which has six members (an even number). The two middle numbers can be found by rearranging the set in order and taking the fourth and fifth numbers. From greatest to least, the set is 9, 8, 5, 4, 2, 1, so the median is the mean of 5 and 4. The mean is $(5 + 4) \div 2$, or 4.5.

Mode

The third measure of central tendency is the **mode**. This measure is simply the data item that occurs most in the set. Since 20 hours occurs four times and no other data item occurs more than once, the mode for the part-time workers is 20.

The mode is often used to show typical behavior. If you were applying to the company for a part-time job, the manager might tell you, "The typical part-time worker works 20 hours a week."

Sometimes two different data items occur the same number of times, and both occur more often than any of the other data items. In this case, there are two modes, and the set of data is called **bimodal**.

MATHEMATICS

1. What is statistics?

_____

_____

_____

2. What are the different types of averages called in statistics?

_____

_____

_____

3. How do you find the mean of a set of numbers?

_____

_____

_____

4. How do you find the median when the number of members in a set of numbers is even?

_____

_____

_____

5. Explain how you would find the mode of a set of data.

_____

_____

_____

6. What do you call a set that has two modes?

_____

_____

CRITICAL THINKING

1. If the same number of workers are employed by a company each month, which measure of central tendency is most appropriate for comparing the average salary from month to month? Explain.

_____

_____

_____

2. A personnel director wants to give a young executive an idea of how her salary ranks among the company's other executives. With which measure of central tendency should the young executive's salary be compared to be most meaningful?

_____

_____

_____

3. The median of a set of five numbers is much smaller than the mean. Explain what this tells you about the set.

_____

_____

_____

A. Use the table below to find the information asked for in each problem.

Records for the Acme Corporation			
Worker	Hours Worked	Salary per Hour	Weekly Salary
Mathew Smith	35	6.20	217.00
Ana Martinez	28	8.40	235.20
Tyrone Brown	40	8.80	352.00
Marie Sokoloski	35	7.20	252.00
Jean Gastineau	21	6.00	126.00
Ahmed Salaam	35	7.20	252.00
Walter Klecko	42	6.00	252.00
Naomi Simms	60	6.40	384.00
Umeko Tanaka	35	6.00	210.00
Marc Rutledge	14	7.20	100.80
Eduardo Fuentes	0	7.20	0.00
Rita Danelo	35	7.20	252.00

1. What is the mean number of hours worked? _____

2. What is the median number of hours worked? _____

3. What is the mode of the number of hours worked? _____

B. Tell which measure of central tendency you would use for each situation, and why.

1. You are looking for a model, a typical person, to represent your product. You know the typical heights of people who use your product. You want a model of average height.

   _____

2. You are purchasing a large order of shoes for your shoe store. You know the sizes of shoes that people buy, and you want to order extra pairs of the most popular size.

   _____

3. You are designing a passenger airplane, and you know how many passengers it will carry. You need to know the weight of the average passenger to determine the weight when the plane is fully loaded.

   _____

Reading-Writing Connection

On a separate sheet of paper, keep track of how many hours you watch television each day for a week. Then find the mean, the median, and the mode for your TV-watching time. Write a summary of your findings.

Skill: Accented Syllable and Schwa

> When words contain two syllables, one of the syllables is stressed, or accented, more than the other. In most dictionaries, the **accent mark** (') is placed at the end of the syllable that is said with more stress. For example, the first syllable in the word *pilot* is said with more stress than the second syllable.
>
> pi' lot

In words with three syllables, the accent is usually on one of the first two syllables. When you are trying to pronounce a word with three syllables, such as *conclusion*, stress the first syllable. If the word does not sound right like the word *conclusion*, say it again, stressing the second syllable.

con clu' sion

A. Say each of the following words to yourself. Write an accent mark after the syllable that should be stressed.

1. doz en	**3.** at tend	**5.** a mount	**7.** suc cess
2. im i tate	**4.** ad di tion	**6.** hi ber nate	**8.** nu cle us

Words of four or more syllables usually have two accented syllables. In the word *territory*, the first syllable has the most stress. This syllable has the primary accent mark ('). The third syllable has more stress than the remaining two syllables but less than the first syllable. The lighter accent mark (') is placed after that syllable. This is called the secondary accent.

ter' ri to' ry

B. Say each of the following words to yourself. Write a primary accent mark after the syllable that has the most stress. Say the word again. Write a secondary accent mark after the syllable that has the second-most stress.

1. e lec tri fy ing	**3.** op er a tion	**5.** dic tion ar y	**7.** dis tri bu tion
2. hel i cop ter	**4.** sat is fac tion	**6.** sal a man der	**8.** trans por ta tion

The vowels *a, e, i, o,* and *u* can all have the same sound. This is a soft sound like a short *u* pronounced lightly. This short, soft *u* sound is called the **schwa** sound. In dictionary respellings, the symbol ə stands for the schwa sound. If you look up the word *vitamin* in a dictionary, you will find it respelled this way.

vīt'ə min

C. Say each of the words below to yourself. Write a primary and secondary accent mark after the syllables that are stressed. Then circle the letter that stands for the schwa sound.

1. ad ver tis ing	**3.** con se quent ly	**5.** at mos pher ic	**7.** in di vid u al
2. e vap o rate	**4.** i den ti fy	**6.** nec es sar y	**8.** jus ti fy ing

Look at the words in the list above. Notice that the schwa sound always falls in an unaccented syllable of a word.

Skill: Fact and Opinion

As you read books, newspapers, or magazines, you can distinguish facts from opinions. A statement of **fact** is information that can be proven to be true. A statement of **opinion** is a personal belief or feeling. As you read the article, think about which statements are facts and which are opinions.

What Is a Paralegal?

Do you know that you can have an exciting career in law without becoming a lawyer? A paralegal, or legal assistant, does many of the things a lawyer does. A paralegal, however, cannot give legal advice, appear in court, or set fees. The duties of a paralegal include drafting, or preparing, legal documents, interviewing clients, and doing research. Most paralegals specialize in one kind of law, such as real estate or litigation, the actual conduct of a lawsuit. However, criminal law may be the most fascinating area of all.

Although law firms hire most paralegals, job opportunities are available in other fields. Corporations, banks, and insurance companies employ paralegals. In the public sector, legal-aid offices, the government, and the courts make use of paralegals. Jobs for legal assistants are also opening up in hospital and school administration and in legal publishing.

There continues to be a sharp rise in the number of paralegals. From 1992 to 2004, according to the U.S. Bureau of Labor Statistics, the number of paralegals more than doubled—from 95,000 to about 224,000 professionals. Although some paralegals who are now employed have had no special training, the competition for jobs will continue to increase. Those people with formal paralegal training will have better chances of being hired in the future.

Hundreds of institutions in the United States offer formal paralegal training. Three main kinds of training programs exist. Junior colleges, as well as four-year universities and colleges, offer two-year training programs. In addition to law-related and legal specialty courses, studies include general education. A few four-year colleges and universities have programs with a major or minor in legal assistant studies. Some universities, colleges, business schools, and special paralegal training schools also offer training programs.

Some of these programs require applicants to have finished at least one and one-half years of college. Other programs accept only college graduates with high grades. Classes may be given full time during the day or part time in the evening. The length of these programs is, therefore, anywhere from three months to two years. Either students study general law with some training in one or two specialty areas, or they specialize in one kind of law. The best training programs include internships so that students get on-the-job training.

Read the following statements, which are based on the selection. On the line before each statement, write *F* if it is a fact or *O* if it is an opinion.

_____ 1. A career in law is exciting.

_____ 2. A legal assistant does many of the things that a lawyer does.

_____ 3. A person with formal paralegal training will have a better chance of getting a legal assistant job.

_____ 4. Hundreds of institutions offer paralegal training.

_____ 5. Legal assistants prepare documents.

_____ 6. The most fascinating area of law is criminal law.

Skill: Using a Dictionary

Each word, abbreviation, prefix, suffix, or group of words that your dictionary explains is called an **entry word**. The entry word and all the information about it is called an **entry**. Most of the dictionaries that you will use include from 50,000 to 80,000 separate entries. These entries are arranged in alphabetical order, with biographical entries alphabetized by surnames, or family names.

To use a dictionary effectively, you need to understand each part of an entry. Study the following.

Syllables: Centered dots in the entry word show where to divide a word when you cannot write it all on one line.

Respelling: Appearing in parentheses following the entry word, the respelling helps you to pronounce the word.

Etymology: Shown within brackets [ ], the etymology explains the origin and history of the word, using symbols and abbreviations. (For example, < means "derived from," and *OE* means "Old English.")

Definitions: Meanings for the entry word are listed together according to their part of speech.

Idioms: Included at the end of the entry may be an idiom, or a group of words with a different meaning from the meaning of the words by themselves.

Use the dictionary entries shown on the next page to answer the questions below and on page 141.

1. What is the last word on this page?
   _____

2. Write the respelling of *eerie*. _____

3. What is the ninth entry word on this page?
   _____

4. What is the fifth adjective meaning of
   effective? _____

5. How long does an eel grow to be?
   _____

6. What key word is given in the pronunciation
   key for the long *o* sound? _____

7. What is the adjective form of the word
   effervesce? _____

8. How would you divide the word *efficiency*
   into syllables?_____

9. How do you spell the plural of the word
   effendi? _____

10. How do you spell the past tense of *efface*?
    _____

11. What phrase is given as an example of the
    second adjective meaning of *efficient*?
    _____

12. What is the origin of the word *effervesce*?
    _____

13. What entry word would you look up to find
    synonyms for *effrontery*?_____

eel (ēl) *n., pl.* **eels, eel**: see PLURAL, II,D,1[OE, *æl*] a snakelike fish with a long, slippery body and no pelvic fins — **eel'like', eel'y** *adj.*

☆**eel·grass** (ēl'gras') *n.* [Fr.] 1 an underwater flowering plant with long, grasslike leaves

eel·pout (-pout') *n., pl.* **-pout', -pouts'**: [OE *ælepute*] 1 a saltwater fish resembling the blenny 2 *same as* BURBOT

eel·worm (-wʉrm') *n.* any of various nematode worms: some live as parasites on plants

e'en (ēn) *adv.* [POET] even **-n.** [Poet. or Dial.] even(ing)

e'er (er, ar) *adv.* [POET] ever

-eer (ir) [Fr. *-ier* < L. *-arius*] 1 *a suffix forming nouns meaning* one that has to do with [*mountaineer*] or one that writes, makes, etc. [*pamphleteer*] 2 *a suffix forming verbs meaning* to have to do with [*electioneer*]

ee·rie, ee·ry (ir'ē) *adj.* [prob.ult.< OE. earg, timid] weird or uncanny, esp. in a frightening way [the *eerie* echoes in the cave] —see *SYN.* at WEIRD — **ee'ri·ly,** *adv.* **ee'ri·ness** *n.*

ef·face (i fās', e-) *vt.* **faced', -fac'ing** [FR. *effacer*< e- (L. *ex.* out) + *face*: see FACE] 1 to rub out or wipe out; erase [to *efface* a memory] 2 to keep (oneself) from being noticed —see *SYN.* at ERASE — **ef·face' able** *adj.* — **ef·face'ment** *n.* — **ef·fac'er** *n.*

EEL
(to 5 ft. long)

ef·fer·vesce (ef'ər ves') *vi.* **-vesced', -vesc'ing** [< L. < *ex-*, out + *fervescere*, to begin to boil < *fervere*, to boil: see FERVENT] 1 to give off gas bubbles, as soda water; bubble 2 to be lively and full of high spirits — **ef'fer·ves'cence** *n.* — **ef'fer·ves'cent** *adj.* — **ef'fer·ves'cent·ly** *adj.*

ef·fete (e fēt', i-) *adj.* [L. *effetus*, exhausted by bearing < *ex-*, out + *fetus*, productive: for IE. base see FEMALE] 1 no longer able to produce; worn out and sterile [an *effete* writer] 2 decadent, soft, etc. [an *effete* society] — **ef·fete'ly** *adv.* — **ef·fete'ness** *n.*

ef·fi·ca·cious (ef'ə kā'shəs) *adj.* [L. *efficax* < *efficere* (see EFFECT) + -*ous*] producing, or capable of producing the desired effect; effective — **ef'fi·ca'cious·ly** *adv.* — **ef'fi·ca'cious·ness** *n.*

ef·fi·ca·cy (ef'i kə sē) *n., pl.* **-cies** [see prec.] power to produce effects or results; effectiveness [the *efficacy* of a treatment]

ef·fi·cien·cy (ə fish'ən sē, i-) *n., pl.* **-cies** 1 ability to produce a desired effect with the least effort or waste; a being efficient 2 the ratio of effective work to energy used in producing it; said of a machine, etc. ☆3 same as EFFICIENCY APARTMENT

☆**efficiency apartment** a one room apartment having a kitchenette and a bathroom

ef·fi·cient (-ənt) *adj.* [< L. prp. of *efficere*: see EFFECT] 1 directly producing an effect or result; effective [illness was the *efficient* cause of her loss of weight] 2 producing a desired effect with the least effort or waste [an *efficient* production method] — **ef·fi'cient·ly,** *adv.*

ef·fective (ə fek'tiv, i-) *adj.* 1 having an effect 2 producing a desired effect [an *effective* remedy] 3 in effect; operative 4 actual, not merely theoretical 5 making a striking impression [an *effective* speaker] 6 equipped and ready for combat [an *effective* unit] —**n.** a combat-ready soldier, unit, etc. — **effec'tive·ly** *adv.* —**effec'tive·ness** *n.*

ef·fec·tu·al (ə fek'chōō wəl, i-) *adj.* 1 producing, or able to produce, the desired effect [an *effectual* plan] 2 having legal force; valid — **ef·fec·tu·al'i·ty** (-wal'ə tē) *n.* —**ef·fec'tu·ally** *adv.*

ef·fec·tu·ate (-wāt') *vt.* **-at'ed, -at'ing** to bring about; effect — **ef·fec'tu·a'tion** *n.*

ef·fem·i·nate (i fem'ə nit) *adj.*[< L. pp. of *effeminare* < *ex-*, out + *femina*, woman: see FEMALE] having or showing qualities that have been thought of as more characteristic of women than of men, as weakness, delicacy, etc.; unmanly: term used only of men or boys —**ef·fem'i·na·cy** (-nə sē) *n.* — **ef·fem'i·nately** *adv.*

ef·fen·di (i fen'dē) *n., pl.* **-dis** [<Turk. < ModGr. < Gr. *authentēs*, a master] Sir; Master: former Turkish title of respect

ef·fer·ent (ef'ər ənt) *adj.* [< L. prp. of *effere* < *ex-*, out + *ferre*, BEAR[1]] *Physiol.* carrying away from a central part; specif., designating nerves that carry impulses away from a nerve center. opposed to AFFERENT

ef·fort (ef'ərt) *n.* [Fr. < OFr. < *esforcier*, to make an effort, ult. < L. *ex-*, thoroughly + *fortis*, strong] 1 use of energy to do something; a trying hard physically or mentally [rowing takes great *effort*] 2 a try; attempt [he made no *effort* to be friendly] 3 a result of working or trying; achievement [her early *efforts* at poetry were not published] —*SYN.*—**effort** refers to an active attempt to do something [make some *effort* to be friendly]; **exertion** implies the general use of much energy, power, or strength in doing something [she feels faint after any *exertion*]; **endeavor** suggests a serious, continued attempt to get something done, usually something deserving praise [a life spent in the *endeavor* to help others]; **pains** suggests taking the trouble to do something in a steady, careful way [to take pains with one's work] —*ANT.* ease

ef·fort·less (-lis) *adj.* making, needing, or showing; almost no effort [she skates in an *effortless* way] —see *SYN.* at EASY — **ef'fort·less·ly** *adj.* — **ef'fort·less·ness** *n.*

ef·fron·ter·y (e frun'tər ē, i-) *n, pl.* **-ter·ies** [< Fr. < L. *effrons*, shameless, barefaced < *ex-*, from + *frons*, forehead] unashamed boldness; impudence; audacity [he had the *effrontery* to criticize the press for exposing his dishonesty] — see *SYN.* at TEMERITY

ef·ful·gence (e ful'jəns, i-) *n.* [< L. prp. of *effulgere* < *ex-*, forth + *fulgere*, to shine: for IE. base see BLACK] great brightness; radiance — **ef·ful'gent** *adj.*

---

fat, āpe, cär; ten, ēven; is, bīte; gō, hôrn, tōōl, lŏŏk; oil, out; up, fur; get; joy; yet; chin; she; thin, *th*en; zh, leisure; ŋ, ring; ə for *a* in *ago*, *e* in *agent*, *i* in *sanity*, *o* in *comply*, *u* in *focus*; ' as in *able* (ā'b'l); Fr. bȧl; ë, Fr. coeur; ö, Fr. feu; Fr. moŋ; ō, Fr. coq; ü, Fr. duc; r, Fr. cri; H, G. ich; kh, G. doch; ‡ foreign; ☆Americanism; < derived from. See inside front cover.

---

14. What key word is given in the pronunciation key for the short *i* sound? _____

15. What is an antonym for *effort*? _____

16. What entry may be used only as a suffix? _____

17. What three words are given as synonyms for *effort*? _____

18. What five key words are given in the pronunciation key for the schwa sound? _____

19. What entry word has two correct spellings? _____

Skill: Reading a Floor Plan

A **floor plan** is a drawing that shows the layout of living or working space. The name and size of each room is marked on a floor plan. To save space, symbols are used on floor plans. For example, 14'1" × 20'0" means that the size of the room is 14 feet 1 inch wide by 20 feet 0 inches long. Note that the width of a room, measured from side to side, is written first. The length of a room is measured from top to bottom on a floor plan, and it is written second.

Study the following floor plan for a house.

House Floor Plan

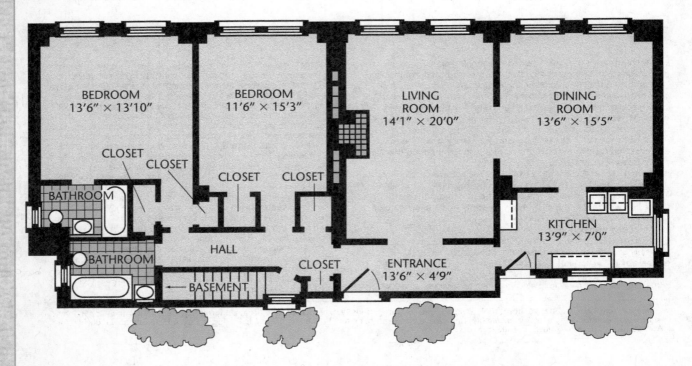

A. Use the floor plan to decide if each statement is true or false. Write *T* or *F* on the lines provided.

_____ 1. There is one bathroom in the house.

_____ 2. The two bedrooms are the same size.

_____ 3. The bedroom that measures 11'6" × 15'3" has one closet.

_____ 4. The kitchen can be entered from three different rooms.

_____ 5. The house has two doors to the outside.

_____ 6. The dining room is 15′5″ × 13′6″.

_____ 7. You enter the bedrooms from a hallway.

_____ 8. You can enter the dining room only from the living room or the kitchen.

_____ 9. A doorway off the hallway leads downstairs to the basement.

_____ 10. The entrance is larger than the kitchen.

_____ 11. The bedroom that measures 13′6″ × 13′10″ is probably the master, or the parents', bedroom, because it has two closets and its own bathroom.

_____ 12. The 11′6″ × 15′3″ bedroom is the smallest room in the house.

B. Complete each of the following sentences using the information on the floor plan.

1. The size of the dining room is _____.

2. Of the dining room and the bedroom located next to the living room, the larger room is the _____.

3. The house has a total of _____ closets.

4. You can enter the living room from the _____ or the _____.

5. The size of the living room is _____.

6. There are _____ windows in the kitchen.

7. The largest bedroom in the house is 13′6″ × _____.

8. The longest room in the house is the _____.

9. The length of the kitchen is _____.

10. The two rooms with the same width are the _____ and the _____.

11. Give the width of the following rooms.

   a. master bedroom _____   **c.** living room _____

   b. other bedroom _____   **d.** dining room _____

12. You can find the width of the entire house by adding the widths of the two bedrooms, the living room, and the dining room that you just recorded. Remember to always add inches to inches and feet to feet. Since 12 inches equal 1 foot, you need to change any measurements greater than 12 inches to feet.

   The width of the entire house is _____.

Environmental Issues

LESSON 39

Skill: Satire

BACKGROUND INFORMATION

The two poems and the cartoon in this selection focus on the environment, presenting future problems in a humorous way. Rapidly growing technology has resulted in both positive and negative environmental effects. In many ways, the future health of our environment depends on the actions we take today.

SKILL FOCUS: Satire

Satire is a literary device that is used by authors to ridicule, or poke fun at, an aspect of human nature or life in general. Almost any subject, from clothing fads to air pollution, can be the object of satire.

Through satire, writers and cartoonists comment on the foolishness or weakness of people, on the policies of different institutions, or on current events. In doing so, satirists also try to persuade people to make changes or improvements. Satire may be gentle, humorous, fierce, or scornful. While often amusing, the subject and intention of satire are always quite serious.

To recognize satire, look for a serious topic treated in a humorous way. Satirists sometimes exaggerate details and events to ridiculous proportions, or they jokingly imitate the language or style of a familiar literary or artistic form.

▶ Read the short poem below. On the lines that follow, explain what the poem satirizes.

The weather today is cloudy,
But don't worry, no rain will fall.
The clouds are really only smog,
And full of pollutants, that's all.

_____

_____

_____

CONTEXT CLUES: Footnotes

When there are no clues near a new or unusual word to help you figure out its meaning, a **footnote** may help to make the meaning clear. A footnote is signaled by a raised number after a word. The raised number tells you to look at the bottom of the page for a footnote with the same number. This footnote gives a brief definition or explanation of the word. Read the following lines.

For the cows have gone dry,
The hay's all awry[1],

[1] awry: wrong, amiss

The footnote for *awry* tells you that it means that something is wrong or amiss.

▶ Read the following lines. Then find the footnote on page 145 for *toxins*. On the lines below, rewrite the footnote, using your own words.

The hay's all awry,
With poisons and toxins[2] that stink.

_____

_____

In this selection, the words *awry*, *toxins*, *grime*, *birders*, *expedience*, *roentgen*, and *phosphates* appear with footnotes. Look for and read the footnotes to understand these words.

Strategy Tip

As you read the following poems and study the cartoon, notice the funny ways in which their creators dealt with serious topics. Think about why satire is more effective than direct criticism.

How Lucky We Are

Anonymous

How lucky we are, how lucky we are,
That our favorite food isn't fish.
For the rivers are brown,
No fish can be found,
We'll look for another fine dish.

So fortunate we, so happy we'll be,
Since milk is not something we drink.
For the cows have gone dry,
The hay's all awry[1],
With poisons and toxins[2] that stink.

What fun there will be—to play, you and me,
With the wonderful three-legged frogs.
They're terribly changed,
By pollution in rain,
And so they hop, one, two—and three!

And who needs the forests? Just huge
    wasted space,
Don't you think it's much nicer this way?
Parking lots are just fine,
With pavement and grime[3],
We can even keep birders[4] away.

Live longer you say? Why bother today?
To reach thirty-five is just right.
No creaky age pains!
No elder care gains!
A cancer will shorten the fight.

The Ingredients of Expedience[5]

Henry Gibson

There's a new recipe for water
That's caught on to such a degree
I now pass it on to others
The way it was passed on to me:
    Into an ocean of fluids   5
    Add a roentgen[6] of fallout or two,
    Aluminum cans, detergents
    (With the phosphates[7] most pleasing to you).
Stir in ground glass, melted plastics,
Any leftovers, sewage, rough waste.   10
Thicken with chemical acids
And mix to a pliable paste:
Mercury, mustard or nerve gas
Well blended with plenty of oil,
Insecticides, powdered or liquid,   15
Then slowly bring all to a boil.
That's it. Oh, yes, one reminder—
And forgive me for throwing a curve—
Fish die, but children prefer it
If you cool before you serve.   20

---

[1] awry (ə REYE): wrong, amiss
[2] toxins (TAHKS ənz): deadly chemicals
[3] grime (GREYEM): filth
[4] birders (BƏR dər): people who watch birds

[5] expedience (ik SPEE dee ənts): the easy way of doing something, usually for personal advantage or self-interest and without regard for the consequences.
[6] roentgen (RENT gən): international unit for measuring radiation dosage.
[7] phosphates (FAHS fayts): salts derived from a kind of acid (phosphoric acid), used in various industrial products.

COMPREHENSION

1. Why does the author in "How Lucky We Are" say he or she feels lucky?

   _____

   _____

   _____

2. Why doesn't the author drink milk?

   _____

   _____

   _____

3. Water (H_2O) is composed of hydrogen and oxygen. In the poem "The Ingredients of Expedience," what does the new recipe include?

   _____

   _____

   _____

4. In the cartoon, what is odd about the message written on the car?

   _____

   _____

   _____

5. Complete each sentence with the correct word.

birders	grime	expedience
roentgen		phosphates

   a. The customer settled for a lower-quality

   product for the sake of _____.

   b. The _____ read the signs along the path directing them to the hawk's nest.

   c. The output of X-ray machines is measured

   in units of _____.

   d. The company used _____ to make fertilizer.

   e. The flood left a layer of black _____ over everything in the house.

1. Explain why there are no fish to be found in "How Lucky We Are."

_____

_____

2. **a.** List ways in which animals have changed in "How Lucky We Are."

_____

_____

   b. In what ways have people brought about the changes described in the first poem?

_____

_____

3. In "How Lucky We Are," how are humans affected by the pollution?

_____

_____

4. **a.** In "The Ingredients of Expedience," what is the result of mixing together all the ingredients in the new recipe for water?

_____

_____

   b. Who do you think made up this new recipe?

_____

_____

   c. What does the poet mean when he says that the new recipe for water has "caught on"?

_____

_____

   d. Reread lines 17–20 of "The Ingredients of Expedience." What is the meaning of these four lines?

_____

_____

5. Consider the meaning of the poem's title: "The Ingredients of Expedience." Who do you think might benefit by having water like that described in the poem?

_____

_____

6. In the cartoon, why is it news that nothing new has been found harmful to one's health?

_____

_____

SKILL FOCUS: SATIRE

The purpose of most satire is to eliminate serious social problems by encouraging people to change their thinking or behavior. To answer the following questions, you may reread the poems and look back at the cartoon.

1. a. What is the subject of the first poem? _____

   b. What is the subject of the second poem? _____

2. a. What is the attitude of the poets in both poems? _____

   b. Do the poets use gentle humor or bitter humor to make their points in these poems? _____

3. a. What method does the first poet use to develop satire? _____

   b. In the second poem, what form of writing does the poet imitate? _____

4. a. In the first poem, what issue does the poet satirize to increase the public's awareness?

_____

   b. In the second poem, what issue does the poet satirize? _____

_____

5. a. How could the problems discussed in the first poem be solved? _____

_____

   b. What action does the poet suggest in the second poem? _____

_____

6. Do you think these poems are meant to be entertaining, persuasive, or both? Explain.

_____

_____

_____

Reading-Writing Connection

On a separate sheet of paper, create a poem or cartoon about an environmental issue in your area. Include humor—either gentle or bitter—and try to be both entertaining and persuasive.

Skill: Making Generalizations

BACKGROUND INFORMATION

"Making a Difference" explores the efforts of four people trying to save endangered wildlife: Pan Wenshi and Lü Zhi of China, Merlin Tuttle of the United States, and Chico Mendes of Brazil. The threat to plants and animals is a result of human factors. One of these threats is the destruction of natural habitats. Cutting down forests or disrupting an ecosystem can have drastic effects on plants and animals in the area, as well as having an effect on all kinds of life throughout the world.

SKILL FOCUS: Making Generalizations

Facts, or information that is true and can be proven, are important in understanding any subject you read about. Specific facts alone, however, cannot provide you with a complete understanding or interpretation of a topic. You must be able to **make generalizations**, or draw principles from a sampling of facts. A generalization is a broad statement that goes beyond the specific information provided by facts. Examine the following facts.

- Pan Wenshi wrote to government officials requesting that they make the Qin Ling mountains panda reserves.
- Wenshi persuaded officials to slow down habitat loss in Qin Ling by convincing them that pandas could die out if no action were taken.
- The Chinese government declared that it would no longer allow people to take wild pandas into captivity.

Based on these three facts, you can make the following generalization: Pan Wenshi's efforts have resulted in increased protection for wild pandas. To be sound and reasonable, a generalization must be based on two or more facts.

▶ Read the facts about bats in the chart at the top of the next column. Then write a generalization based on these facts in the box labeled "Generalization."

Fact 1	Fact 2	Fact 3
Although many believe so, bats do not tangle themselves in people's hair.	Very few bats carry rabies.	Although they will bite in self-defense, bats do not attack people or pets.

Generalization

CONTEXT CLUES: Details

Often the meaning of a word is made clear by **details** provided in the same or nearby sentences. As you read the sentences below, look for detail context clues that help you understand the meaning of the word *beneficial*.

*Bats are, in fact, extremely **beneficial** to humans. They eat tremendous quantities of night-flying insects, including mosquitoes.*

You can figure out the meaning of the word *beneficial* by reading the details in the sentences that follow it. Bats eat harmful insects. From this detail, you can infer that *beneficial* means "helpful."

▶ Read the following sentences. Circle the details that explain the meaning of the underlined word.

*The panda is an **elusive** animal. Because they avoid people, pandas are hard to track or trap.*

In "Making a Difference," look for the underlined words *habitat*, *inbreeding*, and *reserves* to explain the meanings of these words.

Strategy Tip

As you read "Making a Difference," pay attention to the facts and make generalizations based on them.

Making A Difference

Pan Wenshi, Lü Zhi, and the Giant Pandas

At one time, large populations of giant pandas could be found throughout southern and eastern China. Today only about 1,200 wild pandas survive in a few small, scattered areas. Pan Wenshi, a zoology professor at Beijing University, and his colleague Lü Zhi have been studying wild pandas in China's Qin Ling mountains since 1984. Their discoveries about panda behavior, diet, and cub-rearing and their efforts to protect wild pandas offer new hope for saving these rare and elusive animals.

The major threat to wild pandas is not natural predators but humans. Poachers illegally kill pandas for their pelts, which sell for more than $10,000 in Hong Kong, Taiwan, and Japan. A more serious threat, however, is the destruction of the pandas' habitat. Loggers cutting timber and farmers clearing land for fields have destroyed bamboo forests on which pandas depend for food and other resources. In addition, when logging and farming divide forested areas where pandas live, the separated panda populations may be too small to reproduce successfully. In small populations, inbreeding often produces weak offspring that cannot survive.

Pan Wenshi and Lü Zhi hope to save pandas.

To protect what remains of the pandas' habitat, the Chinese government developed a 10-year plan to enlarge the 13 existing panda reserves and to create 14 new ones. As part of the plan, loggers and farmers would be paid to relocate to areas that did not threaten pandas. To Pan Wenshi's dismay, the Qin Ling research area was not included in the plan.

Wenshi decided to take action. He wrote to government officials requesting that they include Qin Ling among the reserves. His request was honored, but Wenshi did not stop there. He next persuaded officials to slow down habitat loss in Qin Ling. In 1994, the roar of chain saws ceased when the government paid timber companies working there to move out of the area. "I think that Wenshi's story is a good example of how the researcher can make a difference," said Lü Zhi. In another major victory for pandas, the Chinese government recently declared that it would no longer allow people to take wild pandas into captivity.

About 130 pandas are now living in zoos throughout the world. Attempts to help save the giant panda through zoo breeding programs have been extremely discouraging. During the past 30 years, fewer than 100 panda cubs have been born in captivity, and most of them died in infancy. Pan Wenshi's and Lü Zhi's studies of infant pandas and their mothers in the wild may help improve the survival rate of panda cubs born in zoos.

Merlin Tuttle and Endangered Bats

Bats are the most endangered land mammals in the United States. Of the 44 species of bats native to North America, 6 species are already on the U.S. government's endangered list and 18 more are candidates for addition.

Since founding Bat Conservation International (BCI) in 1982, Merlin Tuttle has worked tirelessly to protect existing bat colonies and to change people's ideas about bats. For example, bats are not blind. They do not tangle themselves in people's hair. They do not attack people or pets, although they will bite in self-defense, as any wild animal will do. Very few bats carry rabies. People are at far greater risk of contracting rabies from raccoons, foxes, skunks, dogs, and cats than from bats.

Merlin Tuttle is the founder of Bat Conservation International.

✘ Bats are, in fact, extremely beneficial to humans. They eat tremendous quantities of night-flying insects, including mosquitoes, and agricultural pests, such as moths and beetles. Just one little brown bat—the species most commonly found in attics and barns—can consume 600 mosquitoes in one hour. A large bat colony, such as the 20 million Mexican free-tailed bats inhabiting Bracken Cave in Texas, may devour 500 tons of insects in one night. Bats also help hundreds of plant species reproduce, including cactus and valuable fruit trees. Fruit-eating bats are major dispersers of tree seeds. They carry these seeds and spread them in many directions, to places they never would reach otherwise.

As people intentionally kill bats or carelessly destroy their caves, increasing numbers of bat colonies are seeking refuge in abandoned mines. Even there, however, bats are not safe. Although abandoned mines provide excellent shelter for bats, they pose safety hazards for people. Mines regarded as dangerous have been boarded up or filled with dirt, often without thought for bat colonies trapped inside. "BCI sounded the alarm on mine closures," said Tuttle. "A million bats can easily be buried alive, and no one would even know it."

To protect both people and bats, Tuttle advocates closing off mine entrances with grid-like gates that allow bats to pass through but keep people out. Often built jointly by BCI, mining companies, and government agencies, such gates have saved millions of bats. In addition, some closed mines have been reopened and gated to provide new homes for bats. In some areas, local mine inspectors now cooperate with BCI in locating and protecting mines where bats live. In 1994, BCI and the U.S. Bureau of Land Management funded the North American Bats and Mines Project. The project's goal is to educate landowners and managers to survey for bats before closing mines and, if colonies are found, to construct bat-friendly gates.

✔ The largest urban bat colony in North America, numbering between 750,000 and 1.5 million bats, lives in the Congress Avenue Bridge in downtown Austin, Texas. When the bridge was renovated in 1980, thousands of bats that had lost their caves in the Austin area found that the bridge's new crevices provided an ideal roosting site. The people of Austin were horrified at first and demanded that the bats be exterminated.

Then Merlin Tuttle went to work. Through lectures, radio and television talk shows, and educational programs in schools, Tuttle changed people's attitude toward the bats. Now when thick clouds of bats stream out of the bridge every evening, people gather to watch.

After Tuttle spoke at a bridge designer's conference, the Texas Department of Transportation funded major research to design more bat-friendly bridges. "We have about 6 million bats already living in 59 Texas bridges," said structural engineer Mark J. Bloschock, "and we'll be building 15 to 20 new bridges a year that together will accommodate a million new bats."

Chico Mendes and the Amazon Rain Forest

Many environmental activists encounter resistance, physical discomfort, and personal hardship in their fight to protect the world's endangered wildlife. In his fight, Chico Mendes lost his life.

Chico Mendes dedicated his life to saving the rain forests in Brazil.

Mendes was born into a poor, illiterate family of rubber tappers living and working in Brazil's Amazon rain forest. Rubber tappers cut small slits in the bark of rubber trees and collect the latex sap that oozes out. Tapping trees does not kill or injure trees.

By the age of 8, Mendes was already working in his family's grove. After an ex-army officer taught him to read and write at the age of 18, Mendes became convinced that the only way forest workers could improve their lives would be by organizing into a union.

In the 1970s, the Brazilian government started opening the rain forest to development by cattle ranchers, timber and mining companies, and farmers. Unlike rubber tappers, these developers destroy forests as they clear the land. The vast fires used in their "slash-and-burn" clearing method release huge quantities of carbon dioxide into the atmosphere and eliminate the plant life that normally consumes this heat-trapping gas. Amazon deforestation thus contributes to the greenhouse effect that threatens to alter Earth's climate through global warming.

Realizing that the rain forest and the rubber tappers' way of life were in danger, Mendes created a rural workers' union. Besides raising money to build schools and medical clinics, Mendes pioneered the use of nonviolent tactics to block deforestation. Whenever work crews with bulldozers and chain saws threatened a parcel of land, Mendes called together rubber tappers and their families to form a human barrier against the machines. These peaceful blockades are estimated to have saved 3 million acres of rain forest.

Mendes fought to have large sections of the rain forest set aside as "extractive preserves," areas that could be used only for harvesting renewable resources such as rubber. He also helped persuade the Inter-American Development Bank to stop funding for a highway extension being cut through the rain forest. As a result of Mendes's efforts—and the international fame and support he was beginning to receive—the Brazilian government finally designated 5 million acres of rain forest for permanent preservation.

Mendes's successful efforts earned him the hatred of ranchers and developers determined to exploit the rain forest. Five times Mendes survived attempts on his life. When new death threats were made in 1988, Mendes was assigned police guards to protect him. However, on December 22 of that year, as he stepped out of his back door while his two guards played dominoes inside, Mendes was struck down by a shotgun blast. He died before reaching the hospital. Today his union colleagues carry on his work.

Shortly before he was murdered, Mendes wrote in a letter to a friend: "I wish no flowers after I die, for I know they would be taken from the forest."

1. How many giant pandas survive in the wild today? _____

2. What organization did Merlin Tuttle found?

   _____

3. What is an "extractive preserve"?

   _____

   _____

4. Underline the cause in each of the following statements. Circle the effect.

   a. When logging and farming divide the forested areas where pandas live, the separated populations may be too small to reproduce successfully.

   b. Bat colonies seek refuge in abandoned mines because people have carelessly destroyed their caves.

5. Reread the paragraph with an ✗ next to it. Underline the sentence that states its main idea. How many major details support the main idea? _____ Circle those details.

6. Write the letter of the correct meaning on the line next to each word.

   _____ habitat

   _____ inbreeding

   _____ reserves

   a. reproduction among animals of the same kind

   b. type of area in which a particular kind of animal lives

   c. protected areas set aside for certain animals

CRITICAL THINKING

1. Explain why developers hated Chico Mendes.

   _____

2. a. Conclude why abandoned mines are boarded up or filled with dirt.

      _____

   b. How does blocking or filling mines affect bat colonies?

      _____

   c. What is the advantage of using grid-like gates to close off mines?

      _____

3. Read the paragraph with a ✔ next to it. Then write a sentence that describes its main idea.

   _____

4. Describe Chico Mendes's attitude toward the Amazon rain forest.

   _____

1. Underline the statement below that is a generalization. Then circle the letter of each statement that supports the generalization.

   a. Loggers and farmers have destroyed the pandas' habitat.

   b. Most panda cubs born in captivity do not survive.

   c. Humans are the major threat to giant pandas in the wild.

   d. The Qin Ling research area was not originally included in China's panda protection plan.

   e. Poachers kill pandas for their valuable pelts.

2. Locate three facts in the text to support the following generalization.

   Generalization: Harvesting renewable resources in the rain forest is better for the environment than developing the land.

   Facts: a. _____

   b. _____

   c. _____

3. Write a generalization for the following group of facts.

   Facts: Chico Mendes formed a union for rural workers.

   He raised money to build schools and clinics.

   He fought to have large sections of rain forest set aside as "extraction preserves."

   Generalization: _____

4. Write a generalization about Merlin Tuttle and the closings of abandoned mines. Give at least two facts to support the generalization.

   Generalization: _____

   Facts: a. _____

   b. _____

Reading-Writing Connection

What animals or environments are threatened in your area? What could be done to save them? On a separate sheet of paper, write a letter to the editor of a local newspaper in which you present the facts and your suggestions.

Skill: Understanding Chemical Formulas

BACKGROUND INFORMATION

"What Is in the Air?" discusses the elements and compounds that are found in the air. It explains how elements combine to form compounds that create hazardous reactions. It also explains the concept of chemical symbols, formulas, and equations. The air we breathe contains several elements and compounds that occur naturally as well as chemical compounds created by people.

SKILL FOCUS: Understanding Chemical Formulas

Chemical symbols, formulas, and equations are all shorthand ways of conveying information in science. A **chemical formula** is a way of stating what elements have combined to form the compound. An **element** is a pure substance. A **compound** is made of two or more elements. A chemical equation is a shorthand statement that shows how elements and compounds react chemically with one another. When you read chemical formulas, be sure that you understand the following.

- the meaning of each letter and number symbol
- the relationships among the symbols in a formula
- the meaning of the formula as a whole

▶ Look at the symbols in the table of elements below. Then answer the questions that follow.

Table of Elements

					He Helium
B Boron	C Carbon	N Nitrogen	O Oxygen	F Fluorine	Ne Neon
Al Aluminum	Si Silicon	P Phosphorus	S Sulfur	Cl Chlorine	Ar Argon
	As Arsenic	Se Selenium	Br Bromine	Kr Krypton	

1. What does the symbol C stand for?

_____

2. If a scientist wrote the symbol Al, what element would he or she mean? _____

3. What is the symbol for argon? _____

CONTEXT CLUES: Synonyms

A **synonym** is a word that has the same or almost the same meaning as another word. When a synonym appears near an unknown word, it can make the word's meaning clear. In the sentences below, look for synonym context clues that help explain the meaning of the underlined word.

Scientists have identified 90 different elements that are found in nature. They have <u>synthesized</u> 19 others in the laboratory. Together we know of 109 elements that either occur naturally or have been made by scientists.

If you don't know the meaning of the word *synthesized*, the word *made* in the next sentence can help you. The words *synthesized* and *made* are synonyms.

▶ Read the sentence below. Circle the word that is a synonym for the underlined word.

It <u>indicates</u>, or shows, that two molecules of the compound are formed as a result of the chemical reaction.

In "What Is in the Air?," the words *composed*, *decreases*, and *nontoxic* are underlined. Look for synonyms in the text that help explain the meanings of these words.

Strategy Tip

As you read "What Is in the Air?" study the chemical symbols, formulas, and equations carefully. Be sure that you understand how they are being used.

What Is in the Air?

The air around you is full of different **elements** and **compounds**. An element is a pure substance that cannot be broken down into different substances by ordinary chemical means. A compound is a substance made up of two or more elements. In recent years, many elements and compounds in the air have become harmful due to pollutants.

Chemistry Basics

Early in the study of chemistry, scientists assigned symbols to the elements as a shorthand way of referring to them. Scientists have identified 90 different elements that are found in nature. They have synthesized another 19 in the laboratory. Together we know of 109 elements that either occur naturally or have been made by scientists. Carbon, oxygen, copper, iron, and gold are a few examples of naturally occurring elements.

The table in Figure 1 shows the symbols for some common elements. Symbols are one or two letters long, with the first letter always capitalized and the second letter lowercase. Some symbols come from the element's name. For example, O stands for oxygen. Some symbols come from their Latin names. For example, Na stands for sodium because the Latin name for sodium is natrium.

Elements and Compounds in the Air

Air is made up mostly of nitrogen (N) and oxygen (O). These two gases are elements that make up about 99 percent of air, with oxygen being 21 percent and nitrogen 78 percent. The other 1 percent is composed of carbon dioxide, carbon monoxide, ozone, nitrogen oxides, neon, helium, methane, and argon. In addition, air contains a small amount of water, which is a chemical compound.

Chemical Formulas

Water is made up of two parts hydrogen (H) and one part oxygen (O). Its chemical formula is below.

$$H_2O$$

A chemical formula shows the composition of an element or a compound. In the above formula, the numeral 2 is called a subscript. It tells you that for every atom of oxygen in the compound, there are two hydrogen atoms. An **atom** is the smallest unit of an element. Because water is made up of hydrogen and oxygen, it is also referred to by the scientific term hydrogen oxide.

Element	Symbol	Latin Name If Different	Element	Symbol	Latin Name If Different
Argon	Ar		Nitrogen	N	
Carbon	C		Oxygen	O	
Chlorine	Cl		Platinum	Pt	
Copper	Cu	cuprum	Phosphorus	P	
Fluorine	F		Potassium	K	kalium
Gold	Au	aurum	Silicon	Si	
Helium	He		Silver	Ag	argentum
Hydrogen	H		Sodium	Na	natrium
Iron	Fe	ferrum	Sulfur	S	
Nickel	Ni		Zinc	Zn	

FIGURE 1. This chart lists elements, their symbols, and their Latin names (if they have one).

Subscripts are not always required in order to write the formula for a chemical compound. Carbon monoxide, for example, contains one carbon atom and one oxygen atom. It is written as follows.

$$CO$$

Carbon monoxide is a gas. It is colorless and odorless, as well as poisonous. It occurs when carbons burn with too little air. Carbon monoxide <u>decreases</u> the amount of oxygen in the blood. When anything reduces the amount of oxygen in the blood, people who have heart trouble may face serious problems. Carbon monoxide is usually produced from stoves that burn wood or coal, but it can also be produced when farm fields are burned. Car exhausts also release carbon monoxide, although not as much as they did in the past. Today's vehicles limit the amount of pollutants released into the air.

Carbon dioxide is a gas that is one part carbon to two parts oxygen. It can be written as below.

$$CO_2$$

Unlike carbon monoxide, carbon dioxide occurs naturally and is <u>nontoxic</u>. This nonpoisonous gas is part of the natural order of the environment. Animals breathe in oxygen and exhale carbon dioxide. Plants absorb carbon dioxide and release oxygen. Carbon dioxide is a harmless gas that is a very important part of air.

Have you ever driven by a factory when suddenly the smell of rotten eggs filled the air? What you smelled is a gas called hydrogen sulfide, which is two parts hydrogen to one part sulfur.

$$H_2S$$

When hydrogen sulfide burns, a chemical reaction occurs, turning it into a new chemical compound, called sulfur dioxide.

$$SO_2$$

Sulfur and sulfur dioxide are among the major contributors to air pollution. They occur when coal is burned extensively. Many cities, including New York and London, have experienced air-pollution problems because of sulfur.

Sulfur dioxide also leads to the problem of acid rain. Water vapor in the air eventually falls to the ground as rain. If too much sulfur dioxide is in the

This photo shows pollution in a city skyline.

air, it mixes with the water vapor, producing sulfuric acid. It then falls to Earth in acidic form, or acid rain.

Chemical Reactions and Equations

When water and sulfur dioxide mix, they create a reaction, forming sulfuric acid. This can be shown in a chemical equation.

$$H_2O + SO_2 \rightarrow H_2SO_4$$

The equation can be read as "water plus sulfur dioxide yields sulfuric acid." The formula H_2SO_4 shows the chemical composition of sulfuric acid. It contains two hydrogen atoms, one sulfur atom, and four oxygen atoms.

The substances on the left side of the arrow in the equation are called **reactants** (ree AK tənts). Reactants react, or combine, with one another. The substance to the right of the arrow is called the **product**. The product is produced, or created, by the reaction. The arrow is the symbol for *yields* or *forms*.

The Ozone Layer

Every summer, we hear warnings about the Earth's disappearing ozone layer and how dangerous this is to our skin. The reason is that ozone—which is actually three oxygen **molecules**, or O_3—acts as a protective layer around the Earth, shielding it from the sun's harmful ultraviolet rays. A molecule is the smallest unit of a compound.

Many harmful gases dissolve after a short time or wash away with rain. However, one particular chemical compound can linger in the air for years—chloroflourocarbons, or CFCs. Released from aerosol sprays, air conditioners, and refrigerators, CFCs cause the ozone to break down.

To counteract the harmful ultraviolet rays that seep through the ozone layer, many people use zinc oxide on their skin. The following equation states that two molecules of zinc, each of which has one atom, unite or react with one molecule of oxygen.

$$2Zn + O_2 \rightarrow 2ZnO$$

The subscript 2 tells you that each molecule of oxygen is composed of two atoms of oxygen. The combination of these three molecules (two zinc plus one oxygen) forms two molecules of zinc oxide.

The formula for zinc oxide (2ZnO) shows its chemical composition. Each molecule of zinc oxide is composed of one atom of zinc that has joined with one atom of oxygen. The number 2 is called a **coefficient** (koh ə FISH ənt). It indicates that two molecules of the compound are formed as a result of the chemical reaction.

Because chemical symbols are the same in all languages, formulas and equations can be understood by scientists everywhere, and ideas and discoveries can easily be communicated. Pollution in the air we breathe is a global concern. The universal language of chemistry allows scientists and environmentalists around the world to work together to solve pollution problems.

COMPREHENSION

1. What information does a subscript in a chemical formula give?

   _____

   _____

2. What is a chemical equation?

   _____

   _____

3. Describe the difference between a chemical symbol and a chemical compound.

   _____

   _____

   _____

4. Explain what reactants do in a chemical equation.

   _____

   _____

5. Complete each sentence with the correct word.

   decreases   nontoxic   composed

   a. Water is _____ of hydrogen and oxygen molecules.

   b. Fewer CFCs in the air _____ the chance of the ozone layer breaking down.

   c. Unlike carbon monoxide, which can be harmful, carbon dioxide is _____.

CRITICAL THINKING

Circle the letter of the correct answer.

1. The number of atoms in H_2SO_4 is _____.

   a. 6   b. 4   c. 7   d. 8

2. In the chemical equation $2H_2O \rightarrow 2H_2 + O_2$, the coefficients are _____.

   a. the 2s in front of the Hs

   b. the 2s following the Hs

   c. the 2s following the Hs and the 2 following the O

   d. the 2 following the O

3. What is the chemical reaction that causes acid rain?

   a. water mixes with sulfuric acid

   b. water mixes with sulfur dioxide

   c. water mixes with carbon dioxide

   d. water mixes with oxygen

A. For each chemical compound listed, identify the elements and give the number of atoms for each element. Use Figure 1 on page 156.

1. H_3PO_4

_____

_____

_____

2. Na_2O

_____

_____

_____

3. $SiCl_2$

_____

_____

_____

4. Fe_2O_3

_____

_____

_____

5. SiO_2

_____

_____

_____

6. SO_4

_____

_____

_____

B. Write the formulas for the following chemical compounds. Use Figure 1 on page 156.

1. 1 sodium
   1 fluorine

   _____

   _____

2. 1 potassium
   1 nitrogen
   2 oxygen

   _____

   _____

3. 2 hydrogen
   1 carbon
   3 oxygen

   _____

   _____

4. 1 sodium
   1 nitrogen
   3 oxygen

   _____

   _____

5. 3 potassium
   1 phosphorous
   4 oxygen

   _____

   _____

6. 1 potassium
   1 chlorine
   3 oxygen

   _____

   _____

7. carbon monoxide _____

8. carbon dioxide _____

9. water _____

Reading-Writing Connection

Use the chart on page 156 to look up the symbols or equations for foods that you use daily, such as salt, sugar, and soda water (used in soft drinks). On a separate sheet of paper, write their chemical formulas and write a paragraph that explains what the symbols in the formulas mean.

Skill: Reading Equations

BACKGROUND INFORMATION

"Solving Equations" is about how algebra is becoming more and more important in the workplace. It is a very useful tool for determining unknown facts by using facts that are known. Many jobs now require the understanding of relationships among numbers and facts, which is the major focus of algebra. The Algebra Project, founded by civil rights activist Robert Moses, has helped many inner-city students find better careers. The core of the Algebra Project is field trips, which introduce math concepts to the students by relating them to everyday activities. The goal is to assist students in inner-city and rural areas to achieve a better understanding of mathematics and to provide them with the problem-solving skills that are necessary for entry into the economic mainstream.

SKILL FOCUS: Reading Equations

When you solve a word problem, you use a plan that is stated in the form of a math sentence, or an **equation**. These equations involve unknown numbers, represented by letters called **variables**, such as x, n, R, or t. A variable is a symbol for a number that has a value that can change or vary. To solve the equations, you must find numbers for the variables.

To solve most simple equations, you use the operations that are *opposite* to the ones shown in the equation. For example, in the equation $n - 4 = 5$, where subtraction is shown, you would use addition to solve the equation. You would add 4 to each side of the equation, $n - 4 + 4 = 5 + 4$. This results in $n = 9$. As another example, suppose the equation was $\frac{n}{3} = 2$. Since the equation shows division, you would use multiplication to solve it. You would multiply each side of the equation by 3, $\frac{n}{3} \times 3 = 2 \times 3$. This results in $n = 6$.

Problems can involve equations that include negative numbers or have negative numbers as the solution. You can solve these equations in the same way as other simple equations. Just keep in mind the methods of adding, subtracting, multiplying, and dividing negative numbers.

▶ Look at the equations below. First figure out the operation that you need to use. (Remember that it will be the opposite of the operation shown in the equation.) Write the name of the operation on the line. Then solve the equation.

1. $3 + n = 5$

_____

2. $3(n) = 15$

_____

WORD CLUES

The word *equation* comes from the word *equal*; an equation is a statement in which two numbers or quantities are equal. Two equations that are **equivalent** have the same solution. *Equivalent* means "equal valued." The equations $3 + n = 5$ and $n = 2$ are not the same, but they are equivalent because n has the same value in each of them. Therefore, the equivalent equation $n = 2$ is called the **solution** to the original equation, $3 + n = 5$.

> **Strategy Tip**
>
> As you read each equation in "Solving Equations," notice the signs of operation: addition, subtraction, multiplication, and division. Also be alert for negative numbers in equations.

Solving Equations

The plan for solving many word problems includes one or more equations, depending on the number of steps in the problem. An **equation** is a statement that two numbers or quantities are equal. The branch of mathematics that includes solving equations is called **algebra**.

In algebra, equations use various letters, such as N, x, y, or p, as **variables**. The object of solving equations is to find the numerical values of the variables. A solution to an equation, then, is found when an **equivalent** equation is produced. An equivalent equation shows the variable isolated, or set apart, on one side of an equation and a number on the other, such as $N = 3$. In other words, the equation is true when N has the value 3. Equations are equivalent when the same variable in both has the same value.

Read the following problem.

Calvin is 4 years older than twice his sister's age. If Calvin is 16, how old is his sister?

You need to write two different expressions that describe Calvin's age and then combine the expressions into an equation. (An equation states that two expressions are equal.) The solution to the equation will be an equivalent equation that tells his sister's age.

Let x equal the sister's age. The two expressions for Calvin's age are $2x + 4$ (4 years older than twice his sister's age) and 16. Therefore, the equation is as follows.

$$2x + 4 = 16$$

To solve the equation, first subtract the number that was added, 4, from both sides of the equation.

$$2x + 4 - 4 = 16 - 4$$

$$2x + 0 = 12$$

Then divide both sides by the number 2, that is used as a **factor**. Factors are numbers that form a product when multiplied together. Here 2 is a number that is multiplied by x, the variable, to produce the product 12. So you divide both sides by 2.

$$\frac{2x}{2} = \frac{12}{2}$$

$$x = 6$$

These two steps produce an equivalent equation of the following form: $x =$ "some number."

The equation $x = 6$ is equivalent to the original equation, but it is in a form that directly tells you the value of x. Therefore, Calvin's sister is 6 years old.

Read the following problem.

Lucia told Carlos that if it were three times as cold as the thermometer showed and then got one degree colder, or $-1°$, it would be ten degrees below zero, or $-10°$. What was the temperature?

An equation with negative numbers is solved in the same way as any other simple equation. When a negative number is added to the product, the effect is the same as subtraction. So $3x + (-1) = -10$ is the same as $3x - 1 = -10$. The equation is as follows.

$$3x - 1 = -10$$
$$3x - 1 + 1 = -10 + 1$$
$$3x = -9$$
$$\frac{3x}{3} = \frac{-9}{3}$$
$$x = -3$$

The thermometer showed $-3°$.

Read the following problem.

If Mei-yu used to have five times as many trading cards as she now has plus three more, she would have the same number of cards as if she had three times as many cards plus five more. How many cards does she have now?

Let x equal the number of cards now. The equation is as follows.

$$5x + 3 = 3x + 5$$

MATHEMATICS

First you subtract $3x$ from each side of the equation to get the variable expressions all on one side.

$$5x - 3x + 3 = 3x - 3x + 5$$
$$2x + 3 = 5$$
$$2x + 3 - 3 = 5 - 3$$

$$2x = 2$$
$$\frac{2x}{2} = \frac{2}{2}$$
$$x = 1$$

Mei-yu has only one trading card now.

COMPREHENSION

1. What is an equation?

_____

_____

2. When is a solution to an equation found?

_____

_____

3. What is another way of writing $3x + (-1)$?

_____

4. If two expressions with variables occur on different sides of an equation, what should your first step be in solving the equation?

_____

_____

5. Is there any difference between $5 + (-3)$ and $5 - 3$? Explain.

_____

_____

CRITICAL THINKING

1. To solve the equation $3x = 12$, would you multiply or divide both sides of the equation?

_____ By what number? _____

2. To solve the equation $-4x = -32$, would you multiply or divide both sides of the equation?

_____ By what number? _____

3. Suppose you multiply both sides of an equation by two different numbers. Why does this result in an equation that is not equivalent to the original equation?

_____

_____

SKILL FOCUS: READING EQUATIONS

Solve each equation. Use the space to the right of each equation to work it out.

1. $x + 7 = 10$

_____

2. $x - 3 = 15$

_____

3. $7x = 56$

_____

4. $4x - 12 = 24$

_____

5. $x - 9 = -2$

_____

6. $3x + 3 = 12$

_____

7. $3x + 15 = 12$

_____

8. $25 = 39 - 2x$

_____

9. $x + 8 = 15$

_____

10. $4x + 6 = 22$

_____

11. $3x - 7 = 23$

_____

12. $42 - x = 28$

_____

13. $16 = 24 - x$

_____

14. $65 = 75 - 2x$

_____

15. $5x + 4 = -21$

_____

16. $9 = -6 + 5x$

_____

17. $3x + 4x = 49$

_____

18. $5x - x = 24$

_____

19. $-24 = 7x - x$

_____

20. $8x - 3x = 20$

_____

21. $5x + 7 = 3x - 5$

_____

22. $x - 5 = 3x - 1$

_____

23. $5x + 3 = 2x - 9$

_____

24. $24 = 16 + 4x$

_____

25. $-12 = 2x - 2$

_____

26. $3x + 3 = x + 9$

_____

27. $10x + 1 = 8x - 3$

_____

28. $x - 7 = 2x - 17$

_____

Reading-Writing Connection

In your own words, explain to a partner the meaning of equation and equivalent equation. Then together on a separate sheet of paper, set up and solve an equation based on a real-life situation. Make sure you know certain facts and want to find out other facts. Then write a paragraph summarizing your work.

Skill: Making Inferences

Sometimes you can **infer**, or figure out, information that is not stated directly in a selection.

Read the following selection about two female pioneers.

Pioneers in the Sky

In 1948, Blanche Stuart Scott made history. She was the first woman to pilot a jet airplane. Yet this was only the latest in a lifetime of firsts. She was born in 1892 to a prominent family in Rochester, New York. Always adventurous, she became an expert ice skater and took up bicycling as a trick rider. As a teenager, she terrorized Rochester with one of her first automobiles. When she was about 18, she became the first car salesperson in New York. Soon after, she persuaded an auto manufacturer to sponsor her to be the first woman to drive across the country. The year was 1910, and there were only 218 miles of paved roads in the United States!

On her trip across the country, she saw a demonstration flight by Orville Wright and one of his students. She was captivated by the idea of flying, and by October of that year, she was the first woman to become a professional pilot. In those days, most planes were flown around fields in exhibitions. One day, angry at her boss, she made a 60-mile round trip to another town and back. Newspapers called it the first long-distance flight by a woman. In 1919, as part of Glenn Martin's Flying Circus, she agreed to test new airplanes that Martin built. Blanche Stuart Scott was the first woman test pilot.

Christa McAuliffe never dreamed of glory, but of what she could do for others. Described by a friend as "your basic, ordinary person," McAuliffe was a mother, a wife, and a dedicated social studies teacher from Concord, New Hampshire. Then on July 19, 1985, Vice President George Bush named 36-year-old McAuliffe to be the "first private citizen passenger in the history of space flight." Overcome by such an honor, she deftly commented, "It's not often that a teacher is at a loss for words." Overnight, the name Christa McAuliffe became known, and American schoolchildren were filled with pride and anticipation.

In preparation for her journey into space on the spaceship *Challenger*, McAuliffe trained for many months. While in space, she was to broadcast two live lessons on television to the nation's schoolchildren.

Finally on January 28, 1986, after several days of poor weather conditions, the *Challenger* took off. However, 73 seconds after takeoff, the spacecraft exploded, killing all seven members, including the popular social studies teacher, who, nevertheless, was a pioneer in the frontier of space travel.

Put a check mark next to each of the statements below that can be inferred.

Blanche Stuart Scott

_____ Blanche Stuart Scott loved adventure.

_____ Cross-country travel was difficult for anyone in 1910.

_____ It was easy to learn how to fly in the past.

Christa McAuliffe

_____ Christa McAuliffe accomplished much in her life.

_____ Only trained astronauts should travel in space.

_____ Christa McAuliffe served as a model for American schoolchildren.

Skill: Cause and Effect

Many ideas that you read about in textbooks are connected by cause and effect. A **cause** is a reason, condition, or situation that makes something happen. An **effect** is the result or outcome of a cause. Several causes can bring about a single effect, and several effects can result from a single cause.

Causes and effects are usually directly stated in a selection. Sometimes, however, you have to infer, or figure out, a cause or an effect.

As you read the selection, try to understand how the ideas are connected. Think about the causes and the effects of particular actions.

The Great Blackout

At 5:15 P.M. on November 9, 1965, the lights suddenly went out—first in Toronto, next in Boston, and then in New York City. Before anyone knew what was going on, 30 million people in eight states and some of Canada were in the dark. Never before had there been such a massive blackout.

Somewhere north of New York City, the complex power network that supplies electricity to the Northeast broke down. Nobody is sure exactly how the power failure happened. A big city's rush hour demands extra power. During such periods of high demand, a power system may not be able to supply enough power, and it borrows power from a neighboring system. That is what the power systems of the northeastern net did on the day of the blackout. Even with borrowing, however, the failing systems could not generate enough power.

Linked to the net and guided by computers, each electric system began to fight for more electricity. A chain effect followed. After trying to borrow power from neighboring systems and finding none, each system was forced to shut off its power, resulting in a blackout. Toronto failed at 5:15 P.M., Rochester, New York, at 5:18 P.M., and Boston at 5:21 P.M.

Within minutes, all the communities still connected to the net were drawing on one system, Consolidated Edison, a giant utility serving New York City and Westchester County. During the rush hour, Consolidated Edison usually transmitted

New York shown during a power failure; the car headlights are the only source of light along 42nd Street.

300,000 kilowatts into New York City to run elevators, commuter trains and subway cars, electric stoves, and television sets. On the day of the blackout, Con Ed pumped that power out to other systems. Within minutes, automatic safety devices stopped the straining Con Ed generators.

At 5:28 P.M., New York elevators stopped hustling thousands of people to the streets. Those inside were stuck. Many people who hadn't yet embarked on elevators walked down many flights of stairs in the dark or by the light of matches.

Commuters on the streets, in subways, and in airplanes immediately felt the impact of the blackout. Because drivers had to drive without traffic signals and street lights, police set out flares on busy highways. Commuter trains couldn't leave the stations without power, and stranded, tired riders ended up sleeping in their seats. One by one, police and firefighters led 600,000 to 800,000 people who were stuck on subways from the cars' emergency exits. By midnight, 90 percent of the subway riders were out.

Because stranded people grew exhausted as the dark night wore on, they flopped down on hotel-lobby chairs and floors. Some weary commuters even slept in reclining barbershop chairs. Luckily there were no aviation disasters; the moon was bright and airport personnel guided every plane to a safe landing.

People remained calm and they listened to battery-powered radios. Radio stations switched to emergency generators, so they stayed on the air with continuous coverage. Television stations required too much power to transmit.

The 1965 Northeast blackout became a perfect story for people to tell to their future grandchildren.

Answer the following questions based on the cause-and-effect relationships described in the selection.

1. Give two effects for each cause listed below.

   a. Cause: Elevators hustling thousands of people to the street suddenly stalled.

   Effect: _____

   Effect: _____

   b. Cause: Stranded people grew exhausted as the dark night wore on.

   Effect: _____

   Effect: _____

2. Give two causes for each effect listed below.

   a. Cause: _____

   Cause: _____

   Effect: There were no aviation disasters.

   b. Cause: _____

   Cause: _____

   Effect: Some communities were able to maintain power.

3. When effects are not directly stated, they have to be inferred, or figured out. Answer each of the following questions by inferring an effect.

   a. What might happen if people continued to use more and more electrical appliances and neglected to turn them off when they were not in use?

   _____

   _____

   b. What would happen if the whole country were eventually hooked together in one power network and a failure occurred in one system?

   _____

   _____

Skill: Synonyms and Antonyms

The word *synonym* comes from two Greek word parts: *syn,* meaning "together," and *onyma,* meaning "a name." A **synonym** is a word having the same or nearly the same meaning as another word. For example, *hurry* is a synonym for *rush.*

The word *antonym* comes from two Greek word parts: *anti,* meaning "opposite," and *onyma,* meaning "a name." An **antonym** is a word that is opposite in meaning to another word. As an example, *clean* is an antonym of *dirty.*

A. Underline the word that is the best *synonym* of the italicized word. If you don't know the meaning of the word, look it up in a dictionary.

1. *pledge*
   a. vote   **b.** promise   **c.** joke   **d.** wealth

2. *brood*
   a. flock   **b.** alloy   **c.** stream   **d.** jewelry

3. *skeptic*
   a. bones   **b.** doubter   **c.** instrument   **d.** measurement

4. *client*
   a. noise   **b.** slogan   **c.** smartness   **d.** customer

5. *uncouth*
   a. divide   **b.** careless   **c.** open   **d.** crude

6. *relic*
   a. relief   **b.** satisfaction   **c.** remains   **d.** happiness

B. Underline the word that is the best *antonym* of the italicized word. If you don't know the meaning of the word, look it up in a dictionary.

1. *proud*
   a. humble   **b.** aggressive   **c.** tired   **d.** unclear

2. *retired*
   a. quiet   **b.** arrive   **c.** respond   **d.** working

3. *migratory*
   a. mild   **b.** seasonal   **c.** permanent   **d.** plain

4. *amateur*
   a. vagueness   **b.** professional   **c.** beginner   **d.** affectionate

5. *typical*
   a. usual   **b.** powerless   **c.** exceptional   **d.** copied

6. *likely*
   a. probable   **b.** overdo   **c.** admire   **d.** impossible

Skill: Analogies

An **analogy** is a comparison. It shows that a relationship between one pair of words is similar to the relationship between another pair of words. For example, the relationship between *apple* and *fruit* is similar to the relationship between *spinach* and *vegetable.* In other words, an apple is a kind of fruit, as spinach is a kind of vegetable.

One way to express an analogy is to use words.

   Apple is to *fruit* as *spinach* is to *vegetable.*

Another way to express an analogy is to use dots for the words *is to* (:) and *as* (::).

   apple : fruit :: spinach : vegetable

Each word pair in this analogy contains a specific item and the category to which it belongs. Other relationships can show cause and effect (such as earthquake : destruction :: germ : disease) or part to whole (knob : door :: handlebar : bike).

Read the incomplete analogies below. On the first line, write the word that completes the analogy. Then, on the line at the right, identify the relationship of the words as *cause and effect, part to whole,* or *item in a category.*

1. sleeves : shirt :: wings : _____   _____
   a. engine   **b.** airplane   **c.** flying   **d.** clothes

2. terrier : dog :: dogwood : _____   _____
   a. animal   **b.** lilac   **c.** tree   **d.** green

3. attic : house :: finger : _____   _____
   a. hand   **b.** toe   **c.** nail   **d.** basement

4. drawers : bureau :: spokes : _____   _____
   a. bristles   **b.** bedroom   **c.** clothes   **d.** wheel

5. sweater : clothing :: dictionary : _____   _____
   a. book   **b.** library   **c.** store   **d.** encyclopedia

6. bath : relaxing :: shower : _____   _____
   a. clean   **b.** invigorating   **c.** towel   **d.** water

7. iris : eye :: stem : _____   _____
   a. leaf   **b.** flower   **c.** pupil   **d.** summer

8. canary : bird :: poodle : _____   _____
   a. mammal   **b.** dog   **c.** breed   **d.** collie

LESSON 47

Skill: Improving Reading Rate

A good reader is able to read at several speeds, depending on the material being read. When reading difficult or unfamiliar material, a good reader reads slowly. For example, social studies, science, mathematics, and poetry may be more difficult to read than most stories. So these materials are read more slowly. Even some literary selections can be difficult. Sometimes it is necessary to reread a paragraph to understand a complex idea. A good reader slows down when words or sentences are difficult or unfamiliar. A good reader also stops to read diagrams and maps, which require increased attention and make a slower **reading rate** necessary.

The following selection can be used to check your reading rate. Use a watch or a clock with a second hand to time yourself. Start right on a minute, such as five minutes past ten o'clock. Write your starting time at the beginning of the selection, and then read the selection. Write your ending time at the end of the selection.

A Spear for Omar

Starting time _____

Twelve-year-old Omar knelt at the bottom of a small dugout canoe and let his hand drift in the balmy water of the Red Sea. He loved this hour of the day. It usually made him feel peaceful and happy. Today, however, there was no peace in Omar's heart, for he had failed again.

Omar's father was the best at spear fishing from Suez all the way down to Port Sudan. Omar's brother, Abdel, promised to be as excellent as his father. At 15, Abdel was already exceptionally skillful with the spear and fearless in skin diving.

Abdel went to the sea daily with his father, and his catch contributed much to the support of the family. Omar accompanied his father and brother each day. He did whatever he could to help, but he had not yet learned how to spear fish. He was even afraid to dive. Abdel poked fun at his fear of drowning.

Omar's father was more understanding. "You'll learn in time," he said to Omar, "and when you do, I'll give you a beautiful spear of your own."

Yet this night, as the three rowed home, the spear seemed very far off. As usual, Omar had failed miserably in his diving. He was discouraged and deeply troubled.

The next morning, Abdel and Omar traveled to the sea alone. Abdel gripped his heavy spear immediately, shot far down into the water, and came back with an unusually large fish.

"How about you coming down?" he asked Omar.

"I will . . . I will in a minute," replied Omar a bit unwillingly as Abdel plunged down for another fish.

Suddenly Omar became aware of something happening. As he looked to the right, a huge shark emerged from the deep water and began circling the boat. Omar scanned the clear, deep water for his brother. About 15 feet below, half hidden by a ridge in a coral reef, was Abdel.

Omar uttered a cry of horror. His brother's hand had been caught in a mammoth clam, and he was trying desperately to free himself.

Omar felt his mouth go dry as he fearfully lowered himself into the water. He did not turn his head when the shark moved in closer. Without any outward sign of his deadly fear, he plunged straight downward.

Never before had Omar dived so deep as that, and he felt as if his lungs would burst. For a second, everything looked black. Then he saw his brother in front of him with his hand stuck in the clam. Abdel, almost out of breath, looked at Omar with horror-stricken eyes.

Omar acted quickly. With deft fingers, he pried the stubborn clam loose from the coral. He left it attached to Abdel's hand because he didn't want to waste precious time.

The monstrous shark swam toward them. Trying to ignore the great fish, Omar grabbed Abdel by the armpits and started upward. Suddenly the shark's murderous yellow eyes seemed to focus directly on Omar. The shark came in closer, its powerful, fanlike fins almost brushing against him.

In desperation, Omar did what his father had taught him to do in such an emergency. He let go of Abdel with his right hand and slapped the shark across its pointed nose. Relentlessly he struck again and again.

For a long moment, the shark seemed stunned. Then it churned about in confusion, finally turning toward the deep water.

Omar grabbed Abdel with both hands again, swam swiftly to the top, and pushed him into the canoe. He whipped out a knife with a strong handle and chipped away sections of the shell. Abdel winced with pain, but Omar worked feverishly until he pried the clam open.

"It's only a flesh wound and will heal rapidly," Omar said. He wrapped his dry shirt around Abdel's arm to stop the bleeding. Abdel opened his eyes weakly and smiled at Omar with gratitude and admiration.

"Thank you, my brother," he said. "Thank you."

The next morning, when Omar awoke, he discovered a spear next to his sleeping mat. His father stood looking down at him, with warm approval and affection in his eyes. Omar jumped to his feet, gripping the spear tightly in his hand.

"You will be fine at spear fishing, my son," his father said. Omar lowered his head, a great surge of happiness rising through him.

Ending time _____

To find the total time it took you to read the selection, do the following. (1) Subtract your starting time from your ending time. (2) Divide the number of words in the selection by the remainder expressed in seconds.

For example, if it took you 4 minutes and 3 seconds (4 × 60 + 3 = 243 seconds) to read the selection, you would have read 3 words per second (729 ÷ 243 = 3). (3) To find the number of words per minute (WPM), multiply your rate per second by 60. Your answer would be 180 WPM.

Words in selection: 729

	Hr.	Min.	Sec.
Ending time:	____	____	____
Starting time:	____	____	00
Total time:	____	____	____

No. words: 729 = ____ × 60 = ____ WPM
No. seconds: ____

To check your understanding of the selection, underline the answer to each question.

1. What is the setting of this selection?
   a. the Caribbean Sea
   b. the Suez Canal
   c. Port Sudan
   d. the Red Sea

2. Why was Omar discouraged at the beginning of this selection?
   a. His father had poked fun at him.
   b. He had caught only a few small fish.
   c. He had not yet learned how to spear fish.
   d. He had lost a special spear.

3. What promise did Omar's father make?
   a. He promised to teach Omar to swim.
   b. He promised to take Omar to the city for a week of sightseeing.
   c. He promised to give Omar a spear of his own one day.
   d. He promised to let Omar fight a shark.

4. How did Omar know there was a shark nearby?
   a. Omar could see the shark in the water.
   b. The shark began circling the boat.
   c. His brother warned Omar about the shark.
   d. The shark attacked the boat.

5. Why didn't Abdel return to the boat?
   a. His hand was caught in a clam.
   b. He was busy spearing a large fish.
   c. He thought he should stay hidden in the coral reef until the shark went away.
   d. He was too afraid to swim near the shark.

6. What did Omar do when he reached Abdel?
   a. He gave Abdel a supply of oxygen.
   b. He pried the clam loose from the coral.
   c. He took a knife and cut the coral loose.
   d. He took Abdel's knife and stabbed the shark.

7. How did Omar deal with the shark?
   a. He attacked the shark with his knife.
   b. He ignored the shark, and it swam away.
   c. He hid behind Abdel until the shark left.
   d. He kept slapping the shark across the nose.

Skill: Using an Index

The quickest way to find specific information in a text or reference book is to use the **index**. An index alphabetically lists the important topics of the book. The index is usually located at the end of a text or reference book.

On the next page is part of an index from a world history textbook. Look at the index, and find the main topic or entry, **Agriculture**. The subtopics that follow the entry are arranged chronologically, that is, in the order in which they happened. This kind of arrangement is common to history books since the contents of such books are usually arranged chronologically. In this entry, for example, the most recent event in agriculture, the Green Revolution, is listed last.

The numbers after each topic or subtopic are the page numbers on which related information is found. Numbers separated by dashes indicate that the information begins on the page before the dash and ends on the page after the dash. Numbers separated by commas show that information appears only on the pages for which numbers are given. Study the index on the next page. Then answer the questions on the lines provided.

1. On which page(s) would you find information about the Alliance for Progress? _____

2. How many subtopics are listed under the topic Architecture? _____

3. On which page(s) would you find information about Konrad Adenauer? _____

4. How many pages does the book have on Arabic numerals? _____

5. On which page(s) would you find information about the Algonquin Indians? _____

6. On which page(s) would you find a map of Albania? _____

7. On which page(s) would you find information on the American Revolution? _____

8. On which page(s) would you find a picture of Greek architecture? _____

9. On which page(s) would you find a picture of Ajanta? _____

10. If you wanted information about agriculture in medieval Europe, which page(s) would you not read between 175 and 180? _____

11. Which topic comes between *Appeasement* and *Apprentice*? _____

12. On which page(s) would you find a chart about agriculture in developing countries? _____

13. On which page(s) would you find a footnote about annulment? _____

14. On which page(s) would you find a map of the climate in Africa? _____

Italicized page numbers refer to illustrations. The *m*, *c*, or *p* preceding the number refers to a map (m), chart (c), or picture (p) on that page. An *n* following a page number refers to a footnote.

Skill: Reading a Budget

A **budget** is a plan that shows how much money you will receive, or your income, and how much you will spend, or your expenses, in a given period. To plan a monthly budget, you must first know how much money you receive each month. Although you may receive more income by working overtime or getting a raise, your income usually doesn't change each month. Next you must figure out your expenses on a monthly basis.

Many expenses, such as rent, loan payments, and insurance payments, are the same each month; they are **fixed expenses**. Other fixed expenses, like electricity, may not be the same amount each month. However, you know when these costs must be paid and about how much they will be.

Other expenses may change each month; they are **variable expenses**. The cost of clothing, for example, is a variable expense because you may spend more on clothing in some months than in other months. To plan a budget, you must estimate, or guess the amount of, your variable expenses. The best way to estimate these expenses is to record how much they are for a few months and then find the average for one month. Last of all, you should determine how much money you can save each month. The amount you can save will vary from month to month also.

The following monthly budget shows how Wayne's income will be used during the month of May. Wayne shares an apartment with two friends, and he needs to budget his share of expenses along with his individual expenses. Study his budget carefully.

Wayne's Budget for May			
Fixed Expenses		**Variable Expenses**	
Rent ($\frac{1}{3}$ share)	$210.00	Gasoline and car repair	$85.00
Electricity ($\frac{1}{3}$ share)	22.00	Food ($\frac{1}{3}$ share)	120.00
Car loan payment	150.00	Telephone ($\frac{1}{3}$ share)	11.50
Car insurance	75.00	Clothing	60.00
Money owed to Dad	25.00	Summer swimming	
	$482.00	pool membership	50.00
		Entertainment	120.00
			$446.50
Total fixed expenses	$482.00	Monthly income after taxes	$1,007.25
Total variable expenses	+446.50	Monthly expenses	−928.50
Total monthly expenses	$928.50	Savings	$78.75

A. Fill in the circle next to the phrase or sentence that correctly answers each question.

1. How much money does Wayne receive each month?
   ○ $928.50   ○ $482.00   ○ $446.50   ○ $1,007.25

2. What are some fixed expenses on Wayne's budget?
   ○ rent, telephone, and food   ○ telephone, car loan payment, and gasoline
   ○ rent, car loan payment, and electricity   ○ rent, clothing, and food

3. Why is entertainment listed on the budget as a variable expense?
   ○ The amount spent on entertainment changes from one month to another.
   ○ The same amount is spent on entertainment every month.
   ○ Wayne spends a lot of money on entertainment.
   ○ Wayne doesn't spend money on entertainment.

4. How much money is Wayne planning to spend in May?
   ○ $482.00   ○ $446.50   ○ $928.50   ○ $1,007.25

5. What one expense does Wayne have in the month of May that he will probably not have in any other month of the year?
   ○ clothing   ○ swimming pool membership   ○ entertainment   ○ food

6. What is the greatest single expense on the budget?
   ○ food   ○ fixed expenses   ○ electricity   ○ rent

B. Complete Wayne's budget for June by using the information from Wayne's May budget. Then answer the questions to the left of the budget.

1. Which expenses stayed the same for both months? Why?

   _____

   _____

   _____

2. In which month was Wayne able to save more money? Why?

   _____

   _____

   _____

Wayne's Budget for June		
Fixed Expenses		**Variable Expenses**
_____	_____	Gasoline and car repair $60.00
_____	_____	Food ($\frac{1}{3}$ share) 100.00
_____	_____	Telephone ($\frac{1}{3}$ share) 13.00
_____	_____	Entertainment 80.00
_____	_____	Dental check-up 45.00
_____	_____	CD player repair 85.00
		$383.00
Total fixed expenses _____		Monthly income
Total variable expenses _____		after taxes _____
Total monthly expenses _____		Monthly expenses _____
		Savings _____

CONTEXT CLUE WORDS

The following words are treated as context clue words in the lessons indicated. Each lesson provides instruction in a particular context clue type and includes an activity that requires you to use context clues to find word meanings. Context clue words appear in the literature, social studies, and science selections and are underlined or footnoted.

CONCEPT WORDS

In lessons that feature social studies, science, or mathematics selections, words that are unique to the content and whose meanings are important in the selection are treated as concept words. These words appear in boldface type and are often followed by a phonetic respelling and a definition.